BREAKING INTO NEW HOLLYWOOD

A CAREER GUIDE TO A CHANGING INDUSTRY

ADA TSENG AND JON HEALEY

SIMON & SCHUSTER PAPERBACKS

New York Amsterdam/Antwerp London
Toronto Sydney/Melbourne New Delhi

Simon & Schuster Paperbacks
An Imprint of Simon & Schuster, LLC
1230 Avenue of the Americas
New York, NY 10020

First Simon & Schuster paperback edition August 2026

Interior design by Carly Loman

Manufactured in the United States of America

1 3 5 7 9 10 8 6 4 2

Library of Congress Cataloging-in-Publication Data is available.

ISBN 978-1-6680-5003-3
ISBN 978-1-6680-4998-3 (pbk)
ISBN 978-1-6680-4999-0 (ebook)

From the experts at the *Los Angeles Times* comes a definitive guide that explores and demystifies dozens of careers for those hoping to break into the entertainment industry.

Everyone loves a captivating Hollywood rags-to-riches story. Take Charlize Theron, who was on her last paycheck and in a heated discussion with a bank teller when a kind stranger—who happened to be a talent agent—stepped in to help her cash an out-of-town check. Or consider Rosario Dawson, discovered right on her front porch by filmmakers looking for fresh talent for *Kids*. And then there's Leonardo DiCaprio, the son of a secretary and a writer and distributor of underground comics, who saw acting as a way out of poverty.

But that's not how it usually happens for the tens of thousands of people who work in the entertainment industry. For many just starting out, and even those already in the business, the road can feel mysterious and overwhelming. From actors and directors to behind-the-scenes heroes like managers, grips, and sound designers, *Breaking Into New Hollywood* is here to uncover the many opportunities for newcomers hustling in what the *Los Angeles Times* calls the "company town"—and beyond.

This practical guide offers invaluable insights on navigating the industry today. How has working in film changed in the age of streaming? How are professionals thinking about AI? Even with the rapid rise of YouTubers and social media stars raking in millions of views and competing for traditional movie theater audiences, there are still more job opportunities than ever for those eager to start a career in film and TV. *Breaking Into New Hollywood* is an up-to-date road map for aspiring stars wanting to make a living in front of the camera, but it's also for those passionate about being part of a collaborative, creative community like no other.

For the Hollywood dreamers, may this be the first step toward finding your path.

CONTENTS

CONTENTS

INTRODUCTION

The magic of Hollywood has many guises. Couture-clad stars offering witty sound bites on a red carpet. The laughter, murmurs of outrage, or romantic sobs elicited from a crowd of strangers by a story shared on a flickering screen. The digitally enhanced conjurings of castles, deep space, stampeding dinosaurs, and the feeling of actual flight.

But the real magic takes place in a crucible, an alternative universe that can occupy a dim and echoing sound stage the size of an airport hangar or a tiny local tire shop on the corner of two busy streets in the sun-scorched San Fernando Valley.

In my decades covering the entertainment industry, I have spent a lot of time visiting sets. Big and small, on lots and locations, for film and television and music videos. In Los Angeles, it isn't unusual to simply stumble on one—a local restaurant turned into a cinematic crime scene, the exterior of a nearby school ablaze with "sunlight" at 9:00 p.m. as "students" flood out its doors, a trio of famous actors strolling down a downtown street as Star Waggons and enormous vans take up all the parking spots.

It is always an amazing sight—the forest of cameras, monitors, boom mics, and lighting equipment. The rivers of power cords snaking along the floor. The army of people moving in a complicated dance of production.

Gaffers and best boys adjusting dollies, setting up lights and electrical rigging, sometimes hundreds of yards overhead. The set dressers and production designers making adjustments. The writers tweaking scenes, the script supervisor taking notes and distributing new pages. The cinematographer and camera operators consulting with the director to frame the shot. The makeup artists and costume designers grooming the actors in between takes, the prop masters handing out weapons or protest signs or whatever is required for extras in battle or crowd scenes.

The production assistants, their hands inevitably full with water bottles, clipboards, lunch orders, or someone else's phone; the crew members with their rainbow assortment of duct tape; the grips moving every single piece of equipment that needs to be moved. Stunt performers, background actors, and stand-ins waiting for their call.

Hundreds of highly skilled and dedicated people completing thousands of tasks, making endless on-the-spot decisions to produce each and every scene of each and every film and TV series.

When I visited Disney Studios during the filming of *Pirates of the Caribbean: At World's End*, Soundstage 2 was surrounded by pirates eating their lunch, checking their messages, chatting among themselves. Inside, Johnny Depp, Keira Knightley, Orlando Bloom, and Geoffrey Rush acted out an on-deck scene, surrounded by hundreds of burning candles. As the scene progressed, an assistant director warned everyone to move away from the metal tubes that surrounded the ship set. "In a few minutes, those are going to burst into flame," he said, asking that orange safety cones be put in place. When none could be found, a crew member positioned himself safely in front of the tubes, arms outstretched. "I'll stand here. I'll be the cone."

And he did, until the scene was wrapped. Magic.

On the set of another film, a child actor walked across the floor at the instruction of a sound director. "His shoes are very squeaky," he told one of the child's assistants. "They're just tennis shoes," she replied. "Well, they are very squeaky tennis shoes," he said. "Get him new ones."

And the costume department produced several pairs of non-squeaky shoes. More magic.

Now as more behind-the-scenes footage is available, everyone can watch Emilia Clarke be turned into Daenerys Targaryen or the cast of *Bridgerton* practicing Regency dance steps. But being there, and seeing the pool of light in which the scene is being shot, the tape marks on the floor, the set built so the camera can peer invisibly through a bookshelf, all surrounded by widening rings of equipment and the people who control it, is inevitably astounding.

For several years, I covered the Oscars from backstage. Never mind all the big stars, power players, and award-winning films being honored on Hollywood's most glamorous night—the Oscars is a three-hour live TV show with a million moving parts and no room for error. Yes, Ryan Gosling killed it in his "I'm Just Ken" performance in 2024, but he was just one part of an enormous team effort. The choreographer, the music director, the team of dancers, the set designer, the camera operators, the costume designer, the stage manager, hair and makeup, gaffers and grips and the rest of the crew moving the set around, all to make it seem spontaneous and spectacular.

As jaded as anyone gets about the industry, a day or even an hour on set invariably resurrects the awe and excitement of Hollywood; it's difficult not to want to be a part of it all.

This book is a how-to guide for those who want to be a part of it all. The would-be actors, writers, and directors, of course, but also prospective production and costume designers, makeup and stunt artists, producers, gaffers, grips, composers, and Foley artists.

There are many wildly different paths to a job in the entertainment industry, to becoming part of a working set or one of those who do the work before or after filming begins—the film editors, the sound editors, the agents and publicists. So how does one get started? Is film school required? Theater training? An engineering degree? What skills are necessary? How does one job lead to another? What is the average salary?

How did the people at the top of their professions get and stay there?

Luck, as most everyone featured in this book will say, is always part of it. Talent most certainly is. But mostly it's the work. The willingness to learn the craft of storytelling, from its sweeping vision to its detailed demands. The magic doesn't just happen—the lighting has to be right, the dress must fall just so, the shoes can't squeak, and sometimes someone needs to be the cone.

The real magic of Hollywood is not the glitz or the glamor, the star who was "discovered" walking down the street or posting on Instagram. As you will learn in this book, it's the Foley artist, perfecting the sound of footsteps so the audience can hear the character's pain. It's carpenters in the workshop building the sets, the electrician perched with a light for hours on a twenty-foot crane, or the cinematographer who, like Michael Goi, used car exhaust to create the moody lighting he needed when a piece of equipment failed. It's the set designer combing thrift shops for just the right sofa, and the costume designer making sure the stunt artist's pants don't rip.

As Janelle Carothers says in the chapter on costume design: "I love that you might know what Prada's latest season looks like, but if we're rolling, can you take a piece of bubble gum and fix a hem if you only have ten seconds to do it?"

That's what magic is, after all. Doing an enormous amount of highly skilled work to make it seem like no work has been done at all.

Mary McNamara, Culture Columnist and Critic, *Los Angeles Times*
Winner of the 2015 Pulitzer Prize in Criticism

HOW TO THINK ABOUT ARTIFICIAL INTELLIGENCE AND HOLLYWOOD

Hollywood was created by an innovation in technology: cameras that could record moving pictures. It has been periodically disrupted by technological innovations ever since, including films with sound, VCRs, computer-generated images, and streaming video.

In each instance, the disruption eliminated some jobs while creating others, and many of the people displaced weren't equipped to seize the new opportunities. Although technologies are merely tools, not talents, some talented people were left without outlets for their specific skills.

Some stars of silent films couldn't make the jump to talkies. Digital cameras eliminated a slew of jobs associated with processing and cutting film, and digitally transmitted movies did the same to projectionists.

Artificial intelligence is the latest disruptor, and like many that came before, it has sent panic rippling through Hollywood: It will replace writers! It will replace crews! It could even replace actors!

Writers and actors were so concerned about AI being used to replicate their talents that their unions went on overlapping strikes that crippled the industry for much of 2023. They ultimately agreed to contracts that limited the use of AI but did not bar it completely from the set.

Robert Nederhorst, president of the visual effects (VFX) studio Narrate, offers a bit of perspective. "There are going to be problems with employment," he said, "but that happens every time new technology comes out, period."

Still, it's important not to soft-pedal what this particular new tool could do. It can learn to perform many of the jobs on a film set, then do those jobs faster and at lower cost. AI skeptics worry that these efficiencies will translate into higher profits for production companies and less employment for everyone else.

Tony Vinciquerra fed those concerns in May 2024 when he spoke at an investors conference in Japan while serving as the chief executive officer of Sony Pictures Entertainment. He noted that the industry, which had opened the year with five months of sluggish ticket sales, was still struggling to get box-office revenues back to where they were before COVID-19, especially in the United States. Sony had a number of responses in the works, he said, including this one: "We'll be looking at ways to use AI to produce films for theaters and television in more efficient ways, using AI primarily."

It was a stunning statement, given the months-long strikes the industry had just endured by writers and actors nervous about AI—and the ongoing talks with the AI-averse union representing crew members (the International Alliance of Theatrical Stage Employees [IATSE] reached a new contract agreement a few months later that included benefits for workers displaced by AI). Vinciquerra acknowledged that union contracts would set limits on how the studios use AI, but Sony's goal was clear: to cut costs.

Labor can account for more than half of a project's budget, so "cutting costs" is often shorthand for "hiring fewer people." And like many technological advances that preceded it, AI is taking some workers' places on the film and TV production lines.

But AI represents much more than just a tool studios use to cut production costs. It's a potential revolution in filmmaking—empowering more people to turn their ideas into high-quality video but also replacing human talent behind and in front of the camera with software and virtual actors.

So while some industry professionals see AI as a death knell for many careers, advocates see it as a path to more films and shows being made—potentially far more. That increase will create more jobs, not fewer, they say, although the work performed won't be the same as what's being done on a film set today.

If you're thinking about a career in film and television, you'll need to consider whether AI is your friend, your potential ticket in, or your eventual replacement. That advice goes for just about any profession, but the reckoning appears to be coming more quickly in Hollywood.

The First Wave of AI in Filmmaking

By 2024, AI-powered tools on the market could generate scripts from a brief text prompt, animate images of actors or just spin them out of whole cloth, create voices to read lines of dialogue and write the music to accompany it all. But as promising—or threatening—as the tools seemed, they were not ready to generate a Hollywood-caliber film or TV show.

There were just a handful of high-profile uses of these tools. For example, Marvel's *Secret Invasion* on Disney+ had a surrealistic opening credit sequence that was produced with the help of AI. TV manufacturer TCL used AI to help generate the footage for a film romance, *Next Stop Paris*, that used human writers and actors but still looked and sounded . . . weird. And Coca-Cola released three AI-generated Christmas commercials in 2024 that evoked the look and feel of its previous holiday ads, drawing brickbats from viewers for using software in lieu of human artists.

"Totally synthetic AI media"—that is, a film generated by feeding prompts to an AI, with no actors or human-created sound or sets—was "almost unwatchable" in late 2023, Mike Gioia, cofounder of the AI filmmaking company Pickaxe and an AI filmmaking evangelist, said at the time. But as the Coca-Cola commercials showed, the technology has been improving by leaps and bounds. Ernest Hemingway's words about going bankrupt may well apply to the AI revolution in filmmaking: It happens "gradually and then suddenly."

On the plus side, generative AI tools create text, images, and video "at a rate unfathomably faster" than humans do, Nederhorst said. On the minus side, "there's always something missing. It's never quite there." What's missing, he said, is the message the creator is trying to get across—the intent behind the art.

Where AI has made its biggest inroads is in pre- and post-production. AI tools by the likes of Filmustage, NolanAI, and RivetAI are automating important pre-production tasks, such as coming up with a film's budget. AI is also helping filmmakers create presentations and trailers for movies they're pitching to producers and financiers.

Similarly, AI can speed the process of creating and revising storyboards for a project, making it easier for filmmakers to change directions and incorporate new ideas. Tools are also being developed that use AI to keep track of details of a production in progress, such as recording the camera positions for every shot to ensure continuity.

For VFX artists, who are by nature dependent on computers and software to generate their images, AI-powered tools are letting them work faster and deliver more realistic-looking results at lower cost. For example, instead of spending hours sculpting digital clay to create a convincing model of a rock wall, VFX artists can quickly throw together a rough model and use AI to transform it into something that's Hollywood-grade.

Also progressing rapidly is AI technology that takes images created by humans and animates them, which Gioia called "rotoscoping on steroids." Then there's a hybrid sort of filmmaking that melds AI assets and media with live footage, such as an actor performing in front of a green screen, or making a real actor look like someone else—or even the same actor, years younger.

Such tasks have previously been done with time-consuming and costly visual effects. Gioia predicted that AI-powered techniques will achieve "ninety-five percent of the quality at ten percent of the cost" within a few years.

What Will Happen to Jobs?

The potential jolt delivered by AI seems more severe than, say, the shift to LED lighting. The consulting firm CVL Economics surveyed three hundred entertainment-industry executives about generative AI's effect on employment for a study published early in 2024, and the results were grim.

According to the report, three-quarters of those interviewed said AI technologies had led to jobs being eliminated, reduced, or consolidated. It predicted that more than one in five jobs in film, television, and animation—about 118,500 all told—are likely to be disrupted by generative AI by 2026.

The tasks most likely to be affected are 3-D modeling, character and environment design, voice generation, and cloning and compositing, followed by sound design, tools programming, script writing, animation and rigging, concept art/visual development, and light/texture generation.

In the film and TV industry, about a third of respondents predicted that AI would displace 3-D modelers, sound editors, rerecording mixers, and broadcast, audio, and video technicians by 2026, while a quarter expected sound designers, compositors, and graphic designers to be affected as well. An estimated 15 percent flagged the artists who make storyboards and design the surfaces and materials seen in a video, along with illustrators and animators, as vulnerable to AI.

In the music industry, more than 50 percent of survey participants anticipated that AI would displace sound designers in the next three years, while more than 40 percent saw AI threatening the livelihoods of music editors, audio technicians, and sound engineers. Roughly a third of respondents predicted a similar fate for songwriters, composers, and studio engineers.

Some longtime Hollywood professionals who are incorporating AI into their work, however, are more sanguine. Yes, some jobs will be lost, they say, but by slashing the cost of production, more smaller-scale projects will be green-lit—potentially creating more work for more people.

It also means more people with ideas for films will be able to make them. "This might make it so that in all fifty states in the U.S. and all countries in the world, there are tons of five- to ten-person productions," Gioia said.

Eliot Mack is a former mechanical engineer whose résumé includes designing the original Roomba robotic vacuum for iRobot. Having caught the filmmaking bug when he helped a friend make a student film, he started Lightcraft, a VFX company, to understand how movies were made. "The history of Lightcraft was in many ways a deconstruction of what it takes to make a movie look like a movie, and making it possible for a tiny team to make it happen," Mack said.

Like a lot of professionals who've incorporated AI, Mack envisions a more entrepreneurial approach to filmmaking, with smaller crews, more overlapping functions, and less time elapsing between green-lit idea and finished film. One reason for the faster pace, he said, is that AI can eliminate a lot of the schlepping involved in just getting to the point where the magic happens.

Which is not to say that sets will no longer require grips and electricians. They'll just need fewer people standing around waiting for their turn to do what they do.

AI will also fuel a demand in the film and TV industry for people who know how to use the technology.

"It's definitely a skill set," said Hoyt Yeatman, a writer, director, and VFX supervisor. "The prompting is a very big deal. And it's ever-changing."

But what about actors? Computer graphics are already being used to reduce the need for extras in crowd scenes, and you can find examples of realistic-looking AI-generated characters taking leading roles in short videos online.

Mack, for one, is not expecting to see much use of synthetic actors in the foreground of films and television for at least a century. He has trouble imagining AI replicating the exceedingly small changes in expression seen in great acting, or capturing the spark among a group of actors interacting with a camera.

"It's hard enough to get it, even with the best of conditions," Mack said.

One other thing to bear in mind: Some of the tasks that AI will take over are not being done by anyone today. It's not a job loss if the job didn't exist in the first place.

A good example is Spiideo, a Swedish company that uses AI to replace camera operators for sports broadcasts. In a soccer match, for example, broadcasters use stationary cameras that cover the entire pitch, then Spiideo's technology decides which portion to display, seemingly moving the camera to follow the action. The technology's capabilities are expanding, potentially allowing broadcasters to use it in place of a director too.

Emil Hansson, head of Spiideo Play, said the most likely market for Spiideo isn't the broadcasters carrying the top sports leagues, however. Instead, its low-cost approach could enable broadcasters to televise sports whose audiences are too small today to justify the expense.

The data that Spiideo can gather during a game also opens the possibility for creative new approaches to sports, Hansson said. Everything happening on the field is a data point that can potentially be used to generate new statistics and novel graphics.

How Does AI Change What Would-Be Filmmakers Need to Learn?

It's still a good idea to get a job on a film or TV set to see the various jobs performed and learn about the process as it exists today. Understanding cameras and editing is important too.

But it's also wise to start using the AI-powered tools already on the market. "Get involved and just start making stuff quickly and iteratively and putting it out there," Gioia advised.

The most user-friendly programs are the ones for making short videos. One example is Augie, which uses multiple types of AI to generate videos from as little as a text prompt. "We take whatever you've sent and build a video from that," said Jeremy Toeman, founder of Augie Studio (now part of JWX in Los Angeles).

Augie's AIs turn brief text prompts into scripts, generate virtual narrators to read the lines, then analyze the context to build storyboards and a video, using footage from the client, content from Getty Images, or images generated by Stable Diffusion.

The state of the art today is fine for generating a few seconds or a minute of video, Toeman said, but it's going to take several years for the technology to be capable of producing Hollywood-caliber long-form video. A particular issue for AI is realistically portraying people just having a conversation.

For a deeper dive, Mack suggests learning how to use Lightcraft's free Jetset program (which tracks camera movements to make it easier to integrate visual effects), as well as 3-D modeling programs such as Blender and compositing programs such as After Effects or Nuke (which combine VFX and camera footage into a coherent scene). Lightcraft offers tutorials on its site for all of these programs and more.

"Don't get too wrapped up in what the AI tools are going to be," Mack said. "But learn how to build shots. It turns out that movies are constructed from shots, lots of them."

PART I

ACTING

CHAPTER 1

How to Become an Actor in Film or Television

We see actors everywhere. We see them in our favorite films and TV shows. We see them on talk shows and posters. We see them on red carpets and on their Instagram posts (showing us how they glammed up for the red carpets). We see them win awards. We read their memoirs.

Unlike the hundreds of other jobs in Hollywood that are often so seamlessly tucked behind the scenes that they're invisible, the job of an actor is hyper-visible. It's the job—professionals say—that everyone *thinks* they understand.

But the public often only sees the most glamorous parts of being a celebrity, not the daily grind of a typical Hollywood actor.

When you book an acting role, you get to do all the work that made you want to be an actor in the first place. You break down a script. You learn your lines. You create your character with the help of hair, makeup, and costume people. You discuss your role with the director. You rehearse with your fellow cast members. You deliver the best performance you can muster with the time you were given to prepare and the number of takes you were able to do. Then you hope it's shot and edited in a way that showcases your brilliance, so you can have an easier time booking your next big role.

But it's imperative for aspiring film and TV actors to understand that for most professional actors in Hollywood, the time on a set is very limited.

"People come out of high school and college, they've been acting in theater their whole lives, they've been cast in every single school play, and that's just a very different lifestyle than a working actor," said Ben Whitehair, an actor, active Screen Actors Guild member, and cofounder of Working.Actor, an extensive resource for aspiring actors.

The main part of the job is auditioning. It's the hustle. Many working actors liken the lifestyle to owning a small business. While you're starting out, you have to be your own talent, marketing, customer service, and community outreach departments. Like with any small business, it takes time, energy, and money to get an acting career off the ground.

There is a tremendous amount of luck involved. Get comfortable with rejection that you cannot control—rejection that often has more to do with the superficial parts of you (how you look, your chemistry with another actor, how much you match with someone's idea of a script's character) and less to do with your talent and skills.

In the beginning, you won't book many gigs. You'll need another way to pay your bills that allows you to easily take time off to do auditions or take on small roles. Even when you start landing gigs regularly—a combination of student films, indie films, voice-over gigs, workshops, table reads, commercials and other one-day appearances—none of them, by themselves, will provide a livable wage. But it all adds up, and the reward is that you get to do what you love for work.

Outsiders can easily point out an actor's most high-profile credits on IMDb. For Behzad Dabu, that would be his role as Simon Drake on *How to Get Away with Murder*. But when he made enough money that he was able to quit his safety job as a college admissions administrator, that was a huge win for him.

Many professionals would love for people to stop romanticizing the role of a working actor. What does a typical Hollywood actor really look like? "They can go to the park and grocery store without getting stopped or mobbed," Dabu said. "They bought a house. They raised children. They have a car. And they can afford all of that by being an actor."

What Qualities Do You Find in a Successful Actor?

It might sound obvious, but actors need to love performing. You have to love it so much that you're willing to do things that you don't always want to do to get paid to act. That could include juggling multiple side jobs to support yourself, taking any role that comes your way, or making self-taped auditions not knowing if someone is going to watch them all the way through.

Actors are storytellers. They tend to be good listeners who are highly attuned to all the different ways people communicate and show their emotions. They also tend to be curious about human behavior and psychology, because part of the job is being empathetic and understanding why people do the dramatic things they do.

Actors usually love doing research about different cultures and time periods. They do a lot of that to embody their characters.

And lastly, actors must have really thick skin. Actors who survive in Hollywood have to be very good at managing their emotions. They have to be the type of people who can be extremely vulnerable on camera; give their entire heart, mind, and body to a project; won't get fazed by comments from anonymous strangers who pick apart their looks and performances; and afterward decide that they want to do it again.

How Do You Get Started?

Training—and continuing to train even when you start getting work—is essential. There are many ways to get training. You could get a theater degree at a college or university. (Look up the annual lists of best acting colleges compiled by *Backstage* or the *Hollywood Reporter*. Juilliard, Yale, the University of North Carolina, and Carnegie Mellon are often listed among the top-tier schools.) You could enroll in more intensive acting conservatory programs, like Los Angeles Performing Arts Conservatory, T. Schreiber, Atlantic Acting School, William Esper Studio, the Lee Strasberg Theatre & Film Institute, or Stella Adler Studio of Acting. You could take classes focused on acting techniques, like Stanislavski's Method or the Meisner technique.

There are also classes that teach specific skills, including scene study, character study, auditioning, and improv. There are classes that focus on acting for commercials. There are coaches—including DaJuan Johnson (*Bosch*), founder of Think Bigger Coaching, and Anna LaMadrid (*This Fool*), owner of Put Me On Self-Tape—who specialize in helping actors film self-taped auditions. Modeling classes can help you get comfortable in front of the camera. Learning stand-up comedy can help you nail your comedic timing and find your unique voice.

The goal is to eventually get good enough at your craft that you get booked for roles that will give you on-the-job training. To book these roles, you often need representation—an agent who submits you for jobs and negotiates contracts, and a manager who guides your career.

But first, you need headshots, a résumé, and a reel. So how do you create a reel of work before you've booked anything?

There are national casting networks and websites—including Actors Access and Backstage.com—that list auditions, also known as breakdowns, that you can apply for on your own if you don't yet have an agent. These are typically for smaller projects: short films, commercials, web series, and social media sketches. There are many local networks and Facebook groups that are free. Most opportunities will be found in Los Angeles and New York, but there are growing hubs in cities including Las Vegas, Atlanta, San Francisco, Austin, and Chicago.

The process can be a grind. "Let's say you submit yourself to thirty projects, two get back to you, you do those two auditions, and you don't hear anything. Tomorrow, submit yourself to thirty more projects," Dabu said.

While you're getting used to rejection, make your own content. Actor Randall Park (*WandaVision, Fresh Off the Boat*) regularly directed and starred in his own comedic short films—often featuring alumni from the LCC Theatre Company, the Asian American company he co-founded at UCLA as a student—decades before he got his first professional directing opportunity. Even if you just get your friends together and piece some clips over a few months, you can create a reel to show agents and managers who focus on discovering new actors.

Look for representation that's right for you. A manager oversees the day-to-day operations of your career, while agents help find and secure opportunities, bookings, and auditions. Once you start booking more gigs, you might consider hiring a publicist and an attorney for dealing with contracts.

And lastly, anytime you get the chance to work on set, think about everything you can do in the moment to help yourself get your next role. That means showing up on time, being respectful, and making everyone else's job easier. It means learning how different departments work and connecting with like-minded people you might want to collaborate with in the future.

Don't define yourself (or be defeated) by any individual project. Treat all your experiences—big and small, good and bad—as steps to develop yourself as an artist and build toward your eventual goal. That goal often evolves as you learn more about the industry and yourself.

What Are the Career Paths?

There is no one path and no set timeline for the career of an actor. But there is a general hierarchy. Most working actors start with agents and managers who specialize in getting actors with less experience auditions for smaller jobs, and then eventually work up to the higher-profile agents and managers, who can get auditions for major networks and streaming services.

The only way to fast-track to the top is if a casting director or filmmaker chooses you for a role that's much bigger than the one you did before. But that's out of your control.

Here is a breakdown of the typical acting roles in television:

- Background actor: These actors used to be called extras. They don't have any lines, but they help create the atmosphere of the scene.
- Bit role, costar, or "under-5": This refers to an actor who has fewer than five lines of dialogue.
- Guest star: This is a role that affects plot.
- Recurring guest star: This is a character that affects plot for multiple episodes.
- Top of show guest star: This is when you've become a recognizable actor and your name comes up in the credits at the beginning of the show.
- Series regulars: These are the characters you see in every episode of the show.

There are similar levels for acting in film: extras, featured extras, supporting roles, supporting leads, and leads.

How Do You Make Money? And What Kind of Money?

Getting into the union—SAG-AFTRA—is imperative. Once you get into the union, you agree to stop taking nonunion jobs for any work covered by the SAG-AFTRA contract. Statistically, that limits your options, but union work will offer protections, including health insurance, and set you up for the higher pay you need to have a sustainable acting career.

For most actors, though, it takes at least a couple of years to book jobs that will qualify them for membership. There are two primary routes to get into SAG-AFTRA: You get a job on a union project, or you do work as a member of an affiliated performers' union, such as the American Guild of Musical Artists or the American Guild of Variety Artists.

How do you get a job on a union project if you're nonunion? A producer files a Taft-Hartley form to hire a nonunion actor if they can't find a union one to fill the role. "A common example would be if they need a person who has a particular skill," said Whitehair. "For example, if the character speaks Farsi, they might petition to hire a nonunion actor, and then [the actor] becomes eligible for the union."

SAG-AFTRA has a number of rate sheets that dictate the minimum pay that its members make for a given production. As of 2026, the amount for an episode—a day's work for a performer is worth a minimum of $1,246 and a performer who is hired longer term has to be paid $4,326 a week—might seem high at first glance, but keep in mind that most actors are not booking gigs throughout the year. And it takes a while to book these more well-paid roles, because it takes time to get the type of representation you need to get those types of auditions.

Even established actors might book only two $14,000-an-episode guest star roles a year. Also, most working actors take home only about 40 percent of their check. The rest goes to their agent, manager, and lawyer, as well as the union and taxes.

The reality is that most actors, even if they appear established, have another job that makes them money. They might produce projects, invest in restaurants, dabble in real estate, or start small businesses. Having another source of income isn't a temporary phase or a sign of failure, professionals say. It's a strategy that helps actors sustain their creative career.

Commercials can provide income for actors in between jobs. Actor Brent Bailey (*The Idea of You, The Holiday Dating Guide*), who has shot over one hundred commercials, said he's rarely had to turn down a TV or film role because of a commercial, because the turnaround time is so fast. "If I get offered a really big TV or film role, obviously I'd take that role, but commercials pay so well that it's hard to say no," he said. "You can audition for a commercial this week that shoots next week, and it only shoots for one day."

How much you'll get paid for working in a commercial depends on such factors as whether you're the principal or a background actor, whether it runs on cable or broadcast television, how long it runs, how large its reach is, and, most important, whether it's shot under a union contract. A principal actor could earn up to $20,000 for a national broadcast TV commercial, but only about $1,000 for an ad shot for YouTube.

With the advent of streaming and the decline of traditional advertising, commercial acting is not as lucrative as it once was. But acting in commercials can also be a good opportunity to work with big directors and cinematographers in the business. Bailey shot commercials with both Doug Liman (*The Recruit*, *The Bourne Identity*) and Antoine Fuqua (*Michael*, *Training Day*).

How Is This Career Different from Ten or Twenty-Five Years Ago?

One of the main changes is the transition from in-person auditions to self-tapes. Self-taped auditions were becoming more popular before the COVID-19 pandemic. But when the shutdowns proved how safe and effective those prerecorded versions can be—allowing casting directors to see far more actors, including ones out of town—they've become an industry standard.

Actors suddenly needed to learn the basics of filmmaking, lighting, and sound so that their tapes would be competitive. SAG-AFTRA also put in protections for their members for how many pages actors could be asked to film for first-round self-tape auditions and interviews. It felt like an extra responsibility placed upon actors, who just wanted to act. But some professionals encourage actors to think of it as a new opportunity—a way to take control of the audition and submit their best take.

The marketplace for actors has also changed dramatically. In previous generations, actors put most of their emphasis on training. And while mastering the craft is still important, actors are more focused now on expanding beyond the traditional confines of an actor—and they have more opportunity to do so.

Carolyn Michelle Smith (*The Chi, Familiar Touch*) coaches and mentors young actors, and she said their references for success are actors who also write and produce, like Michaela Coel, creator and star of *Chewing Gum* and *I May Destroy You*, and Quinta Brunson, creator and star of *Abbott Elementary*. Or Tabitha Brown, an actor, author, and media personality who's gained a massive online following with comedic videos about veganism.

Professionals say there are more opportunities to craft your own life and career as an actor than ever before. That said, the abrupt production shutdowns caused by the 2023 actors' and writers' strike was a reminder that it's always important to be prepared for disruptions as a working actor by saving money and having multiple income streams.

What's Some Good Advice?

Be (extremely) patient. Whitehair tells aspiring actors to go on IMDb, the Internet Movie Database, and look up their favorite actor's very first credits—knowing that this credit probably took a while for them to get. Then look at how long it took them to get from their first job to their first *recognizable* job, and you'll see how acting careers almost always take a long time to build and grow.

Don't attach yourself to any one part—or one vision of what your acting career should look like. "It may take longer than you thought it would," Whitehair said. "Daily life might look different than you thought it would. But you can always be an actor. You can always tell stories."

Audition for the casting directors, not for the specific role. Instead of trying to guess what casting directors want, it's better to showcase your personal strengths. Keep in mind that casting directors are not only trying to cast their current project; they're always on the lookout for talent for future projects.

Don't compare yourself to anyone. Actors can feel like they're being pitted against one another, and it's easy to become jealous, especially when people feel like there are limited opportunities. "But for me, I've been in L.A. fourteen years now, and to see people I knew in college or an acting class now be on a show—it's so exciting to me," Whitehair said. "And it proves to me that it's possible. This isn't a 'celebrity.' This is my buddy, my friend."

Don't let anyone tell you that you're too old to start acting. There are roles for all ages. People start their acting careers later in life for all sorts of reasons. They may get distracted by life challenges. They may be afraid of putting themselves out there. They may have been dissuaded from pursuing acting by loved ones.

As in any industry, it's easier to have an earlier start. But having other life experiences can also work in your favor, and one of the benefits of starting to act later in life may be that you have achieved financial stability.

Have a wellness plan. Professionals say that the actor's life is made of extreme highs—when you're on set, living the dream—which can also come with big crashes when the job is over, you're alone in your apartment, and you don't have anything lined up.

Many actors recommend therapy. "We're constantly going through the process of healing and breaking down, and sometimes your body doesn't understand that it's imagination, and it feels real," said actor Annie Gonzalez, best known for *Flamin' Hot* and *Gentefied*.

Have a plan for how to make use of your downtime so you don't spiral, Smith recommended. That's when you should update your social media and all your materials. Make lists of people you've worked with and whom you'd like to work with. See what connections you have. Start thinking about passion projects. Soak up culture. And rest. "Now you see it as a gift of time, not a curse," she said. "The reason it's a gift is because you could be creating your next project."

Find a solid community. Actors Nik Dodani (*The Parenting, Atypical*) and Vinny Chhibber (*Big Sky, For All Mankind*) are cofounders of The Salon, a forum for South Asians in entertainment with a mentorship program for mid-career talent. It started as a social gathering, but they soon realized how crucial it was for actors and creatives—especially in marginalized communities—to have spaces that allow them to have honest conversations about their struggles.

They try to be transparent with their mentees when they first meet. They'll tell them it's a very tough, competitive industry. You need to find people who will validate you when you are being mistreated and help you figure out how to navigate the systems.

Social media and word of mouth are simple ways to find communities that share your culture or goals. Those support systems help you feel confident and safe as you're exploring your own path.

"At the end of the day, you have to be in the driver's seat," Dodani said. "The only person who is going to be thinking about your career twenty-four-seven is you. But it's a lot easier when you don't feel like you're dealing with these struggles by yourself."

Don't let Hollywood be the center of your entire life. Acting is "the type of career where a lot of people fool themselves into putting everything into it," Park said. "They believe that everything has to be sacrificed to be successful in this."

You don't want your relationship with the industry to be an abusive, unbalanced one. Therapist Brian Torres, who works regularly with Hollywood clients, tries to get artists to pinpoint what drives them to act. Is it about telling stories or expressing yourself? Is it about the adrenaline of the stage or the power to change minds? He encourages actors to find other ways to feel fulfilled outside of the often brutal acting grind.

Expect some heartbreak. Park said the reality of pursuing a career in the entertainment industry is that you won't come out unscathed. "I think just by doing it, you get destroyed a little bit," he said. "In life too, right?"

He added, "It makes sense that the funnest job in the world is really hard to get. . . . If you want to experience that much fun for a living, you gotta go through some hoops."

CHAPTER 2

How to Parent a Child Actor

The acting bug can bite at any age, but when it bites one of your kids, you might soon find yourself trying to navigate strange and potentially treacherous waters as you schlepp your child to endless auditions, the occasional callback, and, if your child is one of the chosen few, a string of paying gigs.

Jeff Yang knows this intimately. While his family was living in New York, his then-eight-year-old son, Hudson, came home from school one day and insisted that he wanted to try acting. This newfound ambition apparently emerged after one of the boy's friends had told him she was auditioning to appear in commercials.

Believing that a father's job is sometimes to support the impractical and crazy dreams of his kids, provided that they don't lead down a bad path, Yang began taking his son to auditions. In Hudson's case, the dream proved not to be so crazy. He landed a speaking role in the second movie he auditioned for. Not long thereafter, the producers of the TV series *Fresh Off the Boat* picked him to play Eddie Huang, whose autobiography served as the show's cornerstone.

A role like that will be life-changing not just for the child but for the whole family.

"I basically gave up my job for Hudson's job," said Yang, who was a cultural reporter for the *Wall Street Journal*. His son's work required father and son to move to Los Angeles, and it prevented Yang from continuing in his beat; he couldn't write about two of the most important companies in the field, Disney and Fox, because his son's work created a conflict of interest for Yang.

If you have a child chasing a dream like Hudson's, your family will have to make a lot of sacrifices—especially if you have other kids who are not interested in acting. There will be sibling rivalry, tears shed, tantrums thrown. It can be hard for siblings to accept that their brother or sister gets perks—going to premieres, meeting Hollywood stars—that they don't. Television is a tough gig. Because of the demanding schedule, all of your other plans will be contingent on the needs of the production. That includes family vacations, school outings, graduation ceremonies, and proms.

"All of that ends up being at the whim, to a certain extent, of alignment among hundreds of other people and the warring priorities and schedules that they have," Yang said.

Good productions will try to protect child actors and accommodate their needs. Yet for a family with a busy child actor, the things that make up the typical childhood don't get as much priority as the work a child is doing.

Yang said he doesn't regret giving his son the chance to perform in the series, which ran for 116 episodes over six seasons. But he doesn't minimize the long-term implications of the choices the family made.

"To this day, Hudson wonders what it would have been like to have a traditional school experience. He still, I think, probably has felt more comfortable around adults than people his own age," he said. The time spent on set instead of with his peers left gaps in Hudson's education because of the experiences he missed, Yang said. "School isn't about only attending classes and doing homework." (Hudson Yang stayed the course after the series ended in 2020, when he was sixteen. Among other things, he's starred in his own reality-TV cooking series on the Asian Food Network, *Order Up with Hudson Yang*, and a feature film, *Honor Student*.)

How Does a Child Get Started as an Actor?

As any number of websites will tell you, nailing that first gig will require your child to audition repeatedly in the hope of impressing a casting director enough to be selected.

Kids who want to submit for an audition will need the standard calling cards for actors: headshots, a résumé listing their acting experience and training, and a demo reel (a short video of them performing)—initially, in a school play or just reading lines at home, but eventually in professional gigs. According to Backstage.com, they should also prepare two monologues to perform for the casting team.

Before you pull all that together, though, there are a few things to consider. First and foremost, your child must genuinely want to act.

It's important not to get your own ambitions mixed up with your child's. "Your kid has to be the driver. They have to want to do this," said Anne Henry, cofounder of the BizParentz Foundation, whose three children all acted before moving on to other pursuits.

If you already have a talented young athlete or musician in your home, you may have an inkling about how taxing it can be to support a child actor. You probably also understand that in addition to the rewarding moments in front of a camera, there are a lot of not-so-gratifying things your child will be doing, such as enduring countless auditions and spending hours training for roles they may not get.

"For kids who don't have the desire, the passion, the sense of enjoyment, it's incredibly challenging to continue to make the choices to do this," Yang said. "It's really important for parents not to be pushing them down a path without realizing that the choices made early on take kids down a road of inevitables. The more commitments, the more demands that are made on a child, the more this becomes who they are."

Some child actors have told him while chatting on set that they wished they had been given the freedom to spend less time chasing the acting dream and just be themselves more, because they would have become a different person—and, in some ways, a better one.

Couldn't My Child Break into Hollywood through TikTok?

There's a big difference between performing professionally in front of a camera and filming yourself for a social media post. Being good at the latter doesn't mean Hollywood will beat down your door with offers.

TikTok, Instagram, and YouTube have persuaded countless young people that anybody can make money by stepping in front of a camera. On social media, kids see other kids doing everyday things and somehow attracting huge numbers of followers, then monetizing them. They think they can follow that formula to fame and riches too.

But the reality of the business hasn't changed. The odds remain stacked against those trying to launch themselves into Hollywood stardom off the strength of their TikTok dance moves. Almost all the jobs that pay enough to be profitable still run through talent agents and studios.

Henry also cautions against young children putting their content and image on social media, given the number of predators online. Her organization strongly discourages child actors from using social media in their efforts to be discovered. Besides, she said, it doesn't work—even Justin Bieber, famed for his teenaged YouTube videos, had a talent manager to help him get signed by a major record label.

Multiple sites list open auditions for child actors, including Mandy, Backstage, Casting Networks, and Actors Access by Breakdown Services. However, some of these sites charge fees to view the listings or submit your child's materials to casting directors.

Is Moving to Los Angeles a Good Idea?

For many film, TV, and commercial gigs, Los Angeles is the place to be. But considering the stiff competition for a limited number of jobs, the pros advise against moving before your child has landed a role there.

Instead, they say, families outside of Southern California should let their kids bloom as actors in their hometown. "Don't make extreme sacrifices for something you don't know that you're ready for," Henry said.

Almost every large city has licensed talent agents, managers, theater companies, and places where a child can get good training and experience as an actor without having to pull up stakes and move to Hollywood. There's nothing wrong with swimming in a smaller pool, whether it's in Ohio or in suburban Los Angeles. "You should master that little pool before jumping into that bigger pool," Henry advised.

Chris Smith, national director for the Entertainment Community Fund's Looking Ahead program for young professional actors, said his organization sees many families move to Los Angeles or New York to give their children the chance to act on screen or stage. Moving to the largest, most expensive cities in the United States is incredibly stressful, and the cost, unfamiliarity, and work demands can overwhelm families, he said.

Before going that route, families should research what it will cost to rent an apartment in their new city, how they will get around, and how the move will affect the family members who aren't actors—and who might be left behind.

What Professional Help Does a Child Actor Need?

Most kids get their start acting on student productions or winning small roles through "open calls"—that is, auditions anyone can attend. To vie for bigger parts in higher-level productions, though, you will need professional representation, which for many child actors means a manager and an agent.

The difference between the two is subtle but important.

Managers aren't the ones who book gigs for your child (or rather, they're not *supposed to be* the ones doing that). But they can be the ones who introduce your child to writers and producers; who keep an eye on the roles being cast to make sure their clients know about good opportunities; and who can set you up with acting coaches, headshot photographers, and other service providers your child may need. They typically have a small roster of clients, and they're paid up to 20 percent of their client's earnings.

A manager can also help you navigate the thicket of labor laws and financial complications that far exceed anything you'd find in youth sports leagues or high-school marching bands.

Agents are licensed by the state where they practice and have the power to arrange auditions and negotiate contracts for their clients. They will be alerted by producers to "a whole matrix of potential slots and potential roles and potential opportunities" for their clients, Yang said, and they'll steer individual actors toward the ones they deem a fit. They typically collect 10 percent of the money their clients make from the contracts they negotiate.

Beyond managers and agents, there is a laundry list of other professionals out there waiting to help your child blossom—for a fee. Sadly, as in many talent-related industries, scammers abound, as do self-described experts who are more skilled at cashing checks than helping your child land speaking parts.

In California and New York, state law bars anyone in the "talent representation" business—managers, casting consultants, and the like—from promising to obtain gigs for an actor in exchange for an up-front fee. Instead, "talent services" can charge for training and advice, but they must offer refunds and post bonds. Those are important protections against scammers.

California law also requires talent services that work with minors to obtain a permit and pass an FBI background check designed to weed out registered sex offenders. New York has a similar requirement.

Those laws don't apply in other states, which often have little or no legal protections for child actors, Henry said. Nor do they help parents distinguish between capable professionals and hacks.

To find a representative or service provider you can trust, a good first step is to join a community of other parents of child actors. That's because people talk, Smith said—word spreads about talent representatives to avoid.

You'll also need to do your due diligence. That means scouring the web, social media, and online reviews for information on the people you're thinking of hiring. On its website (www.bizparentz.org), BizParentz offers more than thirty-two hundred words' worth of tips and suggestions for how to do this research, advising: "Your child's safety (and your wallet) depend on you."

"Above all," Smith said, "trust your gut. I've heard numerous stories of parents saying they encountered a situation that 'just felt off.' The hope is that parents and kids can trust their instincts and avoid challenging situations before encountering them."

One place to start is Amazon's IMDb.com, which tracks the credits earned by film and TV industry professionals. Look for people who've worked on productions you've heard of, and who have a track record of credits. You'll need to pay for a subscription to IMDbPro to access contact information for managers and agents.

Similarly, if your child is looking to join a theater company, Henry recommends doing a Google search to see if the group has its own performance space and if it has done "recognizable theater productions." Avoid any "pay to play" group that requires you to buy a block of tickets so your child can participate.

One thing BizParentz recommends is to pay for a single session—an assessment or consultation—with an acting teacher to get their thoughts on your child's strengths and weaknesses. "That's when you also can see if you vibe with this person, see if they give you the creeps," Henry said.

But never, ever agree to meet someone at a hotel. That's where most scammers conduct their business, when they're not defrauding people online, Henry said.

While you're evaluating the people you're hiring, you should also be measuring your child's interest and commitment. You're trying to find out whether your child's desire to act will stand up to the demands of the job before you make a major commitment with your checkbook.

Don't think that any one person holds the key to your child's future. "There are a million photographers; there are a million agents," Henry said. "There are so many people who can legitimately help."

What Kind of Feedback Should Parents Give Child Actors?

Avoid critiquing your child's auditions or work; instead, ask how your daughter or son felt about it and take your cues from their response. Trying to serve as your child's acting coach just creates a barrier between a child and a parent, Smith said, adding that it's hard for a kid to tell what role their parents are playing at any given moment when they've taken on more than one.

"The kid may only be a child actor for a few years, but the parental relationship is one that we hope will last their lifetime," he said. "So it can be better to leave the acting notes and critiques to their acting coaches, and instead prioritize that parent-child relationship."

Parents will almost certainly have to help their child handle the pain of rejection.

Auditions can be really challenging for a kid, in part because children have to perform without their parents in the room. Then, when you leave the audition, your child won't know whether it went well or poorly. No one will tell you if your child didn't get hired—you'll hear back only if they get the gig.

Yang called the process of getting roles *Squid Game* for child actors because "it's one of the most cruel and challenging and heartbreaking of competitions." Contrary to what a lot of parents think, he said, it's not a matter of try, try, and try again until your kid gets hired. Most children are cast as part of a family or a group of friends, which means productions are looking for a child whose ethnicity, race, and appearance will match a specific niche. "You can be perfect, but not perfect for the role."

Are There Hidden Costs to Consider?

Even if your child is eager to act, that doesn't mean you have the wherewithal to pursue that ambition. Your family needs to have the structure—and the finances—to be able to take the kid to an audition on a moment's notice, or make an audition tape at night, or head off for weeks to shoot a film.

A mother or father who is a child actor's "primary career parent" could easily spend as many hours in that role as she or he would as a full-time employee. At least one parent will have to be on set with a child actor. Parents who can't make those sacrifices have to be willing to tell their would-be Doogie Howser that the time just isn't right to make a play for film and TV work. Instead, they could focus on building their kid's acting ability at summer drama camp, say, or in community theater.

Canceling soccer games, birthday parties, and vacation trips because you're waiting to book a gig can become problematic for the kids as well as the parents.

There's also a risk of creating a hierarchy among a family's children if the child actor's schedule and commitments always trump those of the nonacting siblings. "Whether you're in the biggest TV show or not," Smith added, "you still need to clean up the room, you still need to take out the garbage, you still have chores to do around the house."

If you decide to pull up stakes and relocate to Southern California so your child can pursue more gigs in Hollywood, Smith said, that's your decision and you need to own it. And if your child decides two years later to drop acting in favor of playing video games, rescuing shelter pets, or pursuing some other hobby, he said, "go see a therapist, talk to your friends, share your loss—but don't take it out on the kid.

"If a child who had been acting decides to change course, that can be really difficult for the family—but it's most likely difficult for the kid too," Smith said. "In my experience, kids who have wanted to stop acting have shared with me that they've sat with the decision for years, but hesitated to share it with their parents for fear of how they would respond and for not wanting to disappoint them."

That's why it's essential for your child to know that the family can always talk about this if it's not working. Giving your child the emotional room to grow into the person they want to become can be not only a positive and affirming experience for the child but also a rewarding one for the family down the road.

What Else Should Parents Do to Help Their Child Actors?

The child actors who've been successful in life, not just in the industry, are the ones who had a robust safety net of parents, other adult role models, and friends outside the entertainment business. They played on a soccer team; they celebrated their quinceañera.

Acting is work, and there will be times when kids don't feel good about their performances. Spending time with friends and hobbies that are distinct from Hollywood, Smith said, "gives them a healthy break and a detachment from it."

But as much as parents may need the help of other Hollywood parents, they also need to be able to hang out with friends who aren't in that circle. Like their children, they need to have hobbies that let them escape from the acting business.

Is School Optional for Working Child Actors?

Not in California or New York. California requires every set to have a state-credentialed studio teacher to help child actors with both their education and their welfare; New York requires child actors to be taught by a certified teacher on set or remotely. In both states, school-aged children have to log at least three hours of schoolwork daily over the course of a week.

But the teachers on set aren't providing the curriculum, said Lois Yaroshefsky, a longtime on-set schoolteacher in California; instead, they expect child actors to bring at least three hours of work from the school they're attending. And if the school won't provide the material, parents should buy textbooks appropriate for their child's grade level.

Under California law, a production can't make children stay late to complete their three hours of coursework. Instead, those hours count against the maximum hours child actors can spend on set, which range from eight and one-half hours for six-year-olds to ten and one-half hours for seventeen-year-olds.

How Does a Parent Avoid Being "That Parent" on Set?

If your child manages to land a spot in a film or TV show, you'll need to know how to behave on set and what's expected of you. There are many practices and protocols that parents need to know, but there aren't a lot of good places to learn about them.

The best resources, Yang said, are other parents. "Find somebody who's been through the process to learn the language of how to tell your children what to expect, emotionally and psychologically, not just procedurally," he said.

In California, parents have the right to be within seeing or hearing distance whenever their child is working, and parents are expected to accompany their children on meal breaks and to makeup and wardrobe sessions. New York law gives parents the right to accompany a child actor under sixteen throughout the workday, or to designate another adult to do so.

The children hired as background actors are supposed to keep their distance from the principal players, as are their families. This group eats last at mealtimes, and the parents will have to supply their own chairs if they want to sit down on set.

"It makes it so much easier on everybody if they come in knowing" what's expected of them, Yaroshefsky said. It also helps if children have been fed before they show up in the morning, rather than trying to squeeze in breakfast on a busy set.

How a child ranks on the call sheet—the daily schedule laying out when each actor needs to be on set—is a frequent source of friction because it's seen as a pecking order. "Please, can you just be happy that your child is on the call sheet?" Yaroshefsky said. "Thousands of children tried out for this job."

What Resources Are Available to Guide Parents of Child Actors?

Here are some places that can help parents handle the challenges of parenting a child actor:

- SAG-AFTRA: The Screen Actors Guild–American Federation of Television and Radio Artists devotes part of its website to young performers and their parents, offering answers to frequently asked questions and some links to useful resources. It's aimed at union members, though.
- Looking Ahead: Developed in part by SAG-AFTRA, Looking Ahead offers several programs for actors ages nine to eighteen

in Southern California and New York City, including industry seminars, individual and family counseling, educational and career guidance, and group activities for kid actors. The L.A. branch is open to young actors who meet at least one of the required thresholds, such as having a professional theatrical contract or being a member of Actors' Equity Association.

- BizParentz.org: Henry and fellow parent Paula Dorn founded the organization to help explain new revisions to a state law that requires a portion of a minor actor's earnings to be placed into a trust until the child turns eighteen. Among a number of other topics, the nonprofit's website offers free information and advice on state laws that protect child actors, as well as tips for how to avoid talent-services scams.
- *Hollywood Mom Blog*: This blog—and its accompanying newsletter and Facebook page—is heavily oriented toward getting gigs for child actors. In addition to including notices of casting calls, it also offers lists of classes and workshops for young actors and of talent services, such as casting counselors and headshot photographers. Unlike the BizParentz site, the blog accepts some advertising.
- The Studio Teachers: A project of the International Association of Theatrical Stage Employees Local 884 in California, this site provides a directory of certified studio teachers and their work histories. It also has a useful chart detailing how much time child actors in each age group must spend with a teacher and how many hours per day they are allowed to remain on set.

CHAPTER 3

How to Become a Voice Actor

As kids in suburban Houston, Stephanie Beatriz and her little sister would entertain themselves for hours with a Fisher-Price tape recorder, doing mock interviews, commercials, and songs in a variety of voices for fictional radio stations.

That inventiveness became the foundation for Beatriz's work in front of a mic as an adult, doing voices for animated TV shows. Imagination, voice actors say, is integral to the job.

The shows and VHS tapes she watched as a child offered not just inspiration but also a safe place to explore all the things that are scary for children, such as growing up and deciding who you want to be in the world.

"It wasn't lost on me as a kid that the heroes of the stories often didn't look like me," said Beatriz, who was born in Argentina and moved to the United States when she was two. "And animation was one place where the heroes in the story sometimes didn't look like anybody I knew, because they were out of somebody else's imagination. That world felt a little more accessible to me."

Years later, Beatriz would gain fame playing an intimidatingly acerbic police officer on the TV series *Brooklyn Nine-Nine.* At the same time, she became immersed in animated worlds again as an in-demand voice actor, breathing life into characters in the cult favorite

BoJack Horseman, Disney's *Encanto*, Amazon Prime's *Hazbin Hotel*, and multiple other projects.

Typically, each voice actor in a cast works individually, like a soloist before a conductor with no other members of the orchestra onstage. The actors have a lot of blanks to fill in, performing not just the lines on the page but also the grunts, groans, and all the other sounds coming out of their characters' mouths.

The ensemble productions Beatriz has been featured in represent just a fraction of the gigs that voice actors perform. Many of the jobs involve reading a script into a microphone at a recording studio for a production that needs a narrator—a radio or TV commercial, for example, or a corporate training video.

Some voice work can even be done from the comfort of your own home, provided that you've invested a few thousand dollars in a recording studio capable of professional-quality remote work.

Whatever the gig, it's a good time to be in this field—although with AI and voice cloning, it's not clear how long the good times will last. The proliferation of cable networks and then streaming services offering original programming has led to an explosion in animated shows in need of voice actors. The demand has also been fueled by the rise of audiobooks, podcasts, serialized dramas, online educational materials, and video games. As the opportunities have expanded, so has the number of people finding careers doing voice-overs.

Which is not to suggest that it's easy to break in. As with anything in the entertainment industry, you'll need skills and perseverance. Having an agent helps too.

What Qualities Do You Find in a Successful Voice Actor?

Narrating an audiobook, providing the voice-over for a video game, performing lines as an animated character, and making a commercial pitch are markedly different pursuits that demand different skills.

But one thing that seems common among voice actors is a fertile and well-practiced imagination.

Beatriz, a theater actress who came to Los Angeles from the Oregon Shakespeare Festival eager to do voice work alongside films and TV shows, usually goes into a session with the script and a couple of images. The sights, sounds, and details that aren't written on the pages of the script? She fills those in with her mind. "It's so fun and so freeing."

For some actors, though, having all those gaps to fill isn't such a good time, said Jen Rudin, an independent casting agent. "If you're not the type of actor who likes to play around and have fun, it's going to be torture for you. It's going to be agony."

Having some experience onstage or in front of a camera helps—even if you're recording audiobooks. As audiobook narrator Chanté McCormick put it, "How else would you know how to approach a book that has sixty characters in it if you're not used to analyzing scripts?"

An acting background isn't as important to the people hiring talent for advertisements. Still, having some experience as an actor can help you understand and connect emotionally with an ad's script, however short it may be.

How Do You Get Started?

A common entry point is freelance gigs found through websites that specialize in voice actors. These include Voices.com, Voice123.com, BunnyStudio.com, StudioCenter.com, and Backstage.com, or, for audiobooks, Amazon's Audiobook Creation Exchange (www.acx.com). There are also less specialized sites for freelancers where you can find voice-over work, including Upwork.com and Fiverr.com. But you can't expect to land a job just because you have a voice like James Earl Jones.

Most professionals say it's wise to invest in some classes on voice acting. An online search will reveal classes on voice acting not just for film and television but also for commercials, audiobooks, video games, and other niches.

McCormick studied theater in college and was aiming for a career in television and film when she went to a seminar on audiobook narration hosted by SAG-AFTRA. Intrigued, she later took a five-day workshop with a veteran narrator to prepare for an audition on Amazon's ACX.

There's no shortage of people, casting houses, and recording studios offering voice instruction online; for an extensive directory of services for voice artists in Los Angeles, New York, Chicago, and regional markets, consult the Voice Over Resource Guide (www.voiceoverresourceguide.com).

Joe Zieja, a former military intelligence officer who's worked in animation, video games, corporate video, and commercials, is a believer in the learn-by-doing approach. But to help fill what he saw as a void in the market, he launched an online educational program, Joe Zieja's Learnvoiceacting.com, to provide comprehensive instruction in different aspects of the business.

In addition to voice-acting techniques, such as breaking down scripts and creating characters, Zieja's sessions cover where to find work, how to build a recording studio without spending tens of thousands of dollars, and how to approach scripts in different genres. One reason he started the classes, Zieja said, was that young actors asked him the same questions over and over about the business and none of those issues was being covered by private voice-acting coaches.

Another good first step would be to check out the numerous Facebook groups that support voice actors. A search for "voice acting" or "voice actors" will yield multiple groups, both public and private, that dispense tips and job leads. Those are potentially rich sources of new connections too. If you're going to take voice-acting classes, it's best to take them from someone whose work you know.

For audiobooks, you should check out the webinars and guidance that the Audio Publishers Association (www.audiopub.org) offers its members and the mentoring programs at Penguin Random House and Macmillan. The audiobook publisher Audible also offers "Mic Check," a series of behind-the-scenes interviews with popular narrators.

One more option is to scour YouTube for guidance. "You can get a college degree in voice-over from YouTube," said Thomas Copeland, who specializes in voice acting for commercials. "You can get a degree in anything from YouTube."

To land a job, you'll need to record a demo—a sixty- to ninety-second MP3 that compiles samples of your script-reading talents. You can find free scripts to record at EdgeStudio.com, including snippets from comedy routines, travelogue narrations, educational videos, TV commercials, and multiple other genres of voice work.

There are plenty of recording studios that offer to help you make a demo. But the fees can run from $1,500 to $2,500.

You'll eventually want more than one demo so you can present different styles and skills to different employers—for example, a demo for commercials, another for animation, a third for audiobooks. The pros offer diverging views on where to make the demo, however.

Some, like voice actor and coach Kathy Grable, say it's worth the money to pay for professional studio time because you want the best sound you can possibly get for your demo. Others insist that you can record yourself at home instead. In fact, many gigs, particularly in the freelance world, require you to do your own recording—your client isn't paying for studio time.

Be forewarned: The gear required to produce broadcast-quality audio at home can cost $2,500 just for the basics. You'll need a high-quality microphone, as well as a computer and an adapter that converts the microphone's analog signals into digital ones. Then you'll need a way to isolate your recordings from the noise of the outside world; some newcomers set up in a closet and use the clothes to minimize noise, while more established artists shell out hundreds or even thousands of dollars for a dedicated recording booth. Finally, if you're working with an engineer and possibly a director in a remote studio, you'll need a special kind of phone line or a program such as Source-Connect from Source-Elements.com to transmit your audio feed without glitches.

You don't have to be a sound engineer, but you do have to know how to use digital recording and editing tools, even when you're working with a remote engineer. You'll also have to make sure your recordings meet the technical specifications set by the company that will publish your work, which can include requirements for volume, dynamic range, sound quality, and even the names chosen for your files.

Nevertheless, the tools don't make the performer. "Just because you have a beautiful sound booth," Rudin said, "that doesn't mean you'll be qualified."

The online freelance job boards invite voice actors to upload their profiles and demos so producers looking for talent can find them. You may have to pay for that service. For example, Voices.com lets you put your profile and samples on the site for free but charges $499 a year to match you automatically with freelance opportunities.

Rudin said voice acting is like any other job in the entertainment industry in that connections are crucial. "Somebody has to open up a door for you."

Even then, it can be tough to break in. Beatriz said that no one really wants to collaborate with an artist who doesn't have a track record of accomplishments to vouch for their skills. "It was really my work on *Brooklyn Nine-Nine* that allowed people to trust that I would be able to come in and perform."

Having an agent can open more doors, especially in Hollywood. Copeland said that when he signed with an agency that specializes in voice-overs for commercials, it elevated him into a higher stratum of work, including national campaigns and TV spots.

You could consult the self-proclaimed "Official Agent List: Actor Talent Agency Directory" at agentlist.org to find names and contact information of agencies that represent voice actors. Or instead of approaching agencies cold, ask your peers, teachers, and employers for the names of agents they trust; try to get colleagues with agents to introduce you to their representatives.

Either way, don't rush to get representation when you're new in the field; the pros say it helps to have a track record as a voice actor before trying to sign with an agent.

Once you do have some professional credits, you'll be eligible to join the National Association of Voice Actors (navavoices.org), a relatively new, dues-supported organization that offers free professional development classes and access to a group health plan, among other benefits. The annual cost is $175.

What Are the Career Paths?

Voice actors often establish themselves by doing a lot of freelance work, then shift into higher-paying gigs with major studios and larger advertisers.

The low-hanging fruit is voice-overs for corporate training and online instructional videos. Voice actors greatly undervalue corporate work because it's not sexy, Zieja said. "Teaching somebody about semiconductors is unglamorous."

These jobs were the key for Zieja to leave the career he'd built in military intelligence and law enforcement and move to Los Angeles to pursue voice work in animation and video games.

Like their counterparts in front of a camera, voice actors can become directors and producers. And in the audiobook world, narrators who enjoy editing audio can become sound engineers for other voice actors.

There's also coaching other voice actors, as Grable and Zieja do.

How Do You Make Money? And What Kind of Money?

Earning a living from voice acting can be a grind, especially at first.

"It's like any gig in acting," Grable said. "You could have a good year; [then] you could have a year that's ugh."

Major studios and advertisers have contracts with SAG-AFTRA that set a pay scale for the various types of jobs voice actors perform, including films and TV shows, commercials, video games, movie trailers, and corporate videos. Those normally pay a set amount for the first use—for example, you would receive more than $400 for an audio commercial played just in Los Angeles—then small amounts for subsequent uses.

The residuals on a heavily used commercial that runs on national networks can be a gold mine. Copeland said a friend did the voice for an Orange Julius commercial and it stayed on the air so long that he paid off his mortgage with the residuals.

Fewer commercials are being run on national TV networks than a decade ago, however. A spot run regionally is far less lucrative for voice actors than one that's broadcast all across the country.

Nonunion projects are not bound by the SAG-AFTRA rates, so they'll pay considerably less for voice talent. As a freelancer scouring for jobs online, Copeland said, "you kind of have to swim through the crap to find the gold."

Freelancers doing audiobooks on Amazon's ACX may be offered a slice of the book sales instead of a fixed fee, but that model is generally reserved for books with iffy sales prospects. "If they know their book is going to sell, they're not going to split the revenue with you," McCormick said. "They'll just pay you the fee."

SAG-AFTRA has contracts with book publishers too, so union pay scales may apply there. Union scale is a floor, not a ceiling. For jobs that require extra work, such as dialect training, the pros advise negotiating a higher rate.

As with just about any job in the entertainment industry, how much you earn as a voice actor will depend mainly on how full your calendar is and how big your clients are. According to ZipRecruiter, job postings for voice actors in 2025 offered $48 per hour on average, with 50 percent of the gigs paying between $38 and $57 per hour.

How Is This Career Different from Ten or Twenty-Five Years Ago?

One huge change is the shift from recording studios to home studios, which has slashed the cost of production and opened the field to more voice actors. As it has been in many other industries, the Internet has also been a boon to freelancers and part-timers, making it easier for them to find and attract gigs.

AI has also emerged as a potential threat. Professionals say it's important to make sure the recording you submit cannot be used for any other purpose without your explicit approval. Otherwise, you run the risk that your voice will be cloned by AI and used to do work that you should have been paid to do.

If you have an agent or the gig is covered by a SAG-AFTRA contract, chances are good that you'll be informed of any potential AI risk. Otherwise, you'll need to examine the contract terms carefully to avoid having your voice cloned and used without your authorization, potentially putting yourself out of business.

The National Association of Voice Actors site offers a sample contract rider for voice actors to use to protect against having their voices cloned and exploited. It also lays out a series of questions that voice actors can ask before signing up for a job that has an AI component; the goal is to find out in advance whether your voice will be used to replace you or other actors on future projects.

As the field has expanded, voice actors have become more focused on the niches created, such as narrating podcasts or mimicking film and TV actors for overdubs. The companies that employ voice actors, meanwhile, are beginning to recognize the need to diversify their rosters.

"All these industries, collectively, are starting to understand their impact on the world," Beatriz said. "How that affects the arts is that there's much more acknowledgment now, I believe, that the heroes in the storytelling that we've seen in television and film are often cast in one way, and the stars of those shows reflect those heroes—white, straight, cis[gender], heteronormative people. That's changing.

"People want to see stories told by everyone. They want to see themselves as the heroes of these stories. The cool, amazing, incredible, hopeful thing I see happening in the arts is that the characters that are the leads are more and more reflecting the people who fill up this world. All the kinds of people."

Copeland said a similar shift was happening in the advertising world. The announcer voice that dominated in previous decades is out, replaced by a more conversational tone—like a neighbor or friend chatting with them. The result is more opportunities for different types of voices.

What's Some Good Advice?

Remember that a good voice is not enough. A distinctive, appealing voice can definitely be an asset. But professionals agree that you won't land a job just based on the quality of your voice. It's the quality of your acting. "This really is an acting job," McCormick said—even when you're narrating a nonfiction book.

Keep in mind that, conversely, your acting skills won't necessarily make you good at voice-over. That's because acting solely with your voice isn't the same as performing in front of a camera.

Build up your skills before making a demo. "Spending thousands of dollars on a demo when you're just starting out is definitely not a way to be prudent in your spending," Rudin said. "It takes practice."

Audition for everything you can tackle. Zieja said he'd auditioned well over forty thousand times from 2013 to 2021. "That's how I figured out what I was good at."

Study the medium. If you want to work in animation, Rudin said, you need to watch as much animation as you can to explore the emotions the actors convey with their voices, while also examining their energy and pacing.

Similarly, Zieja and Copeland advise listening to commercials and trying to mimic what the voice actors do. There are a number of websites, including Edge Studio and Voices.com, that offer free scripts that voice actors can use to practice.

Save aggressively when you're starting out. McCormick advised setting aside enough to cover six months of expenses. Having a cushion lets you be more selective about the jobs you take, Zieja said. He added, "You can only be as picky as your bank account allows you to be."

CHAPTER 4

How to Become a Stunt Performer

More than 70 percent of movies released between 2000 and 2016 featured at least one stunt professional, film data researcher Stephen Follows determined. In Westerns and action and crime films, stunt professionals make up approximately 8 percent of the crew.

Some stunts are flashier—people flying around on wires (in *The Matrix* and *Mission: Impossible*), performing stylized fight scenes (in classic Bruce Lee films), or driving cars under a train, out of a plane, or off a ramp into the ocean (in the *Fast and the Furious* movies). Some are quieter or more intimate; for example, a drowning or domestic violence scene. Some are funny—people often trip or fall in comedies.

The job of a stuntperson is to take a beating, fly across the room, or flip across the table so the actor doesn't have to. Actors often want to do their own stunts, and some do—like Tom Cruise, Keanu Reeves, and Michelle Yeoh. But many don't have the physical training it requires to perform these stunts safely. A stunt performer with a similar look can shoot the riskier parts of the scene, and it'll be edited so seamlessly that most audience members won't be able to tell which shots were done by the actor or the double.

Stunt performing isn't just about the ability to do the gravity-defying stunt. It's also about being able to do it safely over and over again for multiple takes.

The department head of the stunt team, who plans out the action sequences and manages the stunt performers, for decades was known as the stunt coordinator.

But in 2024, the Screen Actors Guild and Directors Guild of America (DGA) approved the first-ever credit of "stunt designer" to give respect and recognition to the creative architects, leaders, and creators of these sequences. The inaugural film credit went to veteran stunt coordinator Chris O'Hara, second-unit director and president of Stunts Unlimited, for his work on *The Fall Guy*, which stars Ryan Gosling as a stuntman.

In 2025, the Board of Governors of the Academy of Motion Picture Arts and Sciences announced a new official category for achievement in stunt design. Films released in 2027 will be eligible for the award at the 2028 Oscars.

Stunt coordinators (or designers) work with the directors to figure out what kind of action is needed for the scene. If they're coordinating a fight scene, it's similar to choreographing a dance. They can make fights look realistic with punches that don't land and swords that are floppy and fake.

They work with the camera department to understand how the action is being filmed. Sometimes the stunt needs to be subtle. Other times, the stunt should have the audience at the edge of their seats. Stunt coordinators also work with costume, hair, and makeup teams, who help the stunt performers avoid injury (extra padding in the pants) and make the stunt look more realistic (dirt in the hair after a nasty fall or blood soaking into a shirt after a stab wound).

And, most important, they're responsible for ensuring the safety of the entire team. Part of that task is hiring the right professionals to handle the technical demands of a scene. Though accidents happen, the stunt performer's job is to make their work look more dangerous than it actually is, professionals say.

As a teenager growing up in Germany, stuntman Ryan Sturz and his younger brother would get junk cars that were about to be disposed of and film their own car stunts. Sturz would put on knee and elbow pads, and his brother would drive into him as he jumped up onto the roof to practice rolling off.

"When I did my first professional car hit, I was amazed at how slowly the car was traveling," he said. "They were probably going ten miles an hour slower than what we had been doing as youngsters."

Despite how it looks, the stuntman profession's fatality rate is nowhere near that of a police officer, airline pilot, fisherman, logger, truck driver, or farmer, according to data from the U.S. Bureau of Labor Statistics. But it can be a risky profession—there were at least 194 serious accidents and forty-three deaths on film and TV sets from 1990 to 2014, according to a study by the Associated Press.

What Qualities Do You Find in a Successful Stunt Performer?

Stunt performers need a strong athletic background. Think gymnastics, martial arts, cheerleading, diving, or motocross—sports in which you develop body awareness, timing, coordination, and discipline.

You should have an adrenaline-seeking personality, but it's not the wild ones who succeed. Stunt performers tend to be very calm, practical, and responsible. They're the type of people who can quickly scan the surroundings and know they need to put pads on any tables with sharp corners.

You also have to be nimble and have solid control of your body as an instrument. Sometimes that means having the dexterity to make small adjustments—for example, turning your head to hide your face from the camera while sticking the motorcycle landing. Other times, it means knowing your body well enough to understand how many safe takes you can perform.

Noah Garret, who doubled for four characters in *Cobra Kai*, had to perform a scene where Robby kicks Miguel over a rail. The character Miguel hits another rail and then tumbles down some stairs. At first, Garret was hooked to a decelerator, a cable controlled by technicians to slow the impact, but the tumble looked unnatural. After assessing the risk, Garret opted to do it without the decelerator and just went for it. A bold one-and-done take felt less risky to him than having to do it multiple times.

How Do You Get Started?

Many people come in with a specialty—whether it's martial arts, high falls, driving skills, or water stunts. But professionals say it's best to be well-rounded, so you can be a versatile asset on set.

You should learn how to do basic fighting and pratfalls. That includes getting punched and falling, rolling over a table, twenty-foot falls, basic wire work (being suspended in the air on wires to simulate flying or falling), swimming, and scuba diving. Movie fighting is mostly about kicks, punches, and throws, so any martial arts that teach those skills will be helpful. Kali is also helpful to learn weapons.

Aspiring stunt performers can also take courses to sharpen their skills. The Stunt Performers Academy, started by veteran stunt performer and designer Banzai Vitale, holds a three-week intensive program in Los Angeles. The United Stuntman's Association runs its International Stunt School in Seattle, Washington, which offers two programs each summer: a three-week stunt performer course and a weeklong aerial course that teaches wire work, high falls, how to use an air ram (which simulates an explosion by catapulting a stunt performer into the air), ratcheting (another technique to launch a stunt performer into the air or into a wall), and rappelling (the skill rock climbers use to scale up and down a mountain).

It's also important to know how to handle a car and drive a stick shift. Sturz took classes at the Motion Picture Driving Clinic fifteen years ago, and after a decade of working in the film industry, he took over the school as owner and lead instructor. The clinic's programs teach aspiring stunt drivers basic skills, including 90-degree slides and the Rockford turn, where the car goes in reverse and then spins 180 degrees before speeding off.

There are also other stunt specialties. In *Eternals*, Sturz did stunt rigging, which is when stunt performers use ropes and pulleys to make people look like they're flying. He also specializes in horse stunts, which are common in Westerns and other period films when riders are falling off their horses. Another specialty is water stunts. In a memorable *Baywatch* episode, stunt veterans Alex Daniels (David Hasselhoff's longtime double) and Brian Keaulana performed a fight scene underneath a boat.

As you train, understand that your community becomes your network. When you meet working stunt professionals, ask them where they train and what classes they are taking. Join them and make friends. They're the ones who will share tips and perhaps pass on a job if they are unavailable.

"It's all about who you know" is even more true in the stunt industry because it's not just about finding people you like working with: Your team's safety is on the line. People hire folks they can trust. Either they'll turn to the people they train with, day in and day out, because they know their skill level—and what they can be counted on to execute safely. Or they'll hire folks someone they trust can vouch for.

You should also create content with other stunt performers. You'll learn camera skills and you can include the footage in your demo reel, a short video compilation you'll need to show off your skills and convince people to hire you.

What Are the Career Paths?

There are different levels of stunt performers. A stunt double matches an actor's look and performs the stunt in place of the actor. Those newer to stunt work on set usually start as one of the nondescript stunt performers; for example, those running away in the background. Specialists are hired for more extreme stunts. If you need someone to be thrown off a one-hundred-foot building, for example, you need a high-fall specialist. There are also people who help with the execution of the stunt. Stunt riggers handle a lot of the technical equipment—including pulling people wearing wires and harnesses to make them look like they are flying.

Many professionals say that your career starts when you join the union. Stunt professionals are represented in SAG-AFTRA, alongside actors, dancers, and other performers. You don't want to take non-union jobs as a stunt performer because of unclear insurance arrangements and the reality of injuries in this work. A common way for stunt performers to join SAG-AFTRA is to work three days as a background actor. (Be sure the work is covered by a union contract.) You may not do any stunts, but you can observe how a set works. You can also get hired for a job that will apply for a waiver to get you into the union.

Once you've gotten enough experience as a stunt performer, a common career track is to move up gradually toward management and filmmaking.

The stunt designer is the department head in charge of hiring the stunt performers, as well as working with the directors, producers, or showrunners to design the action sequences. Just like it takes time for stunt coordinators to trust someone enough to hire them as a stunt performer, it takes time to prove you can handle the responsibility of coordinating.

The coordinator choreographs all the stunts, but if the project demands it, there might be a fight choreographer or water coordinator to handle specific scenes. Normally, there's just one stunt coordinator, but bigger-budget action projects may have several.

In recent years, more stunt coordinators have become second-unit directors, who often help shoot elaborate action sequences. Some, including Chad Stahelski (the *John Wick* franchise) and David Leitch (*Bullet Train*), have gone on to be blockbuster directors.

But for those who prefer to stick to performing, another common trajectory is to take on more acting jobs, especially as you age.

How Do You Make Money? And What Kind of Money?

The 2026 SAG-AFTRA base rates for stunt professionals specifically in the entertainment industry can look fairly high. But for most stunt professionals, even veterans, the work has busy and slow periods.

Stunt performers get paid a minimum of $1,246 per day; the weekly rate is $4,646. Stunt performers who are hired under a guaranteed term of ten to nineteen weeks must make a minimum of $3,715 per week; the minimum for a guaranteed term of twenty weeks or more is $3,091 per week. Performers get paid extra for particularly dangerous or difficult stunts. Stunt coordinators earn a minimum of $1,246 per day or $4,646 per week. Stunt coordinators employed for more than one episode must get a minimum of $1,938 a day or $7,643 a week.

According to 2025 data from the Economic Research Institute's SalaryExpert database, the mean annual salary for a stunt performer in the United States is $57,689. Even successful stunt professionals look for other streams of income. One option is to find a workplace where you'll be meeting a lot of stuntpeople and training with them. For example, you could work in a stunt gym, which provides professional stunt classes, a martial arts studio, or a freerunning gym with a community of people training in parkour and acrobatics.

Another popular job is live performances at amusement parks, such as Knott's Berry Farm or Universal Studios. In shows at the parks, stunt professionals fall off high ledges into the water and dodge fake bullets. Performing consistently in front of an audience is good training. Glassdoor's job site estimates that a stunt performer at Knott's Berry Farm earns $34,000 to $48,000 per year, while the pay range at Universal Studios is $48,000 to $89,000 per year.

Stunt professionals could also consider acting, since they're already comfortable in front of the camera.

How Is This Career Different from Ten or Twenty-Five Years Ago?

Decades ago, there used to be very few women doing stunts. Now, with more female leads, more women are needed for action scenes. As of 2024, only about a quarter of all stunt professionals in SAG-AFTRA were women, but stuntwomen have begun to get more recognition in the industry. In 2020, the documentary *Stuntwomen: The Untold Holiday Story* was released, tracing the history of stuntwomen in the entertainment industry. That same year, the Association of Women Drivers, the first all-female stunt driving team in Hollywood, was formed.

Another advancement is the integration of practical stunts and visual effects. There is some anxiety about whether visual effects will take over stunt performances, but the ability to enhance stunts in post-production can also make risky actions safer and foster creativity.

"There are some stunts that you might have been able to do five times," Garret said, before you get exhausted and it becomes too much of a risk. But if they can put a pad down on the ground and have visual effects get rid of the pad in the scene in post-production, performers can do the same stunt ten to twenty times, but more safely, he said.

What's Some Good Advice?

Learn how to work a camera. It's becoming more popular to have stunt performers help with stunt pre-visualization ("previz stunts"), which is when they film a fight scene themselves to give a director a sense of the action. That's a good entry point for people who want a say in the creative process. You'll learn how the performance happens in coordination with the camera, and that helps performers learn to adjust their movements for the camera.

Commit. Doing stunts has to be a lifestyle, the professionals agree. "Those first few jobs, they are hard," Vitale said. "If anyone is thinking, 'I'm going to give this six months, and if it doesn't work, then I'm going to go,' I tell them, 'You might as well just go now.' It's hard enough to succeed when you're passionate and you absolutely want it."

PART 2

WRITING

CHAPTER 5

How to Become a Writer for Television and Film

The job of a Hollywood writer can be lucrative and fulfilling, if you manage to land one. You're an integral part of conceptualizing films and TV shows that people love—when they're done right. Your stories can make people laugh, ease their stress, get their pulse pounding, or scare the living daylights out of them. You're creating characters and scenarios that make people feel seen or help them empathize with others.

But it's imperative for aspiring Hollywood writers to understand that the job is not always about getting to write whatever you want. In most cases, Hollywood writers are hired to help execute someone else's vision. Making a film or TV show is a collaborative process, no matter how much the studio paid for the script. The writer's job is to create the blueprint, not to design and build the house.

Your love for script writing needs to be completely detached from the result. Another way to put it: If you're a poet, short story writer, or novelist, you might work with an editor or publisher to bring your words to your audience. If you're a Hollywood writer, your audience will not read your words. Nothing can happen without your words as a foundation—they may be the first step of the filmmaking process—but the final product is the result of what everybody else in the production builds from your blueprint. The result of your work could look better than you ever imagined. Or it could look nothing like you ever imagined. You have no control over that, as a writer in Hollywood.

And that assumes your script even gets made. Most of your scripts won't. The Writers Guild of America registers about sixty-five thousand scripts a year, and fewer than 3 percent of them get made. In the beginning of your career, you're writing to get better at writing—and to create a portfolio that will get you a job to write more. Even experienced writers don't expect all their work to see the light of day. But even if what you were hired to write gets shelved, you still get paid for your work. It's part of the job.

It's also important to understand that the role of a screenwriter in film is different from that of a writer for television. Film is a director's medium. The dream scenario for a screenwriter is for the screenplay you wrote on your own initiative—a speculative screenplay, or "spec" script—to capture the fancy of a director, producer, or high-profile actor who will help get the project financed and green-lit. But a lot of the time, you will be hired by somebody to develop an idea. Or you'll be hired to rewrite someone else's script. Some writers may be invited to consult on the production or post-production process, but often a writer's work is done after pre-production, the preparation time before filming begins.

Television, on the other hand, is a writer's medium. The lead of a project is the showrunner, the head of the writers' room. The promise of becoming a TV writer is that when you work your way up and eventually become a showrunner, you will have creative control of your project. While film writing can be done in solitude, TV writing is a team sport. Processes vary depending on the genre (multicamera comedy, half-hour comedy, or hour drama), but typically, TV scripts are outlined as a group before being assigned to individual writers. After the draft is written, everyone continues to give notes.

What Qualities Do You Find in a Successful Film or TV Writer?

Being a strong writer is a requirement, but so is being an idea generator. That's true whether you're brainstorming about episodes for a TV show with colleagues in a writers' room or pitching to producers who are trying to develop a project.

The creative process has to be something that drives you in everyday life. It's not just about having a strong work ethic. You must have an insatiable curiosity about the world. Hollywood writers, whether they have a job or not, are always consuming news, watching plays, bingeing TV shows, reading novels, and thinking about what their next story could be.

You have to be persistent. It's hard enough to get a job, but writing jobs in Hollywood are gig work, so you have to find another one after the current one is finished. It's a constant hustle, with recessions and strikes making it even more challenging.

The job also requires resilience. In television, for example, dozens of scripts for pilot episodes are commissioned a year, a small percentage of them are made, and a smaller percentage are picked up, expanded into a series, and aired. Full scenes and episodes could be cut at the last minute due to budget issues. If your best work ends up on the cutting-room floor—or not even filmed—it can be crushing. But you have to keep moving forward and getting excited about working on other projects.

How Do You Get Started?

Write a lot. Start by getting scriptwriting software—such as Final Draft, Fade In, Arc, or Highland—and learning how to format a script. If cost is an issue, Trelby, Story Architect, and WriterSolo are examples of free software, and WriterDuet, which makes it easy to collaborate with a writing partner, offers to assist on your first three screenplays for free.

Read screenwriting books such as *Adventures in the Screen Trade* by William Goldman; *Save the Cat* by Blake Snyder; *Screenplay* by Syd Field; and *Story: Substance, Structure, Style, and the Principles of Screenwriting* by Robert McKee. Scroll through online guides, such as those compiled by Final Draft, ScreenCraft, and No Film School. Go on YouTube to watch Writers Guild Foundation panels, the *Hollywood Reporter*'s roundtable, and the *Los Angeles Times*' *The Envelope* interviews, where screenwriters offer personal stories and advice.

Dissect the scripts of your favorite movies, which can easily be found online on sites such as Simply Scripts, Drew's Script-O-Rama, and StudioBinder. Understand how the writers took a situation and turned it into a story. Analyze whether the characters have agency and what their inner conflicts are. Figure out why certain jokes work and others fall flat. Use all that information to figure out your own writing process. Do you like to start by diving into the dialogue and characters or by mapping out the entire structure of the screenplay? Do you like writing to the sound of music or do you need silence? Do you think better when you pace? Do you need to read your work out loud? It's important to find a sustainable writing process and routine that works for you, because when you're hired, you will often be given a certain number of weeks to deliver a script, and it's up to you to manage that time and meet the deadline.

Make sure your portfolio is eye-catching and unique. Imagine this: An intern or assistant is often the first person reading a pile of screenplays, looking for the best ones to pass on to their bosses. If your screenplay is in a pile of twenty, how will it stand out? It's imperative to capture a reader's attention from the very first page. Hollywood creatives are constantly reading screenplays and scripts. You don't want them to feel like this is a story they've seen over and over again—one anybody could have written.

For TV jobs, there are two types of scripts you need in your portfolio:

- Original sample script: This is your own idea for a TV pilot. Write your passion, the stories you want to tell—and the stories that only you can tell. They will come out better. When you've finished your passion project, write other scripts that can show your range as a writer.
- Spec script for an existing series: This is where you write in the style of a TV show already on the air. Use a current show that you know very well and feel as though you could get hired for.

When Michael Golamco, the screenwriter of *Always Be My Maybe*, and co-founder of the production company Imminent Collision, was trying to break into Hollywood writing, he was a playwright who had collected more than thirty ideas for TV shows. His manager chose ten and told Golamco to write a one-page synopsis on each. Then they picked six of those to expand. They kept whittling it until they nailed down his two best pitches. That's what got him his first writing job, on the prime-time series *Grimm*. It takes years to sell a screenplay or get hired for a show. But it's a numbers game, so you have to keep trying—and be very methodical about it. There are many ways to break in, but here are some common ones.

Working as an assistant. It's difficult to get a job as a writer's assistant because the openings are not always listed. Nevertheless, keep an eye out for postings on sites such as EntertainmentCareers.net, ShowbizJobs.com, LinkedIn, and Indeed, and ask around about secret Facebook groups that act as whisper networks. Those who are hiring often get recommendations and referrals through word of mouth—which is why networking is extremely important.

Gennifer Hutchison—the executive producer of *Lord of the Rings: Rings of Power* who also wrote for *Breaking Bad* and *Better Call Saul*—is an example of someone who went the assistant route. Her first job out of college was as an office production assistant on *Nash Bridges*, which she heard about from a production coordinator who was recruiting recent graduates from her university in San Francisco. From there, she became a production assistant in the writers' room at *The X-Files* and continued to move up.

Being accepted into a writing program. Fellowships abound, but they are very competitive. Early in his career, Lucas Brown Eyes—a writer for *Duster* and *Alexa & Katie*—saw only two fellow Native screenwriters in the industry, and they both came from the Walt Disney Television Writing Program. So he applied and got in. "All of this is kind of like winning the lottery," he said. He was one of eight people accepted to the Disney program, and he remembers that about two thousand applied.

The Writers Guild Foundation has compiled a list of about thirty fellowship programs for screenwriters. Some higher-profile ones include the Academy Nicholl Fellowships, the Black List/Women in Film Episodic Lab, the Film Independent Screenwriting or Episodic Lab, and Sundance Episodic Storytelling Lab. Many big studios, including ViacomCBS, NBC, and Paramount, also run their own programs. There are also fellowships for aspiring writers from underrepresented communities, including ISA Diversity Initiative, National Hispanic Media Coalition Series Scriptwriters Program, the Ojalá Ignition Lab, and the Coalition of Asian Pacifics in Entertainment (CAPE) New Writers Fellowship.

Submitting to screenwriting competitions. There are a lot of them and they usually require a fee, so do your research to determine which ones are worth your time and money. The advantage to the more established, higher-profile competitions—such as Final Draft Big Break Screenwriting Contest or the Black List—is that they are run and judged by veterans in the industry. These are the people who presumably have the power and networks to help you launch your career if your script catches their attention. The Script Lab (thescriptlab.com) has compiled a list of the biggest screenwriting competitions. The site recommends looking into each competition's success stories and considering whether it's a good fit for your particular project.

Writing the script for a project that gets accepted at a festival. Film festivals are one of the places where agents and managers scout new talent and you (and your entire filmmaking team) can get noticed for making a great short film, web series, or feature film.

Having success in a different medium. Earning plaudits as a playwright, stand-up comedian, or novelist can open doors to writing jobs in film and TV.

If all else fails, you can always compete for the writing jobs listed online at places like FilmLocal.com and ScreenwritingStaffing.com. You're not likely to find the next Sundance-winning project there, but it will at least get you started on a body of work.

Ultimately, you need to have your work stand out among the piles (and files) of screenplays that producers, directors, showrunners, agents, and managers are constantly sifting through. So if you're not winning the most high-profile competitions and getting accepted to the most prestigious fellowships and festivals, there are benefits to submitting to niche ones first. Get that experience in a smaller, possibly safer space. Make those connections—it all helps build up to your eventual goal.

You don't have to be represented by a manager or an agent to get hired for a writers' room or sell a script. However, many writers eventually hire a team of representatives once they are on staff or garner some attention to help them negotiate contracts and book gigs. In the beginning, you must take what comes your way. But eventually you can pick and choose things that are creatively compelling rather than just paying the rent.

What Are the Career Paths?

There is no one career path for a film screenwriter. You have to have lots of different screenplays and screenplay ideas, and your path will be determined by how successful your pitch meetings are. You'll want to create screenplay pitch decks, which generally include a one- or two-sentence description called a logline, a synopsis of the plot, an explanation of character arcs, a sense of the visuals, an estimate of the production needs, and the demographics targeted by the story. You may also be creating more comprehensive TV show bibles, which outline the entire vision and trajectory for a series. (For examples of film pitch decks and TV show bibles, you can visit sites like Storydoc, ScreenCraft, and VIP Graphics.)

In television, it's competitive to get your first job, but once you do, there is a hierarchy—and paths forward.

This list of writing positions lays out a common way people move up the ladder:

- Staff writer
- Story editor
- Executive story editor
- Coproducer
- Producer
- Supervising producer
- Co–executive producer
- Executive producer
- Showrunner

Apart from the showrunner and executive producer, all these jobs are similar: Everyone is a writer. The idea is that you move up the hierarchy each year that the show is in production. But with some shows less likely to be picked up for multiple seasons, sometimes you're required to repeat a step if you move to a new show.

How Do You Make Money? And What Kind of Money?

Many creative writers try to get into film and TV writing because of the money. Hollywood can be an extremely profitable industry, so entertainment-industry writers, as a whole, typically get paid more than other writers.

The Writers Guild of America (WGA) negotiates for pay minimums on union-covered productions, which vary depending on the type of work and the type of production. Writers typically receive a set fee for a project, as opposed to being paid for the time it takes to complete the project. As of 2026, the minimum compensation for an original screenplay (which includes delivery of the treatment and first and second drafts) for high-budget films ($5 million or over) is $174,057. For non-original screenplays, the minimum compensation for the treatment, first and second drafts is $147,920. For a low-budget film (under $5 million), the minimum compensation for an original treatment, first and second drafts is $92,724. For non-original screenplays, the minimum compensation for the treatment, first and second drafts is $81,127. There are other rates for when writers are hired to work just on the treatment, revisions, or polishing of the script.

In television, there are various rates for the delivery of a story or teleplay—network prime-time rates are higher than others—as well as minimums for staff writers. A writer who is just starting will make a minimum of $4,743 a week on shows covered by the union contract. Story editors make a minimum of $8,462 a week, while writer-producers who have the title of coproducer or above make a minimum of $9,268 a week. There is a pay increase every year as a writer moves up a level. After you get your first deal and rise through the first couple levels, you can negotiate a salary that's higher than the union scale. This is when hiring representation (an agent or lawyer) may come in handy.

In addition to these minimums, writers can make money from residuals, which are additional payments based on how much the project makes. For films, credited writers get 1.2 percent of the distributor's gross receipts when they are reused in markets outside the multiplex, including television, basic cable, and new media. TV residuals vary widely.

How Is This Career Different from Ten or Twenty-Five Years Ago?

Because streaming platforms have led to an increase in overall content production, the last couple of decades have created more opportunities to write for Hollywood, especially for women and people from underrepresented communities. Writers can also showcase their work through social media and YouTube, and they work with filmmakers and actors to build their own audience.

However, those alternatives to the traditional networks and major film studios result in less job security for writers. Shows on streaming services often produce shorter seasons and require faster turnaround times. Building one's own audience online requires patience and business acumen.

The 2023 WGA strike also pushed Hollywood writers to take the lead in addressing industry-wide concerns over fair compensation for streaming content and AI's potential impact on creative jobs. Writers can now experiment with ways generative AI may make their work more efficient, while fighting for regulations to ensure fair use of the technology.

What's Some Good Advice?

Make friends and connections. Start a writing group or join an existing one. Look for like-minded people who can hold you to your writing goals and give you honest feedback when your script isn't working.

Look up local meetups, events, panels, and organizations. Social media has also helped writers meet one another and get noticed. #PreWGA is a hashtag on social media platforms that connects new writers who are trying to get hired.

Many working writers are known for giving helpful advice, including Hutchison, Franklin Leonard, Tze Chun, Aline Brosh McKenna,

John August, and Scott Myers. Follow and interact with as many writers as you can on X, Facebook, Instagram, LinkedIn, and whatever new platforms you see screenwriters gravitating toward.

One golden rule remains the same, no matter whether you're making connections in person or virtually. Be friendly to everyone, especially those at your same level. In Hollywood, it's all about who you know. These friends will become not only the network that feeds you information about jobs but also the support group that helps you navigate harsh rejections and stressful situations.

Take acting and directing classes. They will help you understand what it's like to say your words as an actor—and what you need to see on a page to direct it.

Have a reliable self-care plan. "I think writing is about managing your anxieties . . . because you spend so much time all alone trying to figure this out," said Golamco. "Anxiety is a constant in the room, and a lot of writers I know deal with that anxiety, no matter who they are."

Focus on your work. Hollywood, by nature, is chaotic. The benefit of being a writer is that your job is to take refuge in the fantasy world you're creating. It's the director, showrunner, or producer's job to figure out solutions to any challenges that may arise. Your job is to write. Hollywood rewards consistency, and in an industry where the results are unpredictable, it's best to focus on developing yourself as an artist. That way you're not defined or emotionally defeated by any individual project.

Learn how to tell your own story. Maybe you'll write it in a screenplay, but even if you don't, your personal story will be helpful when showrunners, directors, or producers are meeting with you to make their final hiring decisions. At that point, the person presumably likes your work and thinks you can do the job, and now all that's left is to understand what different candidates can bring. Brown Eyes tells the story of leaving the Pine Ridge Indian

Reservation in rural South Dakota when he was thirteen with just his mom to start over in California. Know the emotional journey of the story of you, he said. What is your lived experience, and how will that be a unique asset on the show? "That's the final story that gets you in," he said.

PART 3

DIRECTING

CHAPTER 6

How to Become a Director

Steven Spielberg once described his job this way: "I dream for a living." But a filmmaker's dreams don't magically appear on the silver screen. Making a movie or TV show requires the talents of many people, and the leader on the set is the director.

The first task of a director is to go through the script and create a cohesive vision for how to tell the story on-screen. Who are the ideal actors for the roles? What kind of mood should be set with music and lighting? What kind of camerawork is best? Where will each scene be shot? And what will everyone be wearing?

Before the shoot, the director will meet with all the different department heads to make sure everyone is on the same page, while also doing rehearsals with the actors. During the shoot, directors run the set, making sure they get all the shots they need. Afterward, they'll work with the editor and provide guidance to all the post-production teams until they (or the studio or financiers) are happy with the final cut.

Whether it's a student project with classmates or a studio picture with many executives sending notes and visiting the set, the basics of filmmaking are the same. The role played by the director, though, is different on films than it is on TV shows. Film is a director's medium, whereas television is a writer's medium. In film, the entire weight of the production sits on the director's shoulders. Even after the film is completed, the director will be involved in the marketing and distribution. A single project may occupy a director's time for multiple years. In television, the showrunner (the head of the writers' room) is the visionary. TV directors are typically hired for individual episodes, tasked with bringing to life the showrunner's vision, not their own.

Directors can go back and forth between different types of projects—including dramas, comedies, documentaries, reality-TV shows, commercials, music videos, and corporate work—but sometimes they get pigeonholed as a certain type of director. They have to convince others of their versatility to get hired across mediums.

Directors are managers, so they don't have to be skilled at any of the individual filmmaking crafts. Instead, they rely on their teams. But because they have to manage all the crafts, directing is a difficult job to do *well.* While anyone can make a micro-budget film (or self-fund their passion project, if they have the means), directing is also a difficult job to get *paid* to do.

It's one of those jobs where you must invest a lot of time, money, and effort into proving that you can direct in order to convince producers or financiers to entrust a film to you.

What Qualities Do You Find in a Successful Director?

It's common for writers and actors to become directors. Writers might finish a script and want to helm the project themselves. Actors inherently know how to get good performances out of other actors. But other filmmaking creatives can also develop the skills necessary to lead a production. Stunt coordinators can direct action movies. Choreographers can direct musicals. Script supervisors—who help maintain the vision laid out in the script—often become great directors.

Strong leadership and storytelling skills are essential. Directors have to be adaptable, because they're often working with different crews and actors in different environments. They have to be good communicators, because they have to make sure everyone involved grasps what they see for the project and how to deliver it. They have to be confident, because people need to trust their vision—and also because everyone will judge them for every decision they make.

They also need to be able to make tough decisions. Sometimes people have to be fired—swiftly. If members of the cast or crew aren't on the same page, it can create problems for the hundreds of others involved.

And directors need an intense, resilient work ethic. "Almost everyone I know who's successful in the film business is a workaholic," said Richard Wong, director of the comedies *Come as You Are* and *The Valet*. "It's not just about being addicted to work. It's about: Do you think of challenges as fun, or do you think of them as obstacles?"

Here are a couple of good questions to test whether you've got a director's mettle. If you're asked to do a pitch deck for a show, can you not stop working on it, even though you won't get paid a dime unless you get hired and the odds are stacked against you? Do you enjoy the creative process only if everything flows smoothly, or do you relish the creative challenge of working within budget limitations?

"It's like a video game," Wong said. "You've got to jump over a bunch of spikes and have fireballs flying at you. You have to think that the fireballs are fun; otherwise you're going to think it's torture and you're going to quit."

Put another way, it's difficult to maintain a work-life balance as a director. There can be twenty-hour workdays and months spent on a shoot away from home. The job involves personal sacrifice and compromises.

How Do You Get Started?

Film school is a common starting point for aspiring directors to gain basic skills and connect with a community of filmmakers. Some directors also get their start at art schools. Successful graduates have been known to leverage a good thesis film into a gig helming a low-budget feature. And there are programs for aspiring film crew workers that train students to be assistant directors, such as Stockade Works in the Hudson Valley, New York.

Another way to start is to get a job as a production assistant. You'll learn how a film set works, and you can pick a department that interests you and work your way up the ladder. The directorial team often includes assistant directors (depending on the size of the project, there would be a first, second, and third assistant director) and a script supervisor. You could join the camera crew, which is led by the director of photography or cinematographer and includes a camera operator, one or more assistants, and a digital imaging technician.

Fellowships can also help propel your career. Programs vary, but most of them involve classes, training, mentorship, or shadowing—where a fellow can follow a director through the pre-production, physical production, and post-production process. But they're competitive, so be prepared to apply multiple times to multiple programs. Options include the DGA Director Development Initiative, Film Independent's Directing Lab and Amplifier Fellowship for Black artists, Ryan Murphy's HALF Initiative, the Sundance Directors Lab, the CAPE Animation Directors Accelerator, the Los Angeles Latino International Film Festival's Latinx Inclusion Fellowship Series, the American Film Institute Directing Workshop for Women, Fox's Franchise Directing program, and UCLA Extension courses. There are studio-run fellowships too—from ViacomCBS, Disney/ABC, HBO, NBC, Sony, and Warner Bros.—that train specifically for television.

Any job where you can observe how different directors work will be invaluable, but none of them necessarily leads to the job of being a director. The only way to become a director is by directing.

Sujata Day started as an actor; she's best known for her role as Sarah in HBO's *Insecure*. She was inspired by watching Issa Rae create unique, personal stories for young Black women, and she wanted to do the same for South Asian women. At the Sundance Film Festival, she watched Justin Chon's award-winning drama, *Gook*, about the 1992 L.A. riots and cornered the actor-turned-director to ask him how he got his first feature made. He told her he raised money from family and friends—and just did it. Around the same time, Day got an unexpected payout from a development deal that fell through. She took that check and became the first investor in her film, and the first investor in herself as a director. The result: *Definition Please*.

As a new director, you can't wait for someone to hand you a job. You have to create a job for yourself. Write a script or find a writing partner to develop a script with. Find a producer who can help you build the team, raise money, create a budget, and map out a schedule. Start with smaller projects such as short films or music videos to develop your skills, with the eventual goal being a full-length feature that will give you legitimacy as a director—and attract the attention of a manager or agent who will help you navigate your career.

In the meantime, create a portfolio that showcases your unique point of view and range of skills—whether it's getting great performances out of actors, nailing a certain visual style, or showing how your sensibility will be a great fit for a particular show that you'd love to direct one day.

What Are the Career Paths?

Like most of Hollywood, there is no single path and the routes are often not straight lines. It's extremely difficult to get your very first directing gig, and it can continue to be difficult to get your second, third, or fortieth one.

Brian Herzlinger—a director of almost forty films, including numerous Lifetime Christmas rom-coms—was a production assistant on *Chicago Hope* and *Ally McBeal*, itching to direct. After six years working on set, he made his first film, the documentary *My Date with Drew*, for $1,100. It was a hit on the film festival circuit, winning multiple awards, and was eventually released in theaters nationwide. But he didn't get another opportunity to direct for six years. In the meantime, he became a correspondent on *The Tonight Show with Jay Leno*.

Wong was a digital imaging technician on *Arrested Development* when he reunited with his film-school classmate director H. P. Mendoza, to develop a low-budget musical, *Colma: The Musical*. Wong self-funded the $15,000 project. Film critic Manohla Dargis of the *New York Times* selected the film as a Critic's Pick, and Wong was nominated as Someone to Watch at the Independent Spirit Awards.

The film helped him get a manager, but looking back, he wasn't ready to capitalize on the acclaim. Having longevity as a director is largely about being ready for any opportunity that might come your way. And if you're lucky enough to have a window of opportunity—whether it's a meeting with a person who is interested in working with you or a rush of attention from a project that does well—you need to be prepared for it.

To improve their chances, many directors develop multiple projects at once. They take lots of general meetings, a Hollywood term for meet-and-greets with producers and executives. Most of these projects will not be made, and many of the general meetings will not lead anywhere. But directors take these steps to prepare for the possibility that one of the people they meet with could help get one of their projects green-lit.

How Do You Make Money? And What Kind of Money?

The salary range for directors is incredibly wide. Directors of big-budget movies can make more than $10 million per film, in addition to a cut of the profits. At one extreme, James Cameron reportedly earned $350 million for his work on *Avatar*, based largely on sales. But it's common for first-time directors to lose money on their first feature. If you break even on your first film and leverage that release into another job, that's a win.

As much as professionals want to tell aspiring directors they shouldn't work for free, many say that you may have to consider volunteer gigs as chances to invest time in your career as an artist. Even if you aren't getting paid a reasonable rate per hour, is there something else you can get out of it? A connection, a new skill, a credit?

For live-action film and TV directors who belong to the DGA, the union sets minimum payment rates that vary by the budget level of the production. For theatrical motion picture films, the 2026 minimum rate is $23,767 a week for a high-budget production and $16,974 for shorts and documentaries. Kevin Jones, former chair of Chapman University's Dodge College of Film and Media Arts, estimated that a new director could earn $30,000 over two years from a low-budget movie. With that experience, they could break into a festival like Sundance and the next directing gig could pay $250,000.

Until that big break happens, though, most aspiring film directors are juggling other jobs. They might be making money directing commercials, corporate videos, or other freelance gigs. They might be working other jobs in the film industry while they are developing projects to direct.

For television, the DGA has rate cards for a pilot—the opening installment of a series, which is used to sell the show to a network—as well as for individual TV episodes. The rates vary depending on where the show will be televised, how long the episodes are, and what kind of budget the production has. Minimums range from $12,721 an episode for a half-hour nonnetwork show (one that airs on cable, a streaming service, or local station) to $149,243 for a two-hour program on prime-time network television (ABC, CBS, NBC, or FOX). Career sustainability is one of the main reasons that directors want to go into television. Some direct television full-time, but you can also make enough money by taking a few months directing a limited number of episodes and spending the rest of the year working on your passion projects.

Directors also receive residuals, which are extra payments for their work when it's used for reruns, home video, and on-demand. Residuals account for a significant amount of money; the DGA distributes nearly half a billion dollars a year in residuals to members. The DGA negotiates these deals, and there are different formulas depending on how and where the work is distributed or exhibited.

Because there's an implicit understanding in the industry that most films don't get made, studios and streaming services have money built into their budget to develop projects and directors get paid for every movie they are attached to. That means a director might receive $25,000 for officially signing on to direct a film and they get paid for their commitment to the project even if the film never sees the light of day.

How Is This Career Different from Ten or Twenty-Five Years Ago?

There was a time when filmmakers did not want to work in television, even if they were struggling to make a living directing movies. But streaming services such as Netflix, Amazon Prime, and Apple TV+ are all trying to carve out an identity in the entertainment world, and there's an appetite for prestige projects, big-budget productions, and new artistic visions. There are also more opportunities for TV directors, with many more cable channels creating original programming—like FX, SYFY, AMC—and the major broadcast networks investing in programming made specifically for their streaming channels (Disney+, Paramount+, Peacock).

As streaming television has boomed in the last few years, the clout of the movie director has also changed. There are fewer auteurs like James Cameron, Martin Scorsese, or Ang Lee who can command a massive budget. Instead, today the dominant creators are TV super-producers such as Ryan Murphy and Shonda Rhimes—showrunners who hire directors for the material they write and produce.

The advent of digital cameras, editing tools, and online distributors (not just Netflix but also YouTube and Vimeo) has also transformed the opportunities in the field. The barriers to entry have been all but erased, which makes it easier to make and show a film and compete for audiences. Meanwhile, the advent of ever-more sophisticated special effects has made it possible to tell new types of stories and bend reality in new ways, enabling directors to bring to the screen more of what they can imagine.

What's Some Good Advice?

Understand every department's job. So much of directing is making choices, compromising, and negotiating with different department heads. You have to understand people's jobs in order to grasp what they need.

Do some work as a crew member. It helps to have firsthand experience with what turns a crew off, so you're not wasting people's time and losing the trust of the team.

Understand the market. If a certain type of film is drawing most of the financing, you could refuse to make that type of project and try to find money another way. Or you could look at the economic reality of the industry and figure out how to put your original spin on something that is marketable, said producer Angela C. Lee (*Songs My Brothers Taught Me*), who also works as the director of artist development at the arts nonprofit Film Independent. Succeeding that way might give you enough clout to sell a different type of film in the future.

Don't take things personally. If you get rejected, it may not have anything to do with you or your project. It could be due to bad timing or the limited spots available, Lee said. Even if the rejection is because your sensibilities as a filmmaker don't match the producer's, the rejection could be a blessing in disguise, Wong said. Directing a film requires so much time, energy, and sacrifice, you want to get hired for the type of storyteller you are, not one you're forced to be.

PART 4

PRE-PRODUCTION

CHAPTER 7

How to Become a Producer

When the Academy of Motion Picture Arts and Sciences hands out its Oscar for Best Picture each year, millions of viewers peer at the small group of winners in expensive suits and gowns and wonder, "Who *are* those people?"

They're the producers—the ones who got the film made.

Although Hollywood publicists may describe a film or TV series as a passion project for a director or a star, those endeavors often reflect the drive and determination of the project's producer. It's the producer who shepherds the work from script—or even just concept—to screen, then stays with it through its entire life cycle, whether it starts in movie theaters or on television. The process is marked by networking, negotiating, and problem-solving.

One of the producer's most crucial responsibilities is finding something worth turning into a movie or TV series. That's the usual starting point for a producer's work on a project, which can take years to turn into a finished product, if it ever does.

"The way we always started was to find a book, or an existing script, or a writer with an idea that we were excited about. Then we would strategize about how to move forward with that property," said Midge Sanford, whose credits with partner Sarah Pillsbury include *And the Band Played On* and *Desperately Seeking Susan*.

Recognizing material that can appeal to a broad audience is also important. It's not as easy as gauging the prospects of a Keanu Reeves action movie or a black-and-white film with no dialogue—it's judging all the projects that fall in between.

After material is acquired, it goes through development—the process of taking an idea, book, or first draft and turning it into something that has a realistic chance of being shot. That means the projected cost has to be in line with what the investors, studios, and other backers believe is the potential market, which may require revisions and negotiations among the writer, director, and other key players. If the investors think your indie love story has the potential to make $10 million at most, you're not going to be able to shoot scenes for four months in eight different cities on three continents.

In addition to a workable script, the producer has to assemble the talent required to film it, including the director, the actors, and top crew members. The producer also must come up with a budget (which may be the work of a "line producer," a specialist in figuring out how much it will cost to shoot the scenes) and raise money for the production. That could mean selling the project to a major studio or an independent such as A24 or Lionsgate; selling it to a streaming service, although those outlets have been more receptive to finished films; using a sales agent to sell the foreign rights to the project; or lining up private backers, who could be friends, family members, or movie investors identified by your agent.

Assuming everything is still on track and the money has been raised for production, the project moves into the pre-production phase. A key step is figuring out where to shoot the film, with the producer working with a location scout, the cinematographer, and the production designer. That decision will also be influenced by the budget, which may be counting on location-specific tax breaks or other governmental incentives to help cover the costs.

Once filming starts, the producer's main role is ensuring that the work stays true to the filmmakers' shared vision for the project, while also keeping a lid on costs. "The producer has to be sure that you're not going over budget," Sanford said. "The producer is the worrier, the person who is concerned if you don't make your day"—that is, if you don't complete all the scenes the director was scheduled to film.

The problems are almost always about time. The production will be running behind, and an actor may have to leave for another commitment, or the location will no longer be available.

"You may have to say, 'We won't be able to have as many shots,' [or] 'Let's look at the script to see if there are any scenes we can cut.' Whatever you can do to speed the process along," Sanford said. Or maybe the producer will find a way to cut some other line items in the budgets—costumes or set building, for example—to pay for an extra day of shooting.

If a studio has signed on to finance or distribute the film, its executives will be looking at the footage coming from the set every day and potentially raising issues that the producer will have to address. The worst-case scenario is having to replace an actor who isn't meeting expectations, including those of the financier and director. More frequently, the notes will ask for something like a change to a star's makeup or attire. Small details will have to be ironed out, and sometimes the producer will have to fight suggestions that are untimely or poorly conceived.

"Then you would see it all the way through, at times being in the editing room with the director," Sanford said. The producer also weighs in on the marketing plan for the project.

In the case of an independent film, the producer may not have a distributor until after the finished film is shown at festivals. If all goes well, the film will draw enough interest from distributors around the world to more than cover the costs and give investors a reason to plow more money into future projects. If the film doesn't attract any distributors, investors will lose their money.

RadicalMedia cofounder Jon Kamen (executive producer of *Summer of Soul* and the film version of *Hamilton*) said producers are like explorers venturing into worlds unknown, "listening to a creative visionary's ideas for what they want to do, and then figuring out how you can actually do it—whether raising the money to do it, persuading a studio to do it, [or] developing it for sale."

In a nutshell, the producer's timeline goes something like this: Acquire an idea, book, script, or other source material for a project. Recruit a writer to develop a script that can be filmed. Attract a director and other key filmmakers. Create a budget. Sign up talent to validate that budget and boost the project's appeal. Pitch the package to a studio or other source of financing. Revise the budget to match the financing. Hire a lawyer to negotiate the deal. Oversee the production, hire department heads, begin casting, find locations, and set a shooting schedule and other elements as needed to complete the filming. Shepherd the project through post-production, working with the director on the edit and overseeing all the other work done after the shooting ends. Hold test screenings with your target audience, then make final revisions. Submit it to festivals if needed. Screen and sell to distributors. Maybe, get paid.

You may not notice the mark a producer leaves on a film or TV series the way you notice the distinctive style of a director like Sophia Coppola or a writer like Aaron Sorkin. But one of their key contributions, producers say, is ensuring that the film or TV show envisioned by the creative team makes it onto the screen. Which is not to say that everything a producer touches turns into celluloid (or a stream of data). Interviewed early one morning, Phillip B. Goldfine (*Isolation*, *Adrenaline*) said he'd already had a project rejected by a studio and two major streaming services that day. "Everybody's going to say no," said Goldfine, who nevertheless has amassed roughly two hundred film and TV credits.

To be successful, "you never let 'no' be an obstacle," Goldfine said. "You're going to wake up and say, 'How do I get this movie made?' or 'How do I get this television show made?'" (A case in point for

Goldfine: The project that had been rejected by the studio and two streamers was picked up for global distribution by a third streamer a few weeks later.)

Producers say every day at work is a little bit different, but much of the day is spent just talking to people, whether it's friends, colleagues, or studio executives, trying to figure out what they're looking for and whether that matches any of the projects the producer controls and is developing. They may also listen to pitches from people who have ideas for films to see if any are worth taking on. And for each project they have underway, they'll try to find financiers who share the vision of the director. It's about connecting people with the right partners and building from there.

Then there is the time spent networking, which some producers attend to morning, noon, and night. Developing connections with the directors and other talent with whom you'll be making films is crucial.

If they have a film in production, some producers will spend every day on set, attending to the scheduling problems that inevitably arise. Producer Kara Durrett (*Bird*, *Caddo Lake*) said roughly half of her time is spent solving problems involving the crew or with actors who need to leave the set for other commitments before their scenes have been shot.

"No one ever needs you until something goes wrong, and then when/if it does, everyone is looking for you to fix it," she said. "You're just kind of waiting for the problems to happen."

What Qualities Do You Find in a Successful Producer?

The pros frequently point to four traits that producers have in common: being a leader, a collaborator, a negotiator, and an entrepreneur.

Leading means listening and helping the writers, directors, and other key people on a project tell the story the best way. It helps to be a people person because much of this job involves bringing creative individuals together and establishing connections. Similarly, a knack for persuasion is key because a producer must negotiate for so many things—funding, talent, locations, distribution. Finally, you'll need an appetite for risk. In effect, a producer is running a start-up business with the goal, but not the guarantee, of making a return—most efforts die on the launchpad.

"You have to be relentless without seeming relentless," said Carol Baum (*Father of the Bride*, *The Good Girl*). "The people who get the Oscars are the people who've been with [the film] for ten years. They deserve the Oscars for doing it for ten years without getting paid."

Patience and persistence are vital, given how long it takes to bring anything to fruition. So is the ability to multitask and get up to speed quickly on the subjects you're working on. Beyond that, one of the biggest assets is a sense for how to tell a story visually. That includes understanding how to create and develop characters and how to move a story along.

Being a natural organizer and a resourceful problem solver is important too, as is being the sort of person who's curious and asks a lot of questions, because that can help you get to the heart of what's needed to resolve an issue.

How Do You Get Started?

In theory, there's no limit to the number of producers who can work in film and television. If you can get control over a hot book or gain the trust of a blockbuster screenwriter, you're set!

In practice, though, the barrier to entry is the money and talent required to bring a project to fruition. Studios and investors won't throw their dollars at just anybody, nor will directors and writers sign on to a project unless they're confident the producer can get it done. You've got to earn the trust of key players, typically by making contacts and developing a track record of small successes.

Durrett, for example, worked as a producer's assistant on a few films, then started going to film festivals to meet filmmakers in the shorts programs. She'd offer to produce their next short film for free—an offer filmmakers found hard to refuse.

"I made nine shorts in a row, working for free," she said. "I definitely lost money during this time."

About half of the shorts went on to higher-profile festivals, and half of those generated good ideas for feature films. Durrett made one feature, which went to Sundance, which led to her getting pitched more films by other directors. Within a few years, she had three features in the works—one she was finishing, one preparing for shooting, and a third in development.

"Make friends with the people you want to work with," Durrett said. "The connections I've made through Sundance, through South by Southwest, those are the people I still work with today. . . . We can all bring each other projects and bring each other up."

Film school is one place to start building your network. Wherever you happen to be, creating a community with people at your level is extremely important. Once you've made those relationships, maintain them. Find the storytellers and the directors you love. Forge links to the people who have the power to make decisions.

One way to do all those things is to go to work for a talent agency, where you'll almost certainly have to start at the bottom of the career ladder: the mailroom. The idea of working your way up from an agency mailroom may be a cliché, but it isn't far-fetched. If you can grab a spot as an agent's assistant, you will get the chance to do "coverage"—summarizing and analyzing a script's potential for filming—on an enormous number of scripts. That's an opportunity to display your skills in the development arena. If you prove your mettle at coverage, the pros say, you'll eventually be invited into meetings with the agency's clients—writers, directors, actors. That's where you can start making the connections to the talent you'll need to assemble once you begin producing projects.

Alternatively, you could land a job as a producer's assistant, a director's assistant, or something close to it so you can sit in meetings and listen to a project being put together. Being exposed to those decisions from development through the sale of a film or show, Durrett said, "was film school to me."

Another potential starting point is in a manager's office; besides guiding careers, some managers become producers on their clients' movies. In addition, the major studios, production companies, and TV networks all have development teams that have entry-level jobs for assistants, which are similar to the entry-level jobs at agencies and management companies. If you have a good relationship with your boss, you'll be invited to sit in or listen in on meetings, where you'll start to see how it all works and begin building contacts.

If you don't have connections you can tap for an assistant's job, you can find ads for them on entertainment-industry job sites such as Staffmeup.com (which charges fees to access some listings) and Entertainmentcareers.net, but don't overlook generalized job sites such as Indeed, LinkedIn, ZipRecruiter, and Salary.com. A shortcut is just to do a Google search for "assistant producer jobs."

Kibi Anderson, copresident and chair of the Black TV & Film Collective, said the most important thing for new producers is to make connections with writers. To find your way into the field, she said, go wherever you can find writers—for example, at screenings and events held by the WGA, the DGA, Film Independent, or NewFilmmakers Los Angeles. Anderson said her favorite place to find talent is at the Black TV & Film Collective ("We have tons of writers in our membership"), but she also suggested the Gotham Film and Media Institute, the National Hispanic Media Coalition, the Coalition of Asian Pacifics in Entertainment, the Native American Media Alliance, Outfest, and the Inevitable Foundation, which supports screenwriters with disabilities.

Being independently wealthy or a great fundraiser makes it easier to put together the sums of cash large enough to snap up the rights to hot books and scripts, or to attract people with a track record of spotting good material. For people of lesser means, there are programs and fellowships that offer help to get started as a producer. Film Independent has several, including the Producing Lab and Project Involve, which pairs filmmakers with mentors. The Black TV & Film Collective also offers a Black Producers Fellowship that grants eight emerging producers $25,000 in cash and in-kind support to make a short film to take to the festival circuit.

Shira Rockowitz, director of production and artist support at the Sundance Institute's feature film program, pointed to a handful of sources online where aspiring producers can gain expertise: DearProducer.com, a site run by indie film producer (and former Producers Union president) Rebecca Green; NoFilmSchool.com, a how-to site offering guidance for multiple filmmaking disciplines; and Sundance Collab (Collab.Sundance.org), which offers online classes in producing and other filmmaking roles for a fee (with scholarships available).

Rockowitz also cited three books that offer insights from successful indie producers: *Shooting to Kill* by Christine Vachon and *Independent Filmmaker's Manual* by Eden Wurmfeld and Nicole LaLoggia, which include detailed breakdowns of budgets and contracts, and *Hope for Film: From the Frontlines of the Independent Cinema Revolutions* by Ted Hope.

What Are the Career Paths?

It's important to remember that the term "producer" is a catchall that encompasses multiple roles on a project. In fact, a producer's responsibilities are often divided among people with different specialties and titles.

The most basic division of labor, though, is between story-oriented work and budget-related work. Both can be done by the same person, and for low-budget productions, they often are. But if there's a split, the creative producer will be the one who finds and develops the material and recruits the writer(s), director, actors, and key crew members.

The line producer, meanwhile, will develop the final budget for the shoot and handle the nitty-gritty details, such as making sure that all the trucks and crew members arrive on set at the right time, and in the right number. That involves a lot of research—for example, finding out what resources are available in the cities where you're shooting and the cost of the locations you plan to use. Once shooting begins, the line producer and a top assistant known as the unit production manager are coordinating the entire assemblage and moving it from location to location. That's harder than it sounds, because each actor and location will be available in limited windows of time.

Another key difference: Creative producers spend years with individual projects, some of which don't get made. Line producers often come onto projects after they've been green-lit, and they don't have to see it through to the (sometimes bitter) end. The split between the two roles helps manage the workload. But another reason to divvy up the responsibilities is that the financial duties and creative work require different skill sets. You need to understand both sides, but you should also recognize which one is more in your wheelhouse.

There's no one route into these jobs, but Rockowitz cited two of the most common pathways. One is the suit-and-tie path, where you might start at an agency or management company before moving on to a development and production role at a production company, studio, or streamer. The second path begins on a film or TV set. You might start as a production assistant or an assistant to the producer and rise through the ranks, learning the ins and outs of physically producing a movie.

You may also have "executive producers," which on a film used to refer to the people who helped raise money for the production. Now, however, the credit can be granted to an actor or a manager who has enough clout to demand it.

Note: The "producer" title doesn't mean the same thing on a TV series as it does in a movie. In a TV series, the creative decisions are made by the showrunner, who is typically the lead writer and sometimes also the person who came up with the idea for the series. That person typically carries the title "executive producer." The showrunner may be assisted by other producers, including a line producer to oversee the budget.

To help manage the intermittent nature of their paydays, some producers have struck deals to give a Hollywood studio first crack at the projects they develop in exchange for an office on the studio lot and, possibly, a fee. But those deals have been evaporating as studios pare the number of executives they employ.

How Do You Make Money? And What Kind of Money?

Unlike other creatives covered by union contracts, producers have no pay scale. The Producers Guild of America isn't a union; a 1974 consent decree holds that it can't be a labor organization because many of its members have ownership stakes in production companies—in other words, they are management. That's why a few hundred independent producers have formed the Producers Union, which is trying to organize the ranks of feature film producers. The goal is to strike a deal with the major Hollywood studios and streaming companies to set minimum pay rates and require contributions to healthcare and pension plans.

In the absence of a union contract, producers say, there are industry norms. An indie film typically pays a fee of 5 percent of the film's budget, split among all its producers. But this structure doesn't translate into a steady flow of income; producers could work months, even years, on a project before seeing any income, if ever. For bigger movies, producers are paid a flat fee that they negotiate with whoever is financing the film.

That's why Rockowitz recommends that aspiring producers pursue different types of income streams, including short-term and longer-term commitments—for example, producing branded content or music videos, working in post-production, or teaching. These jobs also provide an opportunity to hone one's producing craft and build a network of potential collaborators.

Producers are often expected to sacrifice part of their fee to cover cost overruns or a funding shortfall. Durrett said she tells her directors from the very beginning, "I'm not going to make less than you, we are going to be equal partners on this for years with no pay, and we should be treated respectfully as such." If they object, she said, she tells them that maybe she's not the producer for their project.

How Is This Career Different from Ten or Twenty-Five Years Ago?

One good thing, Anderson said, is that raising money has been democratized by the arrival of Kickstarter and other crowdfunding platforms. Social media has also provided an avenue for creators to develop an audience without Hollywood's help, she said; a good example is Black&Sexy TV, which used crowdfunding to cover the production costs of the episodes they released on YouTube.com and eventually sold to subscribers via their own streaming platform.

The industry's appetite for diverse programming has also grown, as new investors are looking for stories told from a different perspective. Meanwhile, the ranks of producers have broadened beyond white men; they may not mirror U.S. demographics just yet, but women and people of color are no longer singular exceptions, as they were in the 1980s and 1990s.

The rise of streaming services and the evaporation of DVD sales are also changing the landscape in multiple ways.

The economics are different, with fewer opportunities to generate revenue internationally and in future release windows. For example, selling a film to a streaming service can snuff your chances to sell the overseas rights to the project. One of the biggest changes has been in the diminished role that film festivals play in helping producers find distributors for their films. Amazon, Netflix, and Apple arrived with a splash in the mid-2010s, paying vastly more for films than the smaller, established indie distributors had done. Before long, established distributors were dropping out of the business. And by the early 2020s, the streamers were no longer investing much in indie films either—they had their own films in production.

The challenge for indie producers today is to find films that can be made at a modest budget but have a broad enough commercial appeal to produce a return for investors.

"The old world of distribution is crumbling before our eyes," said Peter Broderick, a consultant who helps independent filmmakers design innovative strategies for what he calls the new world of distribution. His clients retain greater control of their distribution, he said, by splitting some of their rights among distributors and retaining others, while also targeting their films' core audiences.

"If you're not meaningfully involved in your distribution, you're going to be really disappointed," Broderick said. "You can't just sit on the sideline and let it happen."

What's Some Good Advice?

Read as many scripts as you can. Lisa Demberg (*The Wedding Veil* series, *Guiding Emily*) encourages would-be producers to have the appetite to give a close read to every script they can get their hands on. That way you'll know what you think works and what you think doesn't. It's important to watch as many productions as you can for the same reason.

Ask to shadow a producer. Paid internships can be tough to land, but there's a work-around—you can also learn a lot just by asking to follow a producer at work. Use IMDb.com to find out who produced films or shows you admire, then see if they'll let you tag along for a bit. If you can't find their contact information through a Google search, a paid subscription to IMDb.com will do the trick.

Don't be above assistant gigs and other jobs that seem menial. You can be the boss on your own small set, or you can be an entry-level person at a place with a much larger reach that could teach you more about the industry. With that in mind, Mallory Schwartz (*Cora Bora, Molli and Max in the Future*) advised that if you can get a job as an assistant at a talent agency, do it.

But don't be a personal assistant. It will lead nowhere, Schwartz cautioned. Be very careful if a job says it will be both personal and professional assistance. "Sometimes, yes, you can go pick up laundry and that will be fine, but you want to be sure they're sharing their knowledge and expertise. That's the benefit to you."

Remember that you don't have to work for free. Schwartz pushed back on the notion that working for free is a necessary step toward a career in entertainment. If you're being paid in other ways, if it's a great opportunity, then you're making a larger investment in yourself and your career, she said. But if it's an unknown writer or director, or a writer or director whose work you don't like, get paid for your time.

Be a joiner. Join any groups of your peers that are related to filmmaking, because that's a good way to gather information. "You meet people; you find out about jobs; you find out about people leaving jobs," Demberg said. If no such group exists, she said, start one. This cadre becomes like a graduating class from film school, competing with one another but also helping everyone rise through the ranks.

Be open about your expectations. Producers often find and foster the talent of a friend who is a novice director, only to be left behind when the film does well. That's why it's important to work with people you communicate exceptionally well with, Schwartz said, and to convey your expectations up front.

Work on a slate of projects, not a single film. "Be working on five, six projects at a time," said Rob Aft, a former production executive. "You're hustling, trying to find people who can make these movies."

Find a mentor. Copy someone else's career, whether you know them or you just watch them from afar, Schwartz said. "You can really get lost if you don't have a road map." Aft suggested getting in touch with people who've made a movie like the one you're trying to make, because many producers enjoy talking about their projects.

At the same time, Schwartz said, don't be a pushover when famous or powerful producers say they want to get on board a project of yours. Their interest is a sign that you've got something good on your hands—and that you have the power to say no. Find out what they have to offer before bringing them in, she said, because the last thing you want to do is saddle your project with a bunch of producers who don't do anything but take credit.

Build a catalog of material that you own. The riches, Anderson said, are in the niches. Streaming platforms are looking for content that appeals to niche audiences, as exemplified by the Elvis Presley Channel, the Dove Channel, and the Hallmark Channel. You may not be able to afford to produce feature-length movies, but you don't need million-dollar budgets for your content either. "If you have the power to speak to an audience in an authentic way," she said, "people will spend money."

Keep in mind that there is power in pausing. Sometimes the friction a project encounters is a signal from the universe that you might need to set it aside for a while. "You may not know what it is, but you need something else," Anderson said.

Make the films you want to make. Don't tell yourself that you need permission from somebody in mainstream Hollywood to make your project.

Don't take a bully for a role model. Many a tell-all account has been written about award-winning executives at production companies and studios who made their workplaces a living hell. But the pros insist that these people are not models for succeeding in Hollywood—it's a business built on relationships, after all—although as some of the industry's best-known bullies have shown, it's also built on box-office revenues and awards.

CHAPTER 8

How to Crowdfund Your Indie Project

William Yu moved to Los Angeles in his late twenties with the goal of becoming a screenwriter. Over the course of a few years, he won screenwriting competitions and fellowships. He then wrote a script titled *Good Boy*, which follows a Korean American aspiring streetwear designer, which was selected for the 2020 Sundance Episodic Makers Lab.

After receiving mentorship from the lab to develop his project, Yu felt he had a clear vision for the pilot. He talked to director friends before deciding to direct the short film himself. The reality facing Yu was that making even a sixteen-minute project takes a lot of money. The online resource Newbie Film School estimated that short films cost between $700 and $1,500 per minute.

Finding the money is usually done by a producer, who hires the director and oversees the project from the very beginning to the end. So for Yu, directing the pilot would require him to produce it—and secure the money to hire a cast and crew, rent equipment, and secure locations, then pay for post-production, promotion, and distribution.

He started a spreadsheet, listing every person he thought he could ask privately for money and a projected amount each might give. He calculated how much more he'd need to cover the rest of his budget.

To raise the remainder of the money, Yu turned to crowdfunding. He had built a Twitter audience of more than thirty-two thousand followers after starting the viral hashtag #StarringJohnCho, which advocates for more Asian Americans in leading roles, so he hoped those who gravitated toward the same mission would consider donating. He knew his screenwriting community would be supportive. He also planned to rally streetwear brands and sneaker shops behind his film.

Yu chose Seed&Spark because the platform provides feedback on each campaign before it's launched. It also allows people who can't afford to support projects with money the opportunity to help in other ways. For example, supporters could "like" a project to help unlock discounts on gear for the filmmaker, or they could offer to let the filmmaker use their property for free.

His spreadsheet became a key tool in the Seed&Spark crowdfunding campaign he launched in 2021. It was where he kept track of every person who contributed, every person who shared, and every person he still needed to contact. Eventually, he raised $17,768, enough for the sixteen-minute short film with Young Mazino in the title role.

But perhaps what has been most valuable of all is that it gave Yu an official directorial debut. In 2023, *Good Boy* screened at film festivals and premiered online on Omeleto, a YouTube channel specializing in short films. He leveraged that success to secure staff-writing gigs on the TV shows *Fight Night: The Million Dollar Heist* and *Brilliant Minds*.

To Crowdfund or Not to Crowdfund

A crowdfunding campaign requires a lot of time and effort. Some producers think of crowdfunding as a last resort. It's way more work than if you can find a few investors—or afford to pay for a project out of your own pocket. But others say that if you need money, you should crowdfund—as simple as that.

"If you could shake the money tree of Hollywood and get financing to make short films, that's great and good for you," said Jim Cummings, filmmaker (*Thunder Road*, *The Beta Test*) and founder of

FilmFreeway's The Short to Feature Lab. "I've never had success doing that, and none of my friends have had success."

Bri Castellini, a crowdfunding and production consultant and host of the podcast *Breaking Out of Breaking In*, said even the lowest-budget films can benefit from some support. Plenty of crowdfunding campaigns aren't seeking to cover the entire budget of a project. Filmmakers might look to cover pre-production costs, festival fees, or travel. Smaller campaigns often do better because supporters are more confident that their money will go toward a tangible result.

There are also benefits to crowdfunding that go beyond money. Castellini encourages filmmakers to think of crowdfunding as audience building first, fundraising second. Treat it as if it were the beginning of your marketing campaign. You're announcing your project to the world for the first time and telling them why they should pay attention and go on the journey with you.

Where to Start

Look at other campaigns that successfully launched films that are similar to yours, and pick a crowdfunding site that fits your needs.

Kickstarter is the most popular crowdfunding site, but it's an all-or-nothing platform—if you don't meet or exceed the fundraising goal you set at the start of your campaign, the site won't collect any of the money your backers pledged. Other platforms, including Indiegogo and Seed&Spark, offer more flexible funding. Additional sites to consider include Wefunder and Patreon. Wefunder matches filmmakers with people looking to make equity investments in new projects. If you're trying to fund multiple projects, Patreon allows users to donate a set amount of money every month, which could work well for filmmakers who are planning to make a series of short films.

One of Patreon's most high-profile success stories is Issa Rae, who used Patreon to finance her web series, *The Misadventures of Awkward Black Girl*, before she created *Insecure* on HBO. Now her HOORAE page is dedicated to supporting other Black creators and funding their projects.

Other examples include actress Angel Laketa Moore (That Chick Angel), who has an active Patreon community for her family-related content; Keith Knight, who started by creating weekly comic strips that eventually inspired the sitcom *Woke*, for Hulu; and the Try Guys, who started an independent media company with the help of their fans from their successful Buzzfeed series.

Preparation Is Key

After you've chosen your platform, you have to put the same amount of energy into the preparation for the crowdfunding campaign that you'd put into any other pre-production for a project. It's not enough to just set up the campaign and hope people will come. Make sure you have enough time to concentrate on promotion.

It helps to build an audience in advance, whether it's through a social media account, YouTube page, or email newsletter. If you don't already have a platform, figure out which communities you need to reach out to, depending on who you are and what your project is about. You'll have a better chance raising money if you're sharing with like-minded people more likely to see the inherent value of what you're creating, as opposed to randomly spamming people.

Will Haines, who worked as the vice president of product and customer trust at Indiegogo, identified three primary groups of backers: those who really want to see the finished work, those who are really interested in the work's cultural or societal impact, and those who want to support the person creating it.

For example, let's look at Kayla Robinson's 2021 campaign for *Ball Is Ball*, a coming-of-age film about a high-school basketball star navigating the aftermath of a sexual assault. It was inspired by her own life experience. She knew it would appeal to several groups: those who survived sexual assault and anyone passionate about the #MeToo movement; people who are interested in women's athletics; and those vested in elevating Black and women filmmakers in Hollywood. And because she worked as an art director at Apple, she had a network of Bay Area filmmakers who'd worked on one another's projects over the years and would support her.

While it'll take time to find your most loyal fans, your communities will likely be the ones who will stick with you through multiple projects.

Have an Outreach Plan

Castellini points to a stat she often shares in her workshops: A direct email has a 20 to 30 percent chance of convincing someone to support a project, whereas a social media post succeeds less than 10 percent of the time. Direct contacts take time and effort, so create a database of potential backers and pace yourself. Keep track of everyone who is engaging with your social media feeds and reach out directly to them.

Cummings recommends learning how to use Facebook Ads Manager to target the right people—fans, advocates, filmmakers, journalists, people into crowdfunding. "You can spend twenty bucks on it and get two hundred and fifty people who otherwise wouldn't have seen your movie" to learn about it, he said.

Figure Out How to Be In-Your-Face without Being Annoying

How can you be politely in people's faces for an extended period of time? It's a tricky balance, but it boils down to finding the folks who will see your pitch as an opportunity, not as a guilt trip.

Ryan T. Husk crowdfunded a *Star Trek: Voyager* documentary in

2021, which became *To the Journey: Looking Back at Star Trek: Voyager*, the highest-funded documentary on Indiegogo. He raised $1.3 million in a month. "If I'm doing a *Star Trek* documentary and I post it in *Star Trek* groups, they're not going to say, 'Oh, this is annoying,'" he said. "They're going to say, 'Whoa, cool, a new *Star Trek* documentary? Where do I sign up?'"

Yu said one of the tips he got from his Seed&Spark mentor was that for every post you make about your project, you should be posting five times about other related topics. He'd post about new sneakers or share other Korean American stories.

Launch Strategically

Run a thirty-day campaign. There are often options to do campaigns that are longer than thirty days, but thirty-day campaigns generally tend to find more success because there is more urgency.

Don't ask for too much money. Husk advises setting your goal at the bare-bones minimum to make the film. "This is totally counterintuitive," he acknowledged. "But if you dangle a carrot way out there, people are going to say, 'That's too far. It'll never happen. I'm not going to waste my money.' Or they'll say, 'Huh, I'll come back when they get closer and see how it's doing.' They're not going to be encouraged to donate.

"But if you're asking for something that's just right over the horizon, just so attainable, then everybody will be motivated. And then you can add stretch goals."

Understand that the first day is by far the most important day of your campaign. Many crowdfunders plan in advance and ask the supporters they've already got commitments from to help them get the momentum going on day one. Once you start to show traction, you're much more likely to get contributions from people who are outside your network. Even if it's the coolest idea in the world, if people see that it has $0, they hesitate. They don't want to embark on a crowdfunding journey that looks like it might be unsuccessful.

Generating momentum from the beginning also makes it more likely that the algorithms on crowdfunding platforms will display your campaign more prominently on the site. It also makes it more likely that it'd get featured in their newsletter and appear higher in search results.

The most popular contribution times are the first week and the last three days of the campaign. The hard part is maintaining the excitement between those two periods. Offering short-term incentives in the middle weeks of the campaign helps—perhaps limited-release behind-the-scenes swag that is first come, first serve.

What's Some Good Advice?

Tell your personal story in your pitch video. Some people use a teaser as their pitch video, but it's better to have the human story behind the film. People want to support a person, cause, or mission, so tell your unique behind-the-scenes journey.

Limit the swag; keep it digital if possible. People forget that it can be exhausting to mail giveaways. You'll spend more time than you'd like at the post office. But if you do offer swag, make sure you take into consideration the cost to design, print, package, and ship the items so you're not losing money.

Tag-team your campaign. No one will care about your project more than you will, and often crowdfunding is a one-person operation. But if you can find a partner to help, it could pay off handsomely. Haines said that campaigns that have more than one person running them tend to raise more than twice as much. "I think that's because maybe you're the creative genius and you're great at the content piece," he said. "Find someone who's good at the other piece."

CHAPTER 9

How to Become a Location Manager

Location managers typically work with the director and production designer to figure out: What does this character's home look like? What does this restaurant look like? What kind of street do they need in this scene?

There's a lot of pride that comes from finding and securing the backdrop—or canvas—of a film or TV project. Lori Balton has scouted locations for *A River Runs Through It*, *Catch Me If You Can*, and *Top Gun: Maverick*. She found the site in Hawaii that would become the kingdom for the antagonist mermaids in *Pirates of the Caribbean: On Stranger Tides*. She helped pinpoint the best location in Yellowstone National Park for the Elephant Graveyard in the live-action *Lion King*. And she traversed the Amazon River, from Brazil to Peru, to provide research for Disney's *Jungle Cruise*.

But just as often, she's surveying alleys in downtown Los Angeles, stepping over dead rats, cigarette butts, and used condoms.

Depending on the size of a property, she might spend anywhere from fifteen minutes to an hour taking photos. Then the creative team will review the options, thinking about what the script requires, how much space there is for the camera and the actors to move, or whether the surrounding noise will be an issue.

For example, Heritage Square is one of Balton's favorite locations in Los Angeles. It's an outdoor architectural museum that features restored Victorian-era homes, a train station, a barn, and a church that were saved from destruction in the 1960s. But it's hard to film there, because it's so close to the loud 110 Freeway. When she needed to find a place to film a small-town neighborhood montage for Disney's *Saving Mr. Banks*—without sound—she knew Heritage Square would be perfect.

"There are other beautiful Victorian jewels strewn about Los Angeles—Pasadena even has a few that are next door to each other—so other places could have worked," Balton said. "But Heritage Square really helps create the feeling of the depth of the town around you."

The location manager's work doesn't end once the perfect location is identified. Next comes the managing portion of the job: prepping the location so the crew can film there. The logistics include pre-production (assembling a team, handling permits, dealing with agencies, getting insurance), to production (finding and securing parking, working with vendors, overseeing the use of police, firefighters, or security), to post-production (if new locations for reshoots are needed).

Shutting down a street for one day to shoot a one-minute Jaguar car crash scene in *Erin Brockovich* took six weeks for location manager Greg Alpert's team to plan.

Shutting down a stretch of the California 73 toll road to shoot a two-minute scene in *The Hangover Part III*—in which Zach Galifianakis buys a giraffe and tows it in a trailer behind his car—required numerous permits, thirty-five California Highway Patrol officers, and four months to plan.

The maps the cast and crew get when they enter a set, the yellow signs to tell people where to go, the filming notifications for residents—those are made by the locations team. Checking the environmental impacts in the places filmmakers want to shoot—that work is also done by locations.

Once the site is chosen, the art department takes over. Balton said when she is on set watching the crew prep it's like watching a magic trick. The set decorators come and move all the furniture and decorations out of the place and replace them with whatever makes sense for the film. After the shooting ends, they move everything back to exactly how they found it.

"I've seen it done so many times, and it never fails to amaze me," she said. "It's like the traveling circus comes to town. We squeeze so much in that house, we do our work, and then when we leave, the house looks exactly as if we were never there."

What Qualities Do You Find in a Successful Location Manager?

Curious people who are always noticing details about their surroundings make for good location scouts. They know why a neighborhood looks a certain way. They know about all these nooks and crannies that other people overlook.

It helps to be a skilled photographer, to know how to analyze a script, to understand lighting, and to be able to visualize how a film camera would move through the location. The directors and cinematographers rely on the location manager's initial photos to picture how they can set up their shots.

Though the job involves exploring new places on your own, it helps to be a people person. You have to knock on doors and persuade people to let you film. You have to be able to negotiate. The location management part is similar to planning an event: setting up contracts with each location and working with vendors. They arrange parking, catering, air-conditioning, security—you name it.

Most people on a film or TV set can exist in a Hollywood bubble, because their job is to be hyper-focused on helping the director or showrunner make the best product. But locations is the one department that must also consider how the production is affecting the rest of the community.

The location manager is the principal liaison between the production and the outside world. You may be knocking on neighbors' doors and getting them comfortable with the fact that there will be filming on their street. You have to be comfortable dealing with all types of people: politicians and residents—sometimes introducing neighbors who haven't met yet—in addition to business owners and unhoused people. Locations is also the department that handles a lot of the complaints, so you have to have thick skin and good communication skills. You'll often be dealing with angry, frustrated people.

"You can't take it personally when a merchant is yelling because they feel that the production has caused them to lose money—or a neighbor doesn't like that they're being held up by the police so the crew can get the shot," said Alison Taylor, veteran location manager and vice president of the Location Managers Guild International, a global nonprofit that supports location professionals. "When you're dealing with the outside world, how the movie goes is not their lives. They don't care. They're not making any money off your movie. They're going to be late for work."

How Do You Get Started?

Online courses on educational platforms including LinkedIn and Skillshare offer tips on how to organize a shoot and how to photograph locations.

The Association of Film Commissioners International offers Location Management 101, an online training course developed in collaboration with the Location Managers Guild International. It covers location research, planning, scouting, budgeting, permitting, photography, laws and regulations, transportation, security, and equipment. Learn more at the Association of Film Commissioners International website.

You can start as a general production assistant and get to know the location team and make sure location management is something you want to do. It helps to have connections, but if you don't have any, you can find a movie or TV set and ask the security guard to direct you to the location manager.

"I wouldn't recommend that for other departments," Taylor said, "but I would recommend it for our department. We are the people who interface with the community."

If you're starting in Los Angeles, the goal is to join the Hollywood Teamsters (Local 399) union, which will help you get your first gig as an assistant location manager. To get into the Teamsters, you need thirty days on union projects, so it's good to be on other location managers' radars when entry-level opportunities pop up. In cities outside of Los Angeles and New York, where location departments are not part of the Teamsters, the job you want is location department production assistant.

The Location Managers Guild International is also a great resource for those starting out. The organization hosts events and offers volunteer and networking opportunities. Taylor also suggests starting in a market outside of Los Angeles or New York—like Atlanta, Cleveland, Detroit, Pittsburgh—if you have the flexibility. It'll be less competitive.

Another strategy is to seek a job outside of Hollywood that has transferable skills. Planning live events—weddings, theater productions, fairs, or concerts—will give you experience working with vendors and site reps and may make for an easier transition into the film industry.

What Are the Career Paths?

There are three main positions: assistant location manager, key assistant location manager, and location manager. When you progress from assistant location manager to key assistant location manager, you're expected to know how to manage your own locations. The location manager hires the team and works with them to report the best options to the director and production designer.

On larger projects, there can be supervising location managers (who manage other location managers), a location scout or researcher (someone hired specifically for the scouting parts of the job), and location department coordinators (who act as the organizational hub and deal with paperwork and budgets).

How Do You Make Money? And What Kind of Money?

Once you get into Local 399, you are eligible for benefits and minimums.

As of 2026, the union minimum for assistant location managers was $2,153 a week. Location manager and key assistant location manager minimums vary, depending on the medium. For studio films, key assistant managers make a minimum of $2,700 a week and location managers make $4,142 a week.

For new one-hour episodic TV series, one-half-hour digital or videotape single-camera dramatic TV series, digital or videotape nondramatic series of any length, and all pilots, key assistant managers make a minimum of $2,862 a week and location managers make $4,018 a week. For long-form TV motion pictures, programs made for DVD, and low-budget theatrical productions, key assistant managers make a minimum of $2,788 a week and location managers make $3,914 a week.

Veterans are able to negotiate for much more. Location managers also get paid a daily rate for the car they're driving.

As of 2025, the Economic Research Institute's SalaryExpert database estimates the average base salary of a film location manager to be $127,836 a year, with an average hourly rate of $61.46. An entry-level location manager earns an average salary of $89,084. It also estimates that the salary potential for film location manager will increase 12 percent over five years.

One of the benefits of working in locations is that once you get booked on to a project, you're often there from pre-production to the end of production, Taylor said, which provides more stability than other departments where people are hired for shorter-term duties.

How Is This Career Different from Ten or Twenty-Five Years Ago?

Technology has made the job easier. Instead of shooting on film and having to give a lot of consideration to every single shot, location scouts can document more easily with their cell phones.

Now there are more virtual scouting jobs. For the 2023 live-action *Little Mermaid*, Balton was hired early on as a researcher to get ideas of what the possibilities were, before they were ready to hire a team to scout in Europe, where the film was eventually shot.

What's Some Good Advice?

Learn about architecture. "If you have a designer saying, 'I want a mid-century modern house,' you have to know what they're talking about," Taylor said.

Familiarize yourself with different parts of cities. It helps to know that Pasadena has different filming rules from the city of Los Angeles, or that Granada Hills has a pocket of Eichler houses. Build your own knowledge base.

Learn how to deal with frustrated people. The job requires managing a lot of relationships, Taylor said. You're trying to be respectful to the people and places you're filming, while accomplishing what the production needs. Alpert said he always has the same goal for each of his projects: "I always want to leave a neighborhood and for them to want us back."

CHAPTER 10

How to Become a Casting Director

It can be difficult to describe what it takes to find the perfect actor for a role on a film or TV show, but casting directors say there's something intuitive about the process. When you find the right match, you can feel it.

In 2021, Libby Goldstein and Junie Lowry-Johnson, the casting directors behind Showtime's *Yellowjackets*, had the challenge of casting teenagers for the 1996 plane crash story line, as well as their adult counterparts. Sophie Thatcher won the role as the younger version of Juliette Lewis's character, Natalie, with her self-tape. Josh Ropiequet, a casting associate for the show, said the producers kept rewatching Thatcher's self-tape the night they received it.

"She so truly was that character," he said. "Even just sitting at her desk on a self-tape."

After fans and critics widely praised the show's ensemble casting, Goldstein and Lowry-Johnson explained that they weren't necessarily looking for actors who looked alike, but for pairs who shared the same essence. Though Thatcher's and Lewis's versions of Natalie have different hair colors (bleached blond versus jet black), their raspy voices and vulnerable performances both embody the destructive character.

Directors and showrunners look to casting directors to find the right actors to bring their stories to life. They're brought on to the project during the pre-production process. The first step is to read the script and have discussions with the director or showrunner about what is needed for each particular character. If it's an action film, they might request input from the stunt coordinator. If it's a musical, they might be asking the choreographer for recommendations.

The casting team will likely have some dream actors in mind, so they'll add them to their wish list. They'll also look through headshots and reels. They're not only considering the stars for the lead roles. They have to find actors who are the best match for every single character who appears on-screen. They'll hold auditions or request self-tapes. If there isn't another actor or reader in the room for in-person auditions, casting directors may be the ones reading opposite the actors—giving them guidance and nudging them closer to what they think the production needs.

There are a lot of considerations that go into finding each actor: For example, does that person have the right look and the right chemistry to pair with the other leads? Does the actor have the skills to pull off any physicality required or the demeanor to endure what might be a challenging shoot? Casting directors also have to juggle actors' availability. They must be aware of the budget and whether the project can afford the actors they've identified.

After all the research, they will provide a curated list of recommendations to present to the project's director, showrunner, or studio executives. Once the actors are chosen, the casting team handles the deal memos and contracts.

Casting directors are always building and updating their actors' databases, so when the next opportunity comes up, they know who to approach. They often tell actors that they are auditioning not just for the role in front of them but for any part that might come up in the future. They're watching movies, scrolling through online content, going to plays, and attending showcases to keep tabs on emerging talent.

When the casting works, it feels like fate. Audiences often give the credit to the directors and the actors. Hollywood, however, understands the large role casting directors play. In 2024, the Academy of

Motion Picture Arts and Sciences added a new Oscar category of casting, for films released in 2025 and beyond.

What Qualities Do You Find in a Successful Casting Director?

Being a casting director isn't a nine-to-five job. People who work in these jobs are always watching TV shows and movies. They go to plays and film festivals on weekends, watch showcases late at night, and scroll through social media to learn about new talent.

Casting professionals need a lot of knowledge about acting and the entertainment industry, so you might consider getting a theater, film, or TV degree.

You should be a people person. Casting directors are constantly dealing with a host of actors, directors, producers, executives, and other casting professionals, working together to identify the best talent for each role. It helps to be organized, because casting directors have to keep track of a lot of names, headshots, demo reels, other people's opinions, and availabilities.

Emmy Award–winning casting director Jessica Daniels, who has cast series for Disney and Fox, likens the job to throwing a dinner party and introducing friends who you think will get along with one another. "There's something about putting together the best cast, where everyone falls in love that is like that," she said.

How Do You Get Started?

Think critically about the film and TV shows you love. What moved you? Which actors make you laugh, cry, or feel angry? Professionals call this the first step toward building your "casting muscle": learning to hone and refine your taste.

A number of colleges and universities have casting programs. The Tepper Semester program at New York's Syracuse University is a semester-long immersion program for casting. The Savannah College of Art and Design (SCAD), the University for Creative Careers, in Savannah, Georgia, offers a casting minor within the film and TV program. Chapman University's Dodge College of Film and Media Arts in Orange, California, offers a casting class with casting director Russell Boast every semester.

The Casting Society of America holds introductory casting panels, available for anyone who's interested in working in casting. Sign up for the Casting Society of America's Global Community list to get updates on events open to aspiring members. You can also sign up for the Casting Society of America job list to learn about upcoming opportunities.

High-school graduates can apply for the society's education and training program, Casting Society Cares Casting Assistant Pathway program, to learn the basics of the casting process—including prep work, auditions, tests, deals, and other paperwork. Go to castingsocietycares.org for more information.

To find entry-level opportunities in your area, search for "casting assistant" openings on employment sites such as EntertainmentCareers.net, Indeed, LinkedIn, and ZipRecruiter. Another route is to contact your local college to inquire about helping to cast student films and micro-budget independent productions.

Most casting jobs are in Los Angeles, though there are various hubs across the country, including New York, Chicago, and Atlanta. Central Casting—the company that handles casting of extras, body doubles, and stand-ins—regularly accepts résumés for team members in their California, New York, Atlanta, and Louisiana offices.

What Are the Career Paths?

In general, the pathway is to go from casting assistant to casting associate to casting director. The roles of each vary depending on the project.

A casting assistant is often tasked with more of the paperwork, including deal memos and contracts. It's common to bounce around and juggle different gigs when you start, and it takes years to get a shot at being a casting associate.

Casting associates get to be more creative and have more input in selecting the actors to pursue. Casting directors manage the entire process and communicate with all the stakeholders to figure out what everyone wants from the role.

The responsibilities of casting directors also will depend on whether they're working on a small independent film, a bigger-budget movie, or a TV show. Although television and film can be divergent career tracks in other entertainment fields, many in the casting industry are able to jump back and forth between film, television, and streaming projects.

Casting directors in independent films often are brought in early in the process, and sometimes the big-name actors they recruit can essentially get the film green-lit. Daniels worked on Desiree Akhavan's 2018 *The Miseducation of Cameron Post*, about a teenager sent to a gay-conversion-therapy center. The film struggled to get funding and was on the verge of falling apart. But then Chloë Grace Moretz dropped out of a big tentpole movie and Daniels's casting team jumped on the opportunity to get her attached. Once they had a star, the project secured financing.

For studio films and TV shows, there are many more people who need to approve the casting decisions—including casting executives. At studios like Disney or The CW, executives often do less of the nitty-gritty work of finding the actors. Instead, they oversee projects to make sure the casting decisions align with their company brand.

Kim Williams—who has worked at Disney, HBO, Paramount, Reuben Cannon Productions, and Tyler Perry Studios— and Daniels have both gone back and forth between working as a casting executive for a studio and a casting director for independent projects over the course of their careers. If you work for an established office, casting can become more of a steady gig. But it's best to think of the job as gig work, professionals say.

"Even when you go to the studio side, where there's the idea of stability, when regimes change, they might want new people," Williams said. "That's just the way things work. Nothing is *forever* forever."

How Do You Make Money? And What Kind of Money?

Casting assistants are not covered by a union contract, and often earn close to minimum wage. Their rate is similar to what production assistants make.

Once you become a casting associate, you're represented by Teamsters Local 399 Hollywood. You don't need any credits or hours worked in casting to join the union, but it often doesn't make sense to join until you get hired as a casting associate. The minimum rate for TV casting associates hired on-call in 2026 was $2,378.00 per week.

The union doesn't set minimums for film casting associates, nor does it set minimums for casting directors in feature film or television, but those rates are generally higher than the minimum for TV casting associates—and they're negotiable. Payments also vary widely based on the budget and work required. Those who are more prominent and in demand typically negotiate for more.

Salary estimates from online databases vary. According to 2024 data from the Economic Research Institute's SalaryExpert database, the average casting associate's gross salary in the United States was $57,810. According to data from Payscale, casting directors in 2025 with less than four years of experience earn an average of $52,000 annually. Those with five to nine years of experience earn an average of $92,000; those with ten to nineteen years of experience average $100,000 and those who've been in the industry more than twenty years average $136,000 a year. SalaryExpert estimated a mean annual salary of $83,727 for casting directors working in the United States.

How Is This Career Different from Ten or Twenty-Five Years Ago?

Nowadays, there isn't a reliance on VHS tapes, and hard copies of headshots in mail crates, because the casting process has moved online. The pandemic shifted auditions from in person to self-tapes and, for actors who make the first cuts, Zoom callbacks.

This was a major adjustment for the industry. The good part is that it gave more actors an opportunity to compete for a role—and there are now greater options for international searches. However, it has added to the burden for casting professionals, who can become inundated with applicants even as they are expected to do their jobs faster than ever.

Since the pandemic, there has been a hybrid of in-person, self-taped, and Zoom auditions.

"There's something about being able to just do it in the room, have that energy and feel that back-and-forth with an actor," Ropiequet said. "And also just giving a note off the cuff and saying, 'All right, let's do it again.' . . . Zoom callbacks are helpful for that, but it's still not quite the same in terms of the end result and the actual feeling of an audition."

What's Some Good Advice?

Take some acting, improv, or directing classes. These skills are helpful during an audition, where often casting directors are reading with actors or encouraging them to try to read the scene in different ways.

"A lot of times I'll have the pages in front of me, but I've done the scene enough that I don't have to look down," said Ropiequet, who has a background in theater. "And there was one time where I was really in it and very much acting from the chair opposite an actor, and she was so taken aback by that, that I had the pages in my lap but didn't even touch them."

Be confident in your unique background and points of view. Daniels said that when she hires her casting team, she's looking for someone who has different interests than she does. "I look to start with a wide lens when approaching talent and material," she said.

Be flexible. People often assume casting directors have more power over a production than they really do. "Yes, we are doing what we can to make sure that we're getting the best actors, in our minds, for the role," Ropiequet said. "But at the same time, we've had to start from square one in a few cases, because one producer or one executive somewhere just can't see it." At the end of the day, casting directors are there to assist the people who oversee the final vision—and you have to let them find their own way.

PART 5

REPRESENTATION

CHAPTER 11

How to Become an Agent

Since the demise of the Hollywood studio system after World War II, filmmakers have largely been freelancers. Even the most celebrated writers, directors, and actors now earn a living one project at a time, rather than counting on a biweekly paycheck from a Universal Studios or a Warner Bros.

The A-listers and rising stars can at least count on their services being in demand (at the moment). For the less celebrated players, life is an endless series of job applications, whether in the form of pitch meetings, auditions, or screen tests.

In most cases, though, they have professional help: an agent, whose job is to obtain gigs for their clients. In exchange for 10 percent of the income from the projects they helped land, agents will promote their clients' talents and star power (real or potential) to the producer, director, or casting director doing the hiring. Agents may also negotiate the terms of the deal and step in to help enforce them if a dispute arises on set.

That's why many people in Hollywood's creative class, particularly those who aren't household names, view agents as indispensable. Actors still have to nail the auditions, writers still have to deliver a winning screenplay, but their agents are the ones finding and even generating the opportunities.

Bear in mind that, with the possible exception of those working with child actors, agents aren't in the career-launching or strategizing business. That's a talent manager's turf. "If an agent decides to work with you, it's because they feel they can make money with you," Steve Stevens Sr. wrote in *So You Want to Be in Show Business*. "It's strictly about dollars and cents."

Agents tend to sign clients after those artists have already started getting jobs. They typically have dozens of clients. And they regularly dump clients who aren't generating revenue. It's an annual process that the wags call drop season, when agents take a hard look at their roster and decide who isn't generating enough business to be worth their time. It works both ways; actors and filmmakers can dump their agents too.

One of the hazards of working at a smaller agency is helping a client become a hot property, only to have the client leave for an agent with more perceived clout. The Association of Talent Agents lists 115 member agencies, but three powerful ones dominate the landscape—William Morris Endeavor (WME), Creative Artists Agency, and United Talent Agency.

Just how transactional the relationship is between agent and client will depend on the parties involved. While there's no getting around the economics of the work—agents don't get paid unless their clients get bookings—some agents say that the job involves creativity as well as salesmanship.

For example, Chris Noriega, a partner at the Verve Talent & Literary Agency, said that if you're working with a writer who is penning a script, you'll be the first person to read and give feedback on it. "You're really there at the ground level with new ideas, and that's really exciting."

Tracy Christian, who runs her own talent agency, TCA MGMT, in Beverly Hills, said the job is 100 percent creative for her. "It's creative in who you sign, why you sign, and how you push them forward. How you help them define a successful career. Especially when you're negotiating a contract, it's about being creative."

Under California's 1978 Talent Agency Act, agents must obtain a state license, which requires a showing of "good moral character," and carry a $50,000 "talent agency bond" to protect their clients against fraud. Among other things, the law also forbids agents to set up shop in a bar, brothel, or casino. To check whether the agency you want to join has a valid license, use the directory on the California Department of Industrial Relations website, dir.ca.gov.

New York has similar rules, requiring agents to be licensed by the state, to be of good moral character, and to post a bond. You can find a list of licensed agencies at the NY Department of Labor website, https://dol.ny.gov/employment-agencies.

California law allows only licensed talent agents to be in the business of "procuring, offering, promising, or attempting to procure employment or engagements for an artist or artists." The line that defines this boundary is blurry in practice, however, as a number of managers seek auditions and book work for their clients.

Agents spend much of their day making new connections in the industry and tapping their existing contacts to find work for their clients. In a typical week, motion picture literary agents will call and meet with clients, talk to executives at the studios they cover, call producers who have deals with those studios, talk to other agents about potential opportunities for their clients, go to lunches with producers and executives to cultivate and nurture relationships, and attend screenings, premieres, and other events.

It's all about the transaction in the short term, but in the long term it's about building durable connections with the people who can make your clients successful—and you in the process.

What Qualities Do You Find in a Successful Agent?

The people who are drawn to this field aren't necessarily film or TV aficionados. Instead, they are fascinated by the industry's inner workings—the dealmaking that powers Hollywood productions and drives the careers of creative people forward.

They also tend to be well educated, ambitious, and competitive—in some cases, ruthlessly so. While the pros say that some of their colleagues are, in fact, sharks, you can't succeed in this line of work without serious people skills. You'll need them both to persuade talented people to sign on as clients and to persuade other talented people to hire them. Besides, Noriega said, "You can only burn so many bridges. This isn't just transactional. You are dealing with the same people over and over again."

You have to be personable—and unafraid. Agency work is not for timid people or wallflowers.

"The ability to deal with a wide variety of personalities, let's just say, is vital," said Amos Newman, founder of Word is Bond and a former partner at WME. Not only do you have to be able to work the room, he said, but you have to communicate and do business with people you may not get along with.

Being an elite schmoozer is necessary but not sufficient; you'll also need an aesthetic sense that people trust. Confidence is important too, confidence in who you are, confidence in what you're saying, and confidence in your ability to seal the deal. Agents also must be resilient and persistent, the pros say, because they hear "no" frequently. And their job is to get to "yes."

"Who hears 'no' more than the agent?" Christian said. "'No, I will not read this script.' 'No, your client can't have the audition.' No, no, no, no, no. You hear it every day in every way, even when they're hiring your client. 'No, you cannot have that billing.' 'No, we're not paying in advance.'"

Agents also should be able to envision and identify opportunities for their clients beyond the acting, writing, or directing gigs for which they're best known. These days, agents are working with clients on an array of pursuits beyond bookings, such as signing endorsement deals, building second careers as a producer, and leveraging their other interests (e.g., their love of hockey or Formula 1 racing) to promote their personal brands.

Durability is important too, given the long hours and relentless demands of the job. "It's nonstop," Noriega said. "You're up super early in the morning, and you're up pretty late at night. Nonstop meetings, phone calls, Zooms, pitches—and then when you have a moment of quiet, you have ten scripts to read. It is tiring; it is *really* tiring. You have to have the energy. For me, the energy comes from having a true passion for the job and what you do every day."

Agents say that it's important to have a "just get it done" mentality, because that's what clients expect. So it helps to be resourceful in handling the challenges thrown at you, and persuasive as you try to sell your clients' services to the market. After all, selling is a big part of the job.

How Do You Get Started?

A common entry point is still a job in a large agency's mailroom. Noriega, for example, was an MBA and former bank executive when he decided at age thirty-one to try his hand in Hollywood, landing in the mailroom of the Gersh Agency in Beverly Hills.

"The idea of going into a mailroom and starting at the absolute bottom was kind of a tough pill to swallow," Noriega said. On the other hand, he said, he wasn't making the jump to Hollywood just to keep looking at spreadsheets—he wanted to do something he was passionate about.

The usual route is to spend several months (and possibly a year or two) in a mailroom, delivering mail and packages, printing copies of scripts, and handling other entry-level tasks. The next step is to fill in for absent assistants as a "floater," then be hired by an agent as an assistant. It typically takes several more months or years for the agency to move you up to a full-fledged agent. Assistants can jump to other agencies if they want to move up faster, just as agents can switch agencies in search of greater decision-making power.

Getting a mailroom job—or, as some agencies call it, admittance into their training program—can be highly competitive, requiring candidates to perform well in multiple interviews at the bigger firms. Having a summer internship at an agency on your résumé is a plus, although the competition for those can be fierce too.

Starting at an agency is a smart move even if you ultimately decide that being an agent isn't for you. Working at an agency puts you in the best position to see everything about the entertainment business—especially if you're at a large agency that represents clients in food, fashion, and other industries outside of film, television, and music.

But let's not sugarcoat what happens to the people who do get their foot in the door. The process of becoming an agent, particularly at a big agency, is often akin to a fraternity hazing that lasts months, even years. Agents say a very small percentage of the people who start down that path make it all the way to the end.

The pros insist that low-level agency employees aren't subjected to the kind of abuse that David Rensin chronicled in his seminal 2003 book, *The Mailroom: Hollywood History from the Bottom Up*. The agents Rensin interviewed told of bosses who delivered withering, almost sadistic criticism of them in front of their coworkers, who yelled at them constantly, who threw or smashed staplers and phones at the slightest upset, and who made seemingly impossible demands just to try to make them quit.

Still, to work your way up, you'll have to do menial jobs for hours on end—preparing breakfast meetings, refueling cars, booking flights, booking tables, sending gifts, cleaning clothes, feeding pets, driving to and from the airport, and so on. You very well may be yelled at when you make a mistake, which you will definitely make. You will be paid a wage well below what a professional should earn (it used to be minimum wage, but it's higher now) and be constantly on call. And even when you're not in the office, you may spend all your free time reading scripts and writing summaries so the agent you work for won't have to.

You'll be tested constantly by your employers—how well you handle stress, how resourceful you are, how you respond to irrational demands. They want to know if you really will do whatever it takes to accomplish what needs to be accomplished.

Some agents will actively train their assistants, but much of the education will come from watching the agents and listening in on their calls (while taking notes). It's about learning the business from the inside—the names, the places, the relationships—and forming your own connections.

Noriega worked for a month or two in the Gersh mailroom, then became an assistant at Gersh for Bayard Maybank, rolling phone calls (that is, connecting your boss to one person after another on the phone, with you doing all the dialing), setting up meetings, and reading scripts. As it happened, Maybank didn't follow the stereotypical agent's playbook of intimidation and aggression, Noriega said—he was down-to-earth, loved movies and reading scripts, and operated with passion, excitement, and positivity.

"So that was like, 'Oh, OK, you could be this way as an agent,'" said Noriega, who became an agent at Verve in 2013, a little more than a year after starting his mailroom stint at Gersh. "You don't have to be like a maniac person."

Nevertheless, people who have worked their way up from mail sorter to assistant to agent say the journey can be demeaning, life sucking, and depressing. Still, defenders of the process say it's not cruelty for the sake of cruelty. Instead, they say, the process is designed to show assistants how demanding an agent's work is, and to weed out the ones who won't be able to handle it.

Christian said that when she got into the business, she assumed that most agents were highly educated people who were extremely well-read and knowledgeable about film. Feeling insecure about her level of expertise, she made it a point to see as many of the American Film Institute's top one hundred films and to churn through a list of the most important books in the Western canon. She told herself not to fake it; she wanted to have meaningful conversations with the creators she admired and wanted her clients to work with. As it turns out, she realized as she rose through the ranks, none of the other assistants had done any of that work. "Then I was less hard on myself."

But her pursuit of knowledge continued. She tried to hang out with writers, directors, and showrunners to learn the mechanics and vocabulary of film and television, so that when she spoke to them about her clients, she was speaking their language. She also relentlessly pursued the people whose work moved her, reaching out via email to praise what they'd done and asking to talk about what they could do for each other.

"I am so glad I built that knowledge base," she said.

Noriega's rise has been relatively quick. He feels lucky to have been assigned to cover HBO as an assistant, which made him the point person at his agency for shows on the network that were hiring writers and directors. That helped him build relationships with the network and producers as well as the agency clients who were trying to land those jobs.

Doing the grunt work of a junior agent well—developing good sources of information at the networks and studios you cover, preparing clients for meetings and auditions, promoting clients for openings that you've learned about—is how you make a name for yourself with senior agents and high-level clients, Noriega said. That, in turn, is how you attract high-level clients and move up in the agency world.

An agent's definition of success can change quite a bit over time, however.

Christian said that when she was thirty success meant her clients made a ton of money and worked on high-profile projects. For her, it was working at one of the biggest agencies, being feared by others in the industry, and getting invitations to all the right parties.

In short? "I would be the female Ari Gold," the character played by Jeremy Piven on *Entourage.*

Today, she said, success still means her clients are making a bunch of money and doing all the right projects, but "by 'right projects' now I mean truly a mix of art and commerce."

It also means consciously deciding whom she wants to be in business with, which means representing artists who are taking chances on independent films and riskier projects, not doing "empty studio film after empty studio film." And it means being respected, not feared.

Christian also feels an obligation as a woman in the field where there isn't a profusion of women to make the path easier for people "who look like me and think like me." That, in turn, will make the industry more profitable and lead to real competition "based on merit, aesthetics, and not nepotism or any other-ism."

What Are the Career Paths?

There are multiple types of agents in the entertainment world, including those who specialize in film and television, the stage, commercials, modeling, voice actors, authors, podcasters, and child actors. Within those fields, agents may also focus on a particular genre. The basic parameters of the job are the same—helping clients find work—but each field has its own players. The people who hire writers, actors, and directors for commercial shoots aren't the same ones who hire for Broadway or for audiobooks or for feature films. Some agencies cross-pollinate, however. For example, at WME, agents can work in multiple fields and genres, including music, television, sports, motion picture, and comedy.

Within an agency, people typically rise from assistant to agent to partner, then move into positions of greater authority within agency management. But there is also a hierarchy among agencies; agents often move from small firms to larger ones in search of higher-profile clients and higher-profile gigs for the clients they already have.

"The belief is, and I encounter this all the time, that smaller agencies are the First Wives Club," Christian said. "When I got into the business, I believed that too—to represent clients the way I wanted to represent them, I needed to move to a larger agency. Now that I've been in the business for a while, I know it's not true." That's because clients are represented by teams of professionals, and if they're all doing their jobs, the client will be successful, she said.

The agency world has consolidated significantly in recent years, and there's been an exodus of top agents to talent management firms where they are free to produce projects. But the work isn't going away; agents remain an integral part of Hollywood's star-making machinery.

How Do You Make Money? And What Kind of Money?

Agents earn a base salary and bonus based on their performance and commission from the deals they close for their clients, so a big part of their success is also based on the fortunes of the talent they represent. Base salaries can start in the five-figure range, but many senior agents make seven-figure salaries.

Having a roster with multiple high-salaried actors or filmmakers can translate into a Maserati and Moët lifestyle. But getting to that point is a tough slog, and once you do, you'll have to worry about rival agents trying to lure away your top clients.

Agents' fees aren't limited by law, other than prohibitions on commissions charged before a gig is obtained or split with the company doing the hiring. But agencies' contracts with the major Hollywood unions bar them from charging more than 10 percent commission for work on productions covered by union contracts.

Some agents also used to make a considerable amount of money by "packaging" clients together for a studio—for example, pulling together a showrunner, a writer, and lead actors for a new TV series—then charging the studio a percentage of the revenue instead of collecting commissions from their clients. But the WGA forced agencies to give up those deals in 2022. In the guild's view, substituting packaging fees for commissions eliminated the agents' incentive to fight for higher pay for their clients because their revenue was no longer based on their clients' income. That's one reason so many agents switched to the talent management side of the business, where they could produce films and TV shows.

How Is This Career Different from Ten or Twenty-Five Years Ago?

Agencies are undergoing cultural shifts, as Hollywood has faced a reckoning over the treatment of women with the #MeToo movement and calls for workplaces to oust bullies.

"We've seen a sea change in HR policies pretty much everywhere, and rightfully so," Newman said. "The tolerance for that kind of bad behavior just doesn't exist. . . . On balance, things are much better now in that regard."

The "frat-boy, white-straight-male fantasy" culture of agencies, and the abuse that accompanied that, led to a brain drain in recent years, Christian said. Big agencies aren't the magnet they used to be for the best and the brightest, who are turned off by the prospect of working sixteen hours a day for five years only to be laid off, or beating the bushes to discover great new artists only to have a partner at the agency steal them, she said.

"Smart people don't want that. This generation says no to that, never mind the racism, the sexism, and all the other-isms that are inherent in that system," she said. "So today it's really about being a balanced person, being an honest person, having a quality of life. All of those things make me a far more effective and better agent, frankly."

Some agencies have also been stepping up their recruitment efforts to diversify their ranks, which historically have been dominated by older white men. The agent population is more multigenerational and multiracial. Still, white men continue to hold the reins at the big agencies, even though they don't wield as much power as they used to.

One structural barrier to people of color has been the extensive demands on assistants—the expensive professional attire, the long hours of overtime, script reading, and movie watching, the costly schmoozing events—while earning minimum wage. "And who could do that? So you didn't have to say, 'No Blacks allowed,' or 'No white men from state schools,'" Christian said. "Just the activity of it was a culling process."

A revolt by assistants during the pandemic brought about a lot of changes, including significantly higher wages. Still, most agencies are based in Los Angeles and New York, where making even $30 an hour isn't sufficient.

The rise in streaming platforms has also caused big shifts in the industry. As TV seasons have gotten shorter, agents have had to work harder to find jobs for their clients. Meanwhile, "all the major buyers go off an algorithm," Noriega said, leaving fewer executives who use their instincts, not data, to judge whether to green-light a project. It also has meant less stability among the decision-making executives, particularly at the streaming companies.

Christian doesn't believe AI is making key programming decisions at this point, just as it isn't writing scripts—it simply isn't good enough at such things yet. And while she argued that the threat posed by AI is real ("This is the start of every horror film. This is it."), she added that it's a mistake to run from technology. The issue isn't the tool, she said, it's how people use it.

What's Some Good Advice?

Be patient. Agents say you don't have to be the youngest and the fastest to build your client list. It's important to take time to develop those skills, because it takes years to learn, Noriega said. "It's a small town and you build a reputation for yourself. It will determine how your career plays out," he said. "You can start signing clients, but you don't really know what you're doing right away. If you mess up, if you make a mistake, that can haunt you. That can affect your credibility out there."

But begin building relationships early. That means going to events, festivals, and even bars and restaurants known to be industry hangouts to make connections.

Believe that your opinion matters. At a big agency, Newman said, "with all those alphas," speaking up can be really hard. But don't be intimidated—just because another agent has more clients and more experience, that doesn't make their ideas any better than yours.

CHAPTER 12

How to Become a Talent Manager

Thanks to HBO's *Entourage*, the public understands the role that talent agents play in Hollywood: They're the folks trying to turn their clients into stars by getting them work on movies and TV shows.

What talent managers do to earn their commissions, however, is more obscure. Sure, there have been some famous ones—Bernie Brillstein, for example, managed Muppets creator Jim Henson and several seminal figures from *Saturday Night Live*; Kris Jenner manages the Kardashian family juggernaut. But even if you recognize the names, you probably have trouble explaining how they've helped their clients' careers.

Think of a manager as a sherpa leading creative people along the rocky path toward a career in the entertainment industry. Need to find dancing lessons, acting classes, or a dialect coach? Call your manager.

Need to find a writing partner with a particular expertise? Call your manager.

Need a photographer for headshots? Suggestions for how to network? Translation of contract terms? Introductions to agents, publicists, and entertainment lawyers? A critique of a spec script? A shoulder to cry on? Call your manager.

Need to pitch your script to a studio or line up an audition for a show? Call your agent. Then call your manager.

A 1978 California law gives licensed agents the exclusive right in that state to engage in "the occupation of procuring, offering, promising, or attempting to procure employment or engagements for an artist." New York has a similar provision. So legally speaking, an agent's job is to line up potential gigs for a client and help win them. A manager's job is to prepare a client to compete for gigs and help decide which ones are worth taking, considering the trajectory of the client's career.

The line between agent and manager isn't as distinct as it used to be, however. In the 1990s and early 2000s, agents who wanted to produce movies and TV shows started to move from agencies to management firms. Though they were now managers, steering careers and pulling together projects, they continued to perform some of the work they used to do as agents, lining up gigs for clients. This prompted some squabbling in the courts over managers crossing into agents' turf, but eventually agents, managers, and clients recognized that they could all work together to advance the clients' careers.

Music managers will book tours. Actors' managers will look at casting calls and pitch their clients. Writers' managers will try to persuade producers to use their clients' scripts. Managers, in other words, help their clients get hired, albeit less directly than agents do. But unlike agents, they're also all about getting their clients *ready* to be hired.

Susan Ferris, chief executive of Bohemia Group, said actors' lives revolve around auditions, so she will coach and read lines with her clients, as well as make sure they have the right headshots and a good social media presence. Sometimes with a more established client, she'll push back against projects that she doesn't think are a good fit, acting as a sort of career conscience.

"It's really about curating their whole profile, whatever that looks like," Ferris said.

It's also about taking the long view, said Craig Rogalski, the head of CK Talent Management. Agents, he said, are like car salespeople focused on the next sale—the cars being the talent they represent, and the next sale being the next deal. But like the owners of the dealership, managers have to worry about their talent being successful for years to come.

Managers tend to represent fewer people than agents do and can exert enormous decision-making power on their clients' behalf, signing checks and contracts for them, hiring agents, and directing publicity. "Some talent managers are very hands-on and give very specific instructions on every little step that you make in the entertainment industry, including exactly what acting teacher and coaches to use, workshops to attend, what photographer to use, where to get your haircut, and so on," former talent manager Wendy Alane Wright wrote on her blog. "Others have much more flexibility and only give you suggestions for these things."

Representation is a team effort, and the client is ultimately the captain of the ship. But it is the role of the manager to oversee the clients' goals and make sure everyone is rowing in the same direction.

What Qualities Do You Find in a Successful Manager?

The field has its share of MBAs and lawyers, many of whom got their introduction to the film and TV business at a talent agency. Still, the pros say you don't need an advanced degree to be a manager; instead, you need to have good interpersonal skills and a deft hand at negotiating. You also need to be empathetic and adept at reading emotions in a meeting room.

As a result, the barriers to entry in the field are low. And with the burgeoning amount of entertainment being produced and consumed, the number of actors, writers, directors, and other creatives continues to grow—which has industry analysts predicting that the demand for managers will grow modestly as well.

Being a good communicator is crucial because a manager is constantly talking to people—checking on their clients, looking for opportunities for them, expanding their own networks. A manager will spend hours on the phone and the computer on calls, email exchanges, texts, and video chats with clients, the people who support them, and the people who might hire them. Managers also seek out in-person meetings to build a network of contacts for their clients, either one-on-one or at screenings and festivals.

Managers don't rely just on their interpersonal skills, though. They also have to know a lot about their clients' field, whether it be music, movies, television, or completely unrelated ventures that clients want to enter. "You should know any business that you're in, backwards and forwards," Ferris said.

Because new managers aren't likely to represent clients who are already stars, they must be able to discover the folks who have that potential—and then help sell them to the industry. That means understanding and being able to convey each client's talent, value, and the qualities that differentiate them. So it helps to be steeped in film and television, as well as knowing what's currently working in the marketplace. Fearlessness and grit are important traits too, as well as a sense for when to speak up and fight for your client.

"I will burn down my . . . agency before I let my client be taken advantage of," Rogalski said. He's seen a lot of agents—in sharp contrast to how he protects his clients—blatantly look the other way in such situations, and also threaten to drop clients who don't do as they wish.

He guards clients against the sort of predatory behavior that prompted the #MeToo movement—behavior that Rogalski thinks is still taking place. That's why his talent contracts have a clause requiring clients to obtain his permission before meeting or being alone with anyone who ranks above them in the industry. The point, he said, is to give clients a rock-solid reason to turn down meetings that make them feel uneasy and uncomfortable, because they can say the meeting would violate their contract with their manager.

How Do You Get Started?

Although Rogalski said that classes in public speaking, debate, and negotiation can be useful, the pros agreed that no books or classes can prepare you to be a manager better than hands-on experience. That's why an internship at a management company would be a good first step.

Rogalski's CK Talent Management, for example, has a two-semester internship for college students enrolled in a program relevant to the work they'd do at his firm. Some who've gone through that program have stayed on with the firm, while many others have moved on to be executives at studios and other talent management companies. Rogalski said his agency's internship program has produced some of the industry's youngest top executives.

Many internships are advertised online and can be found through a Google search for "talent manager internship." Management companies often look for college students willing to work for credit hours or individuals seeking mentorship, not pay. Although applicants with a background in film or marketing may have an edge, the qualifications sought most frequently are organizational and communications skills.

Another possibility is to find a spot as a manager's assistant at one of many boutique management firms. An IMDbPro account will help you find the firms that manage the sorts of talent you might want to represent (that is, actors, directors, and so on). And if you're particularly interested in screenwriters, you can find the names of dozens of them for free by checking out The Black List (blcklst.com), which compiles promising but unproduced scripts each year and includes the names of the managers behind them.

Stephanie Moy was working as a nanny for a casting director when she decided to become a manager. She put a résumé together, applied to management companies across town, and took any opportunity to have a conversation with anyone who was willing to have a conversation with her. She kept at it until she drew some interest. "I think that's really what it takes, that sort of tenacity and relentlessness to keep trying." She's now a manager at M88, representing film and TV actors and actor/writer/directors.

Ferris, who started Bohemia after working for the manager of the rock band Slayer in the early 1990s, strongly recommends learning from an established manager. She suggested spending two years as an assistant. "You sit at a desk for two years, you not only learn; you [might] also learn that this is not what you want to do. I think that's one of the smartest ways to get in there and start working."

The great thing about being an assistant is that you get the opportunity to see how managers do the many things they do, and what they can and cannot say. That includes working with actors, agents, casting directors, production companies, and lawyers. You also can form valuable connections with the assistants in the casting offices, who are working their way up the ladder just as you are.

Most of your time as an assistant, however, will be spent on the decidedly unglamorous work of managing your boss's time—scheduling meetings, placing calls, getting coffee, copying scripts or other paperwork (and reading it all), running errands, making deliveries, fetching meals, and endlessly taking notes.

The pay for assistants is low—job postings in 2025 were offering \$20 to \$25 an hour in California, or up to \$55,000 a year—so you'll want to be sure to find someone willing to help you develop, Ferris said. "There has to be an expectation and understanding on both sides that there's going to be a lot of mistakes."

Bohemia is largely staffed by people who got their start with Ferris, generally without much experience. "If they sit on my desk for two years, I can mold them," she said. "There are a lot of management companies that will do that."

Alternatively, some folks simply start their own management company, then try to recruit clients and help them find work.

Chris Giovanni is one example. After graduating from high school in Woodland Hills, he paired friends who were models with friends who were professional photographers, taking 10 percent of the modeling fee as a commission. Seeing a business opportunity, the nineteen-year-old launched CGEM Talent in Los Angeles with a website and $100 in the bank.

It was not an auspicious debut. He would cold-call casting directors, producers, and TV networks and was "met with a dial tone because they weren't interested."

He built his initial client base by finding a specialty niche: signing models and unscripted TV actors. To find out who was hiring and for what projects, he paid for an account at Breakdown Express to receive synopses of the projects that were being cast, along with the names of the key members of the casting and production teams.

He worked relentlessly to connect with agents, casting directors, and others in the industry, offering to take them to lunch in exchange for guidance. (In addition to Breakdown Express, IMDbPro is a great resource for contact information.) Although most of his emails landed with a thud, a small percentage of the people he reached out to responded and provided valuable tips.

That's how he started building the network that has enabled him to get meetings—not dial tones—for his clients. He still spends a fair amount of time and money schmoozing, buying lunches for people he wants to add to his contact list. "A big portion of my success in being able to get clients in scripted television is the relationships that I developed," he said.

As important as it is to cultivate relationships, so is putting forward clients with real talent. As they become successful, word will spread about the role you played in getting them started, bringing more clients your way and spreading your reputation among industry executives.

Increasingly, managers are starting out in talent agencies—a launching pad for a wide variety of careers in entertainment. That's where you can learn the inner workings of the industry. In addition to developing relationships with creatives, even entry-level agency employees see how all the key players—including producers, directors, writers, and actors—connect there.

What Are the Career Paths?

Most management companies are small operations, often consisting of the principal manager and a few assistants. Assistants can get promoted to managers, and at bigger firms successful managers can be promoted to partners, with a bigger stake in the company.

Managers also say that their client lists evolve over time, as their clients' success attracts bigger names to their fold. But the quest for higher-end clients also leads some managers at small firms to jump to larger firms, just as some actors do. "I think it's the nature of our business," Ferris said. Although Bohemia has grown, signing and holding on to bigger actors, "everybody's always looking to move to the next place."

Another possibility is to move from a management firm to a production company or a studio as a development executive. But many managers have it both ways: They manage clients while also serving as producers on their projects, which can be a natural progression with some clients.

How Do You Make Money? And What Kind of Money?

Giovanni said he didn't go into the business with an eye on how much money he could make; at first, he said, it was "one hundred dollars here, one hundred dollars there, but I stayed persistent with it." After six or seven years, he said, he was making in the low six figures.

"It can take a couple of years, sometimes it can take six months," to earn a living as a manager, he said. "It just depends on how much focus you have on it." Some managers take on side jobs to make ends meet, but Giovanni believes it's important to find innovative outlets for your clients' talents in order to develop more sources of income for them (and yourself).

Managers who sign affiliation agreements with SAG-AFTRA, the actors union, agree not to impose up-front fees or offer contracts with clients that the manager can renew automatically and unilaterally. But the agreements don't limit the size of a manager's commission; those typically range from 10 to 15 percent of the client's gross earnings.

How Is This Career Different from Ten or Twenty-Five Years Ago?

One of the biggest differences is how the focus of the job has broadened beyond steering clients in their chosen fields. Now managers explore a diverse range of opportunities for clients to exploit their fame and creativity while generating new sources of income. An established client's core strength may be in acting, for example, but that actor may want to expand into such things as clothing lines, sports teams, and production companies. All these pursuits feed one another in sort of a business ecosystem now, Moy said.

Managers can't be experts in all the different businesses their clients may want to get into, which means they need good teammates more than ever. It also requires a different approach for every client, even if they're all actors or screenwriters or musicians.

The advent of broadband and digital media has freed managers from having to send out dozens of copies of their clients' résumés, headshots, and tapes. But the same technologies make managers more accessible to clients, filmmakers, and casting directors than they've ever been—for better or worse.

"There's no turn-off time," Ferris said. "There isn't a time zone where I don't have somebody working on something."

The field is diversifying too, with more opportunities for women and people of color. "Back in the old days, the business itself was different," she said. "Women were looked at like, 'Get me some coffee, honey.'"

With audiences fragmented and original programming available from a seemingly endless number of sources, it's become more challenging to predict what people want to watch. "It's harder to have a moment for a client right now because of that," Moy said. "It's like trying to capture lightning in a bottle."

Rogalski believes that the era of the big studios and talent agencies is ending, their power being eroded by streaming services and the shift in how the industry does business. The streaming services are run by tech people who are driven by data and analytics, he said, which is why his firm has an analytics department to help pitch its clients in a language the services understand. Considering the growing role that data and algorithms are playing in how projects are green-lit and cast, more managers may soon be hiring numbers crunchers too.

What's Some Good Advice?

Don't get too close to your clients. "I'm friendly with all of my clients. I'm not friends with all of my clients. And I think that's really important," Ferris said. Being too close, she said, "makes it harder to tell the truth."

Be selective. Giovanni and Ferris said new managers often take on any and every client who comes their way as they try to build their businesses. That's a mistake, they said, and a painful way to find out what sorts of clients you *don't* want to represent.

Follow your gut. "'Nobody knows anything,'" Moy said, quoting writer William Goldman's famous critique of Hollywood, "and there are no rules. Find people, and don't stop looking until you do, that lift you up, that believe in your perspective, that believe in you, and sometimes challenge you."

CHAPTER 13

How to Become a Publicist

An up-and-coming star lands a role on a TV show, suddenly graces the cover of a major magazine, and gains a million Instagram followers. A celebrity is photographed by paparazzi in a park where she just happens to be all glammed up. An actor becomes the face of an emerging social justice movement.

From the outside, it's fun to believe in the Hollywood fantasy that these things just magically happen. But it takes a lot of work and planning to carve out a public persona and to get that story in front of a large audience. That's where a publicist comes in.

In Hollywood, some publicists work for talent—that is, actors, directors, and other people who work in front of or behind the camera. Some are hired by studios or streaming services. Others promote specific films, TV shows, or digital media projects.

Unlike advertisers who pay others to run their promotions, publicists specialize in "earned media." Their role is to pitch ideas and persuade people (media, celebrities, influencers) to help them share information more widely.

An important part of the work is talking with clients. "What do you want to do? What do you want to be known for? How are we going to get there, step by step?"

There's a stereotype of a Hollywood publicist as someone who crafts fake, media-friendly images for difficult celebrities. Though this might have happened in the past, it's hard for celebrities to get away with it anymore. Contemporary audiences are savvy and will eventually see through most pretenses.

It can come across as gatekeeping, but the job of a publicist is to protect their client's voice and vision. Publicists often sit in on their client's interviews. They can stop journalists from asking certain questions. Part of being a good publicist is figuring out a way to be decisive and stern while still being respectful and professional.

Publicists may provide their clients with media training to limit the chances of salacious headlines based on quotes taken out of context. "When those Twitter alerts start coming through—'So and so said this!' 'And so and so said this!'—that can be very triggering," said Erica Tucker, co-head of talent at AM PR Group.

It's also about knowing what your clients can handle and what they can't. Tucker sees her job as helping people shape their legacies. After all, the behind-the-scenes stories of Hollywood are often written by journalists but nurtured and strategized by publicists.

What Qualities Do You Find in a Successful Publicist?

"Whenever I'm asked this question," said Annalee Paulo, president at 42West, "I jokingly say, 'Publicists are people who like organizing other people's chaos.'"

They're people who enjoy socializing and connecting, but they also need to be good at thinking strategically about their client's image or message. Which publications will help get this story out there? Which journalists will understand the mission of this project? What kind of image does this person want to project in that photo shoot? And what do you do when someone, inevitably, messes up publicly and needs some damage control? It helps to be nurturing, because publicists are guiding their clients through very public and high-stakes moments of their career.

Entertainment publicists should also want to live and breathe entertainment. It's important to watch television and movies constantly, to understand the trends and what your clients' projects are competing against. It is not a forty-hour, nine-to-five job.

Finally, publicists should be good writers, because they devote a lot of their time to composing pitches and press releases. This is why publicity is often an appealing draw for writers in other lines of work who want a more stable job.

How Do You Get Started?

Traditionally, you start with an internship. Tucker had two PR internships in North Carolina, one for the county and another for a university, before moving to Los Angeles for an entertainment PR internship. Paulo landed an internship at MGM Studios after hearing about it from a friend.

It helps to know someone in the business who can connect you with an internship opportunity—though that's not the only way. You can contact college career centers, look up trainee programs offered by big studios, or even cold-call and email organizations. Follow filmmakers and projects you love on social media, and learn about the studios, networks, or production companies that might be hiring. Making friends is key. People get jobs through referral, and often those come from the people you meet in your first internships.

It's also common to start with a communications job in an unrelated field to gain basic publicity skills. David Magdael, whose publicity firm David Magdael & Associates, Inc., mostly focuses on documentary films, began his career doing healthcare-related PR.

Another way to gain experience is to volunteer with the marketing or talent relations department at a local film festival or large community event, such as a concert, a fair, or live theater.

Before he landed a job in entertainment, Magdael volunteered for the L.A. Asian Pacific Film Festival. Through that network, he met Keiko Ibi, then a film grad student, who got nominated for a documentary short Oscar and needed someone to help her with publicity. He took on the challenge. Ibi's surprise Oscar win in 1999 gave Magdael the confidence—and more opportunities—to run publicity campaigns for other projects and eventually start his own company.

What Are the Career Paths?

If you want to become a Hollywood publicist, be prepared to spend two to three years as an assistant to a publicist, doing a lot of grunt work. You'll order a lot of coffee and salads, but you'll also learn how the industry works.

While different companies have different titles, the next step is generally coordinator or junior publicist, then publicist, followed by senior publicist, director, vice president, then president.

It's also possible to jump among focuses, because there is a lot of overlap. For example, someone who has experience as a celebrity publicist is probably also quite familiar with how to run media campaigns for film projects.

When Tucker was at her previous company, she had to decide whether to continue moving up the ladder or start her own company. She launched Ascend PR Group in 2015 with only one client: actress Yara Shahidi of *Black-ish* and *Grown-ish*. She helped Shahidi develop her platform advocating for girls' education while also promoting her persona as a young fashion icon.

Coming from the film festival world, Magdael understands that many projects don't have a lot of money but need help. As the head of an independent company, he has the flexibility to support certain projects even if there is less financial gain.

A larger company, however, will likely expose you to a broader range of projects and a greater variety of opportunities.

How Do You Make Money? And What Kind of Money?

Agencies charge clients a monthly retainer—anywhere from $2,000 to $25,000 a month, depending on the publicist's experience and needs of the job. Their publicists generally make a base salary with a 5 to 15 percent commission tied to the client fees and a bonus tied to profit.

According to ZipRecruiter, salaries for celebrity publicists in 2025 ranged from $28,620 to $87,341 a year. The Indeed job site estimates publicity assistants earned an average of $48,365 annually and celebrity publicists earned $54,000 to $94,500. Talent.com estimated that the average PR salary in Hollywood was $75,460 per year.

Bigger companies such as studios and streaming services generally pay more. According to 2025 data from the job site Glassdoor, Netflix publicists made an average of about $136,000 annually, while Disney publicists were paid $68,000 to $126,000.

How Is This Career Different from Ten or Twenty-Five Years Ago?

There used to be a limited number of print and radio outlets that had the power to drive box-office sales, so the job was more straightforward. Now there are hundreds of niche online media outlets, podcasts, and influencers that may have more effect than traditional media on whether or not audiences tune in to see a new show.

There are also many more ways to get attention. Publicists might recommend buying ads on social media, setting up virtual Q&As, hosting in-person receptions, or planning specific outreach to other movers and shakers to keep the buzz going while working on getting more mainstream recognition.

Magdael said the pace has also increased. "Everyone is trying to stay ahead of the game, but the game keeps getting faster and faster," he said.

The subject matter has changed along with the pace. It used to be controversial when celebrities weighed in on political or social issues. There was more of a divide between the role of an entertainer and the role of a thought leader or activist. Today, younger fans want to know what stars stand for. A lot of Tucker's work is about not just promoting her clients' films or TV shows but also connecting them with the right organizations, so they can use their fame to highlight social causes that are important—and personal—to them.

"You can't just be on a red carpet talking about yourself anymore," Tucker said. "Brands are attaching themselves to talent with something to say. . . . Even networks, they want people who care about our global community, that have a voice, someone who cares."

What's Some Good Advice?

Be proactive. Tucker remembers one of her proudest moments early in her career, when she successfully pitched a story on Jay Ellis to the *New York Times* when he was a guest star on *Masters of Sex*. "Showtime was like, 'You know, he's just a guest star.' I'm like, 'Yeah, so?'" she said, laughing. "I didn't care, but it was like, 'The audacity!'"

She was an assistant, it was a holiday weekend, and everyone had left, so she did everything herself. And it worked. "I was really proud to get that moment," she said. "It gave me the confidence to really keep going. That's what was pushing me to be better and go harder."

Remember that the stars are not your friends. It's tempting and fun to go out and party with your clients after a big awards show or film festival premiere, but it's important to remember that you're there to do a job.

Keep in mind that you aren't the star. Being a publicist is a behind-the-scenes career. But even if you don't get any of the attention or accolades, "you'll have a lot of great cocktail stories," Paulo said.

PART 6

CAMERA, LIGHTING, AND IMAGERY

CHAPTER 14

How to Become a Cinematographer

Sometimes when you're watching a film or TV show, you can't help but notice what the camera is doing.

Take, for example, the movie *Birdman or (The Unexpected Virtue of Ignorance)*, which is told through what appears to be one long take—as if the filmmakers hit the "record" button and, two hours later, had their movie. Members of the Academy of Motion Picture Arts and Sciences gave cinematographer Emmanuel Lubezki an Oscar for that work.

More often, though, the camera's positioning, movement, and focus are unobtrusive. And that's by design. What you're trying to do with the camera and lighting is amplify the emotions the actors, director, production designer, and writer bring to the scene.

"It's like you've turned it up to eleven," said Shane Hurlbut (*We Are Marshall, Terminator Salvation*).

By way of illustration, he pointed to the 2001 teen romance *Crazy/Beautiful.* To underline the actors' portrayal of the characters falling in love, Hurlbut said, he chose shots that gradually narrowed the space between the two of them until, from the audience's vantage point, there wasn't any left. No one watching the film is going to say, "'Wow, you see the gap between the characters is narrowing,'" Hurlbut said. "But you're going to feel that while watching the movie. What defines the art of cinematography is being obsessed with those subtleties."

To work as a cinematographer (or director of photography, as the position is also called), you'll have to know a lot about cameras, lenses, lights, and other technical aspects of the job. But the pros say the work isn't about technology, it's about storytelling. Specifically, it's about helping the audience connect with the story as it's envisioned by someone else—the director in the case of a film, the showrunner in a TV series.

The cinematographer helps decide how scenes will be lit, where cameras will be placed, what they'll focus on, and where they'll move. In essence, the cinematographer is the person in charge of the audience's point of view—how it will see the story being told. It's more than just choosing camera angles and shot composition.

"With the director, you're deciding which shots are going to be photographed," said Erik Messerschmidt, whose work on *Mank* won an Oscar in 2021. "You're deciding which pieces of a scene are going to make their way to the editing suite."

There's meticulous planning involved in every scene of every shoot. But cinematographers need to be able to improvise too.

Michael Goi (*Avatar: The Last Airbender*, *American Horror Story*) offered this example from a nighttime shoot some years ago. The plan was to film a car in an alley using lights mounted on a hydraulic boom called a condor, but the hydraulics failed. So Goi called for a four-foot fluorescent tube light to be placed behind the car, turning the car's exhaust into a moody light source. "It was actually a much better idea than I originally had," he said.

Because the cinematographer is the head of the camera department, the post is anything but an entry-level job. But if you're someone who loves to take pictures, the pros say, there are numerous starting points and multiple ways to work your way up the ladder.

What Qualities Do You Find in a Successful Cinematographer?

First and foremost, you have to be a storyteller.

After that, a cinematographer needs to understand the technology and the techniques involved. Even moving the camera a few inches or switching lenses will change how an audience sees the story. Minor adjustments in color or camera placement can alter the mood of a shot and convey something different about how a character feels.

But being well-versed in cameras and lenses won't, by itself, make you a good cinematographer. Artistic instincts trump technical mastery, the pros say. The creative and storytelling choices you make inform the technology side of a project, not the other way around. Common sense and the ability to pivot on a moment's notice are key assets. That's because a cinematographer will frequently be confronted with unexpected challenges on set.

"Mother Nature can be amazingly beautiful and vicious at the same time," Hurlbut said. "You have the best-laid plans, and then it all changes in an instant. You have to be able to think on your feet very quickly and come up with a plan that unites the team and also continues to fuel the director's vision and move the needle forward."

A big part of the job is people skills—being able to lead a potentially large team of crew members while also collaborating with the director and other key personnel on set. You'll need to communicate well and deal with powerful egos.

Finally, it's helpful to be well organized. As the person overseeing the lighting, camera movement, and filming in every scene, you'll have a lot of balls in the air at the same time, and you can't afford to lose track of them.

How Do You Get Started?

Although their stories are different, the pros typically get their foothold in the industry through a combination of work, luck, and a willingness to take risks.

Arlene Nelson (*Angel City, In Search Of...*) was a production assistant when she landed an interview for a last-minute opening as a camera assistant—a job she'd never done, working with a camera she'd never used. So she spent a few hours at an equipment rental house with the camera ("someone very kind there showed me how to load it") and her copy of *The Professional Cameraman's Handbook*. She said she was honest with the producer about her inexperience, but she got the job anyway.

You don't have to haunt a rental house to learn about the technology involved in the job. Thanks to the Internet, there are abundant resources on Facebook, YouTube, and other sites, including discussion groups for different types of gear and instructional videos from the makers of cameras, lenses, and lights. YouTube is also a rich source of free instructional videos from camera operators.

American Cinematographer magazine also features technical instruction and how-I-did-it insights from shooters. Then there are subscription-based sites like Hurlbut's Filmmakers Academy, which offers online classes in cinematography and other crew jobs. Nelson said the Cine Gear Expo trade shows are good places to learn about equipment, attend seminars, rub shoulders with industry professionals, and potentially talk a company into lending you demo gear for your next project. "It's like you're a kid in a candy store," she said.

Another starting point is film school or, at a considerably lower cost, community college—many of the ones in the cities favored by filmmakers, such as Los Angeles, New York, Chicago, Atlanta, and Pittsburgh, offer classes in various aspects of cinematography. Those studies will also jump-start your networking, connecting you with peers who are trying to get their start in the industry.

Like Nelson, many current cinematographers spent several years holding lower-level jobs on one of the three teams they now oversee: grips, who set up the equipment and move the cameras; electricians, who power and light a set; and camera operators and their support staff. Being on set gives you the opportunity to ask questions, take notes, and listen in on the discussions cinematographers have with other pros.

The difficulties on set can be just as instructive as the times when things are going well. "A film set is an incredible classroom if you're willing to sit and listen and watch," Messerschmidt said. "It's also a melee of disinformation and confusion and frustration for those that struggle to see the forest for the trees."

In his earlier days on set, he would take notes on the relative positions of the actors and the cameras, look at what was shot and what was cut together, then think about how the filmmakers had arrived at that place. On the whole, he said, the educational opportunities are profound, if you're observant. You just have to put in the time.

Pros stress that it's important to get to know others in the business. "Hold on to those relationships," Tommy Maddox-Upshaw (*Opus*, *Empire*) said, because you never know where people will end up. For example, he said he met Gigi Causey when she was a production supervisor on *Straight outta Compton* and he was a second-unit director of photography. But soon she became a production executive at Fox, helping him land the cinematographer's gig for the FX Network TV series *Snowfall* in 2019.

"It changed my career," he said, giving credit to writer-director John Singleton as well.

Another good way to make connections is through online communities such as Women in Film and TV on Facebook and the International Collective of Female Cinematographers. The latter helps members improve their skills, pick one another's brains, and promote themselves.

And then there are internships. The International Cinematographers Guild (also known as IATSE Local 600) partners with several studios that have programs, including Warner Bros. Discovery, AMC Networks, and Sony Pictures, to place interns on productions, giving them training and work hours that could qualify them for union membership. IATSE instructors also work with Hollywood CPR (www.hollywoodcpr.org) in Los Angeles on an affordable training program for camera loaders and digital utility workers, among other entry-level spots on set.

One other L.A. program is ManifestWorks (www.manifestworks.org), which targets people who've been unhoused, incarcerated, or in foster care. ManifestWorks trains enrollees to be production assistants for various departments, then connects them with job opportunities.

What Are the Career Paths?

There's a natural progression from the ranks of the camera and lighting departments to cinematographer. One key to advancing, the pros say, is to start shooting whatever you can and keep at it.

The American Society of Cinematographers offers two kinds of help for shooters. For working cinematographers trying to advance their career, its Master Class program presents five-day seminars taught by veteran cinematographers. These focus on both the technical and interpersonal skills demanded by the work.

A better option for people just starting out is the society's mentorship programs, which annually pair eighty to ninety shooters at varying stages of their career with experienced volunteer mentors. Charlie Lieberman (*Party of Five*, *Heroes*), a cochair of the Master Class committee, said the program has put a special emphasis on working with underrepresented people.

Goi, another cochair of the Master Class committee, said having a mentor is a good way to learn all the relationships among the people involved in a production. "Most everything that's technical in our profession, in our business, you can honestly kind of learn in a book," he said. "What a book and what film school can't teach you is the politics of the business, how the industry runs from a political standpoint, who does exactly what on a set, how do projects get green-lit."

How Do You Make Money? And What Kind of Money?

Expect to spend several years working in the industry before you can make it full-time as a cinematographer, the pros say. At the start of your career, you'll probably take jobs that don't pay much—possibly just meals and lodging, Nelson said. If you're not making a living as a cinematographer after about five years, she added, it's probably time to find a different specialty.

How much you'll earn depends on whether the project is covered by a union contract. The International Cinematographers Guild represents everyone in a production's camera department, from film loaders and their digital equivalents up to directors of photography. Their pay scales are tied to the production's budget and distribution; for films shot by Hollywood studios, the minimum pay for cinematographers is about $5,600 per week, plus contributions to pension and health benefits. Most film and TV production is covered by union contracts, and those jobs are not generally available to nonunion shooters without some special dispensation. Instead, the main sources of nonunion jobs are music videos, documentaries, and extremely low-budget films.

To join Local 600 on the West Coast, you'll have to work either thirty days on union shoots within a year (which, again, is hard for nonmembers to do) or one hundred days of union and nonunion shoots within three years. Then you'll be placed on a roster of professionals maintained by the major studios, after which you'll be eligible for your union card.

How Is This Career Different from Ten or Twenty-Five Years Ago?

Pros say the job is the same at a fundamental level; it's just that some of the tools are different. Digital cameras are lighter and easier to move in ways that seem to defy gravity—think of what you could do with a drone instead of a crane or a helicopter. Lighting has been revolutionized as well, with LEDs emerging as a less power-hungry and more adjustable alternative to the tungsten lights the industry relied on for decades.

Nevertheless, the latest changes in technology—such as the advent of high-resolution cameras in phones—have opened the door to many more filmmakers producing far more works. Checco Varese (*Daisy Jones and the Six*, *Dopesick*) put it this way: Before the piano, there may have been many potential Mozarts. But it wasn't until the piano existed that a Mozart could actually emerge.

Among the potential new Mozarts are kids from around the world in countries rich or poor, he said, who need access only to a computer and a phone or a point-and-shoot camera. "You don't need to go to Hollywood and get the camera and get the lenses and get the film."

Technology is making it easier for young cinematographers to promote themselves too, with DIY streaming sites and social networks helping shooters show off their work.

Just as fundamentally, the pros say, cinematography is becoming less white and male.

"Right now it's definitely different for me," said Maddox-Upshaw, who was once "the only Black face in grip electric" in his union in Massachusetts. But he still remembers the days when he struggled just to get an interview, only to be told that his reel was "too dark," as in, it had too many scenes with Black actors. A lot of filmmakers want to see something in your reel that looks like the story they're about to shoot, he said, which is weird, given that a good cinematographer can shoot any type of story. But a lot of filmmakers want to see their movie in your reel.

Still, the ranks of cinematographers don't mirror the U.S. population. That's true in part because the people with the power to hire—producers, showrunners, and directors—continue to be predominantly white men. The less diversity at the top, the less diversity there will be in the ranks, the pros say.

What's Some Good Advice?

Don't buy a camera. It will probably become outdated well before you've finished making payments on it, said Jasmine Karcey (*The Proposal, No Spectators Allowed*). "It's better to just have a good relationship with a rental house."

Network at film festivals. "It's where you'll see new things," Varese said. You'll also get the chance to pick the brains of the people behind the films shown there.

Reach out to other cinematographers. Kira Kelly (*Insecure*, *Queen Sugar*) said she was hesitant to contact other cinematographers early in her career and now she wishes she'd started sooner. Fellow pros can be a good source of advice on how to handle situations that come up on the job, she said, whether it's a technical challenge or a personnel issue. Maddox-Upshaw said that you should attend any event where cinematographers are speaking about their experiences. Karcey suggested going to seminars and events staged by equipment makers, "where it's basically a free master class" in how the gear works and the science behind it.

Work for an equipment rental house. Hurlbut got his start at a one-stop shop for filmmaking equipment, where he was able to test out cameras and lights over the weekends. "That was a beautiful training ground for me," he said, adding that rental houses are also a good place to learn about set routines and protocols from the key grips, gaffers, and camera assistants who come in. You can find a rental house in any city with an active filmmaking business.

Don't look for shortcuts. "You've got to do your time," Hurlbut said, adding that it's a good idea to work in a variety of genres. "You need to be in the field using these [tools] and understanding what they do to be able to get the necessary experience to move up."

However, know that there is a shortcut into the union. You can join as a digital technician—the digital equivalent of a film loader—without having worked any hours on set. That way you can have union benefits while you work your way up the ranks. After you've put in hours as a cinematographer (or in another position in the camera department), you can apply to be reclassified.

Speak up about your career goal. "You've just got to put yourself out there," Nelson said. "Sometimes it's uncomfortable, it's awkward, it's embarrassing. Then the more you do it, it becomes second nature, and you realize that you're advocating for yourself."

Be prepared for the demands of the job. "Last year, I only slept in my bed twenty-eight times," Messerschmidt said in a late-evening phone call from a hotel room in Philadelphia, where he was filming a TV pilot with director Ridley Scott for *Dope Thief.* "It's really fun when you're twenty-two; it's really hard when you're forty. And you know, it puts strain on your personal life, it changes your relationships, it affects the circumstances of your life in a way that a 'regular job' does not. . . . It doesn't mean it can't be great. In my experience, it is. But it's also challenging."

CHAPTER 15

How to Become a Gaffer

French New Wave filmmaker François Truffaut won an Oscar for *Day for Night*, a 1973 movie about a film shoot and the dramas within its cast and crew. As befits a movie about filmmaking, the title is a nod to a crucial bit of movie spell casting: making daytime on set look like nighttime on film.

The crew member who weaves this spell is the chief lighting technician, better known as the gaffer. But the gaffer does far more than just flip day into night and vice versa. The way a shot is lit helps establish the feel of a room, a storefront, a neighborhood street. It can enhance the realism of the illusion or underline its surreality. And it can set the emotional tone of the story by bathing the character in a certain kind of light, just as it can by shrouding a character in darkness.

Typically, the film or TV show's director and cinematographer (aka the director of photography) will decide how they want each scene to look. Then it's up to the cinematographer and the gaffer to come up with a detailed plan for what types of light to use and where to place them. Some cinematographers will handle most or all of those details themselves; others will cede them to the gaffer. Regardless, the gaffer's job is to carry out the lighting plan and help make the filmed scenes look like the filmmakers intended.

The gaffer also supervises the electrical department, supplying power to the set and overseeing its safe use. Among other things, that means understanding how much power will be needed throughout the shoot, how much electricity the crew can draw from each location without blowing the circuits, and how much power will have to be generated. With or without a generator, the gaffer needs to provide centralized power sources for the crew to plug into.

It's a team effort. The gaffer will supervise the technicians who load and unload lights off the truck, lay power cables, run generators, reposition and focus lights on set, and operate the lighting console. The gaffer will also hire an assistant chief lighting technician (also called a best boy electric, an antiquated term for a role that has no gender) to manage the inventory and the paperwork. Grips will put up the shades and filters that adjust the intensity, color, and shading of the light.

The gaffer's work starts with scouting visits to the various locations to determine what the lighting needs will be and what local power sources are available. That information helps determine the budget request for the project's lighting and electrical needs, as well as the lighting plan for each scene.

The job is part technical, part artistic, said gaffer David Goodman. He illustrated this point with an anecdote from a project he worked on, *Hopeless*, a dark but humor-inflected short film.

Although the story takes place in a home at night, filming was done during the day. It was easy enough for Goodman to hide the daylight by blacking out the windows. The challenge was removing the shadows his lights were creating inside the home. But then Goodman realized the nettlesome shadows actually added to the mood of the film.

"I thought it really went with the feeling of the script," he said, "because the actors' performances were really fun, dark, and kind of psycho."

Goodman talked with the cinematographer and suggested the team make the shadows part of the film's characters. "So whenever we were composing our frames for our shots, if there was an opportunity to put an actor closer to a wall and create a shadow of their movement, we did it," he said.

Even when they're creating shadows deliberately, gaffers usually want their work to be undetectable. Success, gaffers say, is when the scene looks like all the light is natural—not coming from an array of off-camera LEDs.

What Qualities Do You Find in a Successful Gaffer?

At its core, this job is about casting light. So the people who are drawn to it tend to be captivated by illumination.

For example, Andy Day (*The Departed*, *Succession*) effuses about the way light bounces, is refracted and diffused, how the size of the source of light affects the illumination, and how certain lighting techniques have become associated with particular moods or genres, such as high-contrast lighting with film noir. A gaffer helps the director and the director of photography tell a story, Day said, so it's essential to have an artistic sense of what light does and what it can contribute to storytelling.

That's not just an aesthetic requirement—gaffers also must understand technically how to use lights to achieve the desired results. To them, every piece of lighting equipment is like a different color of paint on a palette or a different brush, and they have to know how to mix the various pieces to obtain the filmmakers' desired result.

Gaffers also need to be familiar with cameras, including such things as film and shutter speeds and lens apertures (and their digital equivalents). That understanding goes hand in hand with determining the lights and effects to use to make the end result match the director or showrunner's vision.

As the head of the electrical department, a gaffer needs to know a lot about power and how to distribute it safely to the set. Although some start out as electricians, you don't have to be one to be a gaffer. You just need to know the basics and you'll learn the rest on the job.

How Do You Get Started?

As with many positions in Hollywood, you have to work your way up to becoming a gaffer.

Day was an amateur photographer who, after taking some film courses in college, decided to get a master's degree in film from New York University. Although he was really interested in shooting, Day had a friend who started as a lighting guy and went on to have a pretty good career behind the camera. So Day used his friend's career path as a template of sorts for his own.

He started working on commercials at a company that let production assistants help the unionized crew. "So I got to know a lot of electricians through that and got to hone some of my technical skills and knowledge of electricity, which was important," Day said. "It was almost like an apprenticeship in some way—learn while you earn."

Once he was in the union, Day worked a series of one-day gigs, getting hired off of the union's list of available workers. Eventually, a gaffer he'd worked for as an electrician elevated him to best boy for a string of films in the 1990s, then another gaffer helped him land his first gig as a chief lighting technician on the Jennifer Aniston–Paul Rudd rom-com *The Object of My Affection.*

The pros say that there's no substitute for learning about lighting and electrical equipment from the people you work with on set. "I think that is what's great about the film business," said Eric Fahy (*American Born Chinese*, *Wonder Man*). "If you find the right avenues, it's a very supportive school of constant learning."

There are also training programs and internships that help would-be gaffers and other crew members find entry-level jobs in film and television. These include Hollywood CPR, which focuses on training former foster youth, at-risk young people, and veterans; ManifestWorks, which enrolls people who have been homeless, in prison, or in foster care; Stockade Works in the Hudson Valley, New York; and IATSE Local 728.

If you want to go the DIY route, there's a wealth of material available online from sources such as YouTube and famed cinematographer Roger Deakins's free information-packed site, rogerdeakins.com. There's also the "Box book," more formally known as the *Set Lighting Technician's Handbook* by Harry C. Box.

Entry-level gigs in the electrical department are plentiful on big-budget productions, which typically have large lighting teams. But it may be easier to gain a foothold in student films and lower-budget productions. That's the path followed by Tom Guiney (*Top Chef*, *Mob Wives*), who spent more than twenty years as a gaffer in New York and Los Angeles on reality-TV sets and music videos.

Guiney got his start in the lighting world as a production assistant while studying cinematography in college. His curiosity and willingness to learn got him invited to work on low-budget films, where he got up to speed on the bulk of the gaffer trade. He got his first insights into the role light plays in filmmaking, he said, by talking on set with camera and lighting crews.

Once you've found a place as a production assistant, you should make it known that you're interested in learning more about what gaffers do and how to become one. Guiney said he's typically reluctant to accept a production assistant's help, but he makes an exception for someone who truly shows interest. You can do that by making yourself available to help in any way (even if that means wrapping up cords), knowing when to ask questions, and being observant on set.

Producers looking to fill crew positions often advertise their openings on Mandy.com, which is dedicated to entertainment-industry jobs, and sites with a local focus, such as Craigslist.

It's also crucial to build a network of people who work in film and television. The first step, Fahy said, is to reach out to anybody you know who could help you gain some access to the industry.

One other option is to take a job at a rental warehouse where gaffers get their equipment, which is a great way to learn the nomenclature. There are countless pieces of equipment in the ever-evolving inventory of gear to light sets, and you need to know how to wrap and store them properly. Because the equipment has to be tested regularly, workers at a rental shop can get a sense for what the gear does before they send it out on a job.

It's also a good way to get to know camera, lighting, and grip technicians. Often crew members coming in to pick up equipment will say they need more people and ask if the owner has anyone to spare—or will even ask for you, if you've shown that you know the equipment. Although you might not know a gaffer's routines, you'll know what everything is and can be a valuable last-minute addition to the team.

The demand for gaffers is directly related to the amount of filmed content—movies, TV shows, commercials, music videos, educational or instructional films—that's produced. And although analysts say the growth in streaming may be slowing, the amount of filmed content overall continues to rise.

The emergence of generative AI as a filmmaking tool is the x factor, as it could diminish the use of physical sets and lighting—and the crew members who work on them. If and when that happens, however, remains to be seen. Fahy said there are companies producing technologies that could eliminate the need for *any* lighting workers on set. And digital editing and effects software are working toward the day where filmmakers can add sources of light to an image in post-production, he said, although he added, "The idea is there, but I don't think the technology is anywhere close to being ready."

What Are the Career Paths?

Typically, the first step to become a gaffer is to start as a technician in the lighting department; then you move to assistant chief lighting technician, and then rise to chief lighting technician.

Another entry point is to work as a grip. In the U.S. film industry, grips do much of the physical labor associated with lighting, such as mounting the gear that shades, shapes, and diffuses light. In fact, on productions with smaller budgets the grip and electric departments may be a single unit.

"A grip who understands lighting is indispensable," Day said.

Once you become a gaffer, opportunities open inside and outside the entertainment industry. It's not unusual for a gaffer to parlay their experience into credits as a director of photography and cinematographer. Guiney has hung out his shingle as a gaffer for hire in the Bay Area, working mainly on corporate and marketing videos.

How Do You Make Money? And What Kind of Money?

When you're just starting out, you're probably not going to make much money and will most likely need a lot of roommates. Not only will the work be intermittent, but your daily pay rate is going to be lower than what an experienced gaffer can command.

"The good news is you get time off," Day said. "The bad news is you get time off."

It took Fahy a couple of years to earn enough to feel comfortable about his income. "I sold my car for my first month's rent," he said.

As with many crew jobs, one key to finding more work at higher wages as a lighting technician is gaining entry into the union, which in California is IATSE Local 728. To do so, though, you'll have to work at least thirty days in a single year on jobs covered by a union contract. That's a bit of a Catch-22—film shoots covered by union contracts are required to hire union members unless none are available. The most common way lighting technicians meet the thirty-day requirement is by working on productions that start out as nonunion work, then get converted through an organizing drive.

In New York and surrounding states, you'll want to join Local 52, which requires would-be members to obtain OSHA certifications in construction and aerial lift safety, pay a $1,000 application fee, and pass the local's written and practical exams. Applicants with less than eight hundred hours of work on union shoots or five thousand hours of work at an approved equipment rental house will also have to take the local's eight-week course on electric work.

Once you've worked enough to join the union, your rate will depend on which union contract, if any, is in force on your project. IATSE sets the pay scale for various positions on a crew's electrical team, gaffer included. Union contracts set different pay scales based on the nature of the production and the size of its budget; the agreements that went into effect in August 2026 for Local 728 called for chief lighting technicians to be paid between $60 and $65 an hour, depending on the type of film or TV production involved. Not all productions employ union crews. When there's no contract in play, the producers typically set the pay rate below union scale.

You might have to volunteer your time at first while holding another job or offer a rate of $150 or less for a ten- to twelve-hour workday. No one likes the idea of newcomers working below minimum wage, but it's been a common practice in the industry. It's not uncommon for prospective gaffers to work five years or more in the industry before they can sustain themselves just on this work. That's entirely dependent on how many projects you can line up in a year.

Goodman remembers his father encouraging him years ago not to devalue himself. "He told me, 'What the hell are you doing? Why are you working for all these jokers and working for no money? They're just abusing you,'" he said. He suggested Goodman charge a minimum rate of $300 a day and never go below it, to weed out the people who were taking advantage of him. He told Goodman to embrace saying no.

It was difficult at first to decline offers below his rate, he said, but the payoff was worth it. To this day, Goodman said, he never takes on a new project below his rate, which is considerably more than $300 a day.

How Is This Career Different from Ten or Twenty-Five Years Ago?

The major game changer for gaffers has been LED lights. Powered by batteries or a standard wall outlet, LED bulbs and panels have reduced the need for portable generators and bulky electric cables to power a set. Their efficiency and versatility have saved gaffers money and time, and their comparatively light weight has made life easier for the technicians who have to load, unload, and set them up.

The pace of change in lighting technology has accelerated to warp speed. As recently as the early 2010s, technicians were controlling color and intensity by swapping out bulbs in tungsten and fluorescent lights and adding gel filters. Now each LED is a tiny computer and controlling them involves just a keystroke or a button push on a lighting console. Emulating moonlight or streetlamps today is as simple as programming the right values into the console, rather than mounting filters on the lights.

There's a lot of inertia in Hollywood when it comes to how films are made, so it takes a while for new technologies to be widely adopted. Yet the trend lines are clear, and they point to a future where fewer hands will be needed to light a set.

What's Some Good Advice?

Be prepared for long hours of physically demanding work. "Make sure before you jump in you have a full understanding of the lifestyle, because it is not easy," Day said.

Know what the director of photography wants from you. Goodman said there will be some directors of photography who want collaboration and others who want to tell you exactly what to do. "You have to be able to understand the direction, and you have to be clear with your direction for your crew," he said.

Have a specialty. One skill currently in demand is the ability to program and operate a lighting console. Nevertheless, Fahy said, it's important to keep an open mind about your career and go with the flow of opportunities that come your way.

Study film. You can never know too much about the medium, Day said. "Having a hungry mind and getting your hands dirty and just studying filmmakers, it's really important."

Enjoy the job. Filmmakers say that having a gaffer on board who genuinely enjoys lighting scenes, actively contributing creative solutions or ideas to each image at any given moment, injects energy that's infectious and brightens the overall mood of the team. It also helps you get invited on to more jobs.

Invest in gear. Guiney said investing in your gaffing career means buying your own equipment and keeping it organized. It helps over the long haul too, because it saves you money on rental fees. If you're just starting out, Guiney said, you'll need a kit of commonly used tools, including a circuit tester, voltage and current meters, various gauges of wire, and Setwear-brand pro leather gloves for handling hot equipment. A complete set of essential tools is not cheap; expect to spend $1,000 to $2,000, depending on whether you opt for new or used gear.

Be flexible and creative. Gaffers need to be able to adapt quickly to changes on set, which requires both a command of the technical aspects of the job and a willingness to turn on a dime. Productions are typically under a tight schedule, so it's great to have someone who is calm under stress and who understands how to use time efficiently.

Be selective. "You try to pick good work, and you try to work with good people, and it just begets more of that," Day said. That doesn't guarantee that everything you work on will be a high-quality project, however. "I'm glad that I have *Glitter* on my résumé," Day said, "just for comic relief."

CHAPTER 16

How to Become a Grip

What you see in a film or TV show is the work of a legion of creative people—actors and directors, wardrobe and makeup people, prop makers, and set decorators, just to name a few. Less obvious is the work of the grips, the team of improvising, tool-belted builders and technicians who construct the sets, adjust how they're lit, and move the camera around them.

Their work starts in the days before a scene is shot, when construction and rigging grips put up the set walls, scaffolds, trusses, and platforms that support the lights and cameras. They'll work in tandem with rigging crew members from the electrical department, who install lights and the power for them. Rigging grips might also mount a giant high-definition screen to display a virtual background—a desert extending far into the distance, for example.

After that work is done, dolly grips will lay the tracks or flooring needed to allow a camera mounted on a platform (a "dolly") to move smoothly from mark to mark. During the shooting, these grips will move the camera or, if it's carried by an operator, make sure that person doesn't trip or fall off a raised surface. If a crane is involved, grips will get it into position and, in some cases, operate it.

Other grips on set will position the items that shade, color, or shape the lighting for the scene. Grips are also in charge of on-set safety. And if a last-minute problem crops up with the structure of the set, grips will be the ones to deliver the solution. Finally, when it's time to break things down and put them away, that's the grips' job too.

"It's not a very lofty profession within the industry," said Danny Lang, a veteran rigging grip based in North Hollywood. "I'm never going to be onstage accepting an award for my job."

Grips have a reputation for being the people who do the physical labor on set, and that's part of the job.

"You should be able to carry, like, fifty pounds for an extended period of time," Lang said. "It's like construction . . . and it is super-physical. The bigger you are, the more useful you are." The skills you develop as a longshoreman, a lumberjack, or a construction worker would translate better to being a grip than the things you learn in film school, Lang said.

Still, some situations demand the services of smaller, lighter grips—for example, when a crew needs to get equipment into tight spaces.

The field attracts people from a vast assortment of backgrounds—teachers and high-school dropouts, college professors, people who'd spent years in prison, and professional baseball players. And regardless of size, grips are relied on to be problem solvers on set. That takes creativity and resourcefulness, and it's what makes the grip's job one of the most interesting and varied on a film or TV crew.

What Qualities Do You Find in a Successful Grip?

Being a grip is an entry-level position in the world of film and television, kind of like a production assistant. You can get started without having much knowledge about the industry and still do the work well, if you're a quick study.

"It's skills that are learned on the job, for the most part," said Thomas Davis, former second international vice president of IATSE. While some grips are better than others, he said, the skills aren't unique to an irreplaceable coterie of workers. "Charley Gilleran is probably one of the top five grips in North America. But just because Charley turns a job down, it doesn't mean that job is not going to get done or is really going to suffer."

It's important to be mechanically inclined, given how much construction, carpentry, and even welding you may be asked to do. Davis called it having "mechanical intelligence," explaining, "It's like being on top of a skyscraper and the director saying, 'I want a camera twenty feet out off the edge of this building and looking into the window two floors down.' And you're looking at that and saying, 'How do I build that?' . . . You're not handed a set of prints. This is what they're asking for. You visualize it; then you build it."

An understanding of basic physics is crucial, along with enough aptitude in math to be able to calculate loads and counterweights. And the stakes are high.

"Everything you build, there's going to be people working and walking below it," Lang said of the rigging grips working in the "perms"—the beams in the rafters of a sound stage. "Any mistake you make could be fatal. You have to be serious about what you do; you have to be confident in what you do. . . . You have to be confident enough to ask for help."

Finally, being team oriented and resourceful is important. Grips need to work together to come up with solutions on the fly. Filmmakers will tell you what they want, but it will be up to you to figure out how to deliver it.

How Do You Get Started?

Most grips are hired through recommendations and personal contacts. The recommendation doesn't have to come from a grip, Davis said—any connection in the industry, such as a crew member in the lighting, camera, or sound department, could provide the necessary introduction to the supervisor doing the hiring.

So could a family member. Grips are a little like firefighters in that sense—you'll find plenty of grips who got in through their father or their uncle or their older brother. (And yes, they're usually men; the pros say only 2 to 3 percent of grips are women.)

Another entry point is to work for a company that rents equipment, such as Gilleran's C&C Studio Services on the outskirts of Los Angeles. Being on staff at a rental house will introduce you to crew members and teach you about the equipment they use. Although you don't need to have experience on set to get a job as a grip, having some experience in rigging or moving equipment will give you a leg up.

Chris Trillo, a veteran dolly grip, studied at the PCPA Pacific Conservatory to be a theatrical technical director and worked in repertory theater in the Pacific Northwest, but he went looking for a new career after noting that the best-paid person in the area "was driving a beat-up Volkswagen Beetle—that's all he could afford." After a stint in Bakersfield on a concert stage crew, Trillo moved to Los Angeles to work on student films for free.

"The first few months I was in L.A. I didn't earn any money," Trillo said. "Once they realized I could drive the large trucks and deal with electricity, they started offering me pittance pay."

From there, his income grew rapidly as gigs flowed in through the connections he made on other jobs. "I was looking for work, but work usually found me. I attribute that to the fact that I was useful and I was easy to get along with," he said.

Initially, the work will probably be menial. On your first job, you'll mainly be schlepping equipment from one place to another, hoisting things, or tightening bolts on trusses—in short, duties that require no skill. You will need a set of basic construction tools that will cost about $100. IATSE Local 80 has a list of the tools required on union shoots, including a knife, a crescent wrench, a pry bar, a screwdriver, and a tape measure.

Trillo said the usual entry point is to do low-budget productions and work your way up. "Eventually you will get found by somebody who says, 'You're pretty good; I'm going to put you on my next show.'"

There's no shortage of filmmakers seeking free or low-cost help in Los Angeles, Trillo said. Low-budget productions that won't expect much from you are a good place to start learning the craft, although at some point, he said, you will fail and get fired. Possibly multiple times.

"Treat it like trade school or college. You don't get paid to go to college," Trillo said. "Go do the low-budget productions, get beat up a little bit, which is going to happen, learn the equipment, the lingo." With some luck, you'll come across someone in the industry who'll give you the opportunity to move up.

To find entry-level job possibilities, you can check Backstage, Mandy.com, and Craigslist for productions by students, such as those at the nonprofit American Film Institute in Los Angeles. One of the most important things is just getting out there and gaining experience.

Then there are the programs in and around Los Angeles that train people for entry-level employment on sets. These include Streetlights .org, Hollywood CPR, and the Group Effort Initiative. In addition to helping students form networks with their peers, these programs offer connections to studios and production companies that open the door to finding work postgraduation.

Similar programs can be found across the country at community colleges and trade schools in or near cities with active film and theater industries. For example, there's MediaMKRS in Brooklyn, Stockade Works in the Hudson Valley, New York, Georgia Film Academy programs at schools across the state, and the free Central Illinois Film & TV Production Training program for Illinois residents.

If you're looking to get started in California, Lang said, the first thing you should do is call the union that represents grips there, IATSE Local 80, and give them your name. That will put you on the list of people to call if there aren't enough union members available to meet the demand.

Local 80's counterpart in New York and neighboring states is IATSE Local 52.

The number of grip jobs has expanded in tandem with the growth in streaming and the number of films and TV shows created. Analysts expect that growth to continue at a healthy clip for the foreseeable future. The x factor is whether improving technologies to generate visuals with software and digital displays reduce the need for physical sets—and the grips who build the infrastructure of filmmaking.

What Are the Career Paths?

There are four main types of grips, and their duties are somewhat different.

Construction grips and **rigging grips** are responsible for the infrastructure that supports a shoot. The main advantage to these gigs is the shorter workday (ten hours instead of up to sixteen). It's also a more predictable and less intense routine. It's physically demanding work, however, and it requires a lot of problem-solving as you prepare a location to handle the required equipment for the shoot. Maybe it needs a motorized platform to raise a camera or some lights. Maybe it needs a ramp to traverse some extreme terrain.

And it's not for people who are afraid of heights. Rigging grips are often called to hang motors or engineer structures from the beams in a sound stage's rafters, which might be forty or fifty feet in the air. "The first time I worked up high, I came down and went to the bathroom and just threw up, I was so scared," Lang said.

Production grips work in tandem with the electrical department on the lighting, helping to figure out how to illuminate the scene to achieve the look sought by the director and the cinematographer. They are also on hand to do any extra rigging required after the rigging grips have moved on to the next location, because there will inevitably be a lot of last-minute changes. The hours can be brutal, because you're on set for as long as the director might want to shoot.

Dolly grips get camera operators to where they need to be on set to get the shot that the filmmakers want. Doing so means not just maneuvering the dolly (or, in some cases, the crane) on which the camera is mounted; it's providing a smooth path for the dolly to travel on to minimize bumping and shaking. So dolly grips will lay tracks or smooth flooring for the dolly to traverse. The longer and farther the camera needs to track the action, the more complicated the string of camera movements can be.

"We have to know the scene, the dialogue, where they want to get the shots, where we want to put the camera," Trillo said. "Putting that all together is sometimes really difficult. . . . You're also chasing actors around the set—they're standing; they're sitting; they're running to the doorway," he said. That means dolly grips could have dozens of marks where the camera needs to be at specific points during a scene.

Once you become a journeyman grip doing one of these four types of work, there are two main rungs on the career ladder above you: key grip and best boy.

Key grip: This is the boss of the grips, in charge of all the hiring, the planning, and the specialized rigs required for cars and airplanes. Key grips typically own equipment that they rent to the production for the grip crew to use, generating a much higher payday. A bigger production may have a second key grip to oversee the rigging work.

Best boy: This is the top assistant to the key grip, typically working behind a desk to ensure that the paperwork is handled and that the equipment and grip crew are there when the production needs them. Although you may see some references to "best girl," Davis said, "best boy" is a gender-neutral term.

How Do You Make Money? And What Kind of Money?

A grip's pay depends on whether the project is covered by a union contract. In 2026, IATSE Local 80 members made about $55 an hour as a basic grip on a movie studio's shoot, while grip supervisors made about $3,400 to $3,700 a week. Nonunion work is considerably less lucrative. Lang said his pay for nonunion jobs was a quarter to a third of what he makes in the union.

Different IATSE locals have different entry requirements. For example, Local 52 in New York and surrounding states is open to new members with no experience on film sets, although some experience is recommended. Instead, applicants must have current certifications in construction safety, forklift operation, and aerial lift use and they must pass a written and a practical exam.

Local 80 in California requires you to log thirty days of work as a grip in a single year to qualify for membership. The Catch-22 is that with rare exceptions, union rules do not allow nonunion grips on union shoots. Instead, those jobs are supposed to be performed by people qualified for the Contract Services Industry Experience Roster, which is limited to professionals with at least some experience working on union-covered projects.

Davis said there are a few ways for nonunion grips to accumulate those thirty days. One is to be employed on a production that starts off nonunion and gets organized, because all those days on that production will count. Also, when there aren't enough people on the roster to meet the demand, the production can then hire nonunion workers under a permit system administered by the local.

Getting thirty days through permits is probably not going to happen if you're just a name on the union's list, Lang said. Instead, you'll need a key grip or other connection to help you get your days.

A production may be able to wrangle a pass to hire a nonunion worker who has special knowledge of a technologically advanced production technique. But it's rare that filmmakers will find someone who's so proficient that only their services will accomplish the task at hand.

As the number of streaming services multiplied and the demand for new material exploded, so did the opportunities to become a grip. Membership across IATSE's locals grew tremendously in the late 2010s and early 2020s, mainly because the rosters weren't big enough to handle the growing demand.

In addition to the higher wages, union members who log enough hours of work qualify for health benefits. The union also offers a pension to those who work at least seventy-five days per year on projects covered by union contracts for at least five years.

The health benefits are crucial, considering the toll the work can take on your body. "A camera operator I worked with, Tommy Cox, once said, 'When I look at the crew, I think of *The Walking Dead.* You're all fatally injured in some fashion,'" Trillo said.

Trillo was sidelined for more than a year after herniating a disc on the set of a TV series in September 2022 while helping to lift a dolly. "We're always working hurt," he said. "You're never going to say, 'I'm going to take six months off from work and have this fixed.' . . . There's just never a good time to do that."

How Is This Career Different from Ten or Twenty-Five Years Ago?

The pros say that there's a much greater emphasis on safety. For example, Lang said, rigging grips working in the perms now have to wear harnesses clipped to the structure to prevent them from falling. "You'll get fired if you're not clipped in," he said.

It helps that the lights and modular construction components weigh significantly less than they used to. There's more motorization and automation too—for example, some camera movements are done with a telescoping boom controlled by a joystick instead of a dolly on a track.

On the other hand, the arrival of LED light panels and lighting consoles means that gaffers need less help from grips when it comes to adjusting the lighting in a scene. But there's still a role for grips in setting and removing shades and elevating lights on platforms and cranes.

For Gilleran, one of the most significant changes has been in the atmosphere. The business has become more toxic over the years in terms of the relationship between employers and employees, he said. "Everyone's a disposable worker and a gig worker now." The crew doesn't feel as much like a family as it used to, Gilleran said. "You're not looked after as a team player anymore."

What's Some Good Advice?

Be aware that this is not mindless work. One stereotype that grips hear about their work is that it's on the level of a furniture mover or a jackhammer operator. That caricature ignores not just the math and physics required to build platforms and hang structures safely but also the resourcefulness required to solve the structural problems that grips encounter.

So why do people think grips are dumb? "When you are using your mind," Lang said, "there's no one around to see it from other departments."

Network relentlessly. "Shake everybody's hand, introduce yourself to everybody, and get everybody's number. And give your number to everybody," Lang said.

Be the worker people can count on. "Show up on time. Don't complain. Ask questions, not too many," and learn the equipment, Gilleran said. Soft skills such as reliability and teamwork are crucial for new grips trying to establish themselves. "Your technical skills will get you hired, but your soft skills will keep you working," said Gary Dagg, a retired key grip who teaches grip classes at Hollywood CPR.

Be prepared for ridiculously long hours. "Everybody should be ready for the shock of how long it takes each day," Trillo said.

Absorb as much as you can on the job. Dagg said he counsels students, "Eyes and ears open and mouth shut. You can't talk and listen at the same time." There will be plenty of opportunities to learn new skills on the job if you show interest, he said.

Reach out to key grips. Lang suggested using IMDbPro to find the email address for the key grip on a movie you liked, then introduce yourself and try to form a connection. Similarly, if you come across a location for a film or TV shoot, he said, ask to speak to the key grip. "I would think that most key grips would admire that kind of moxie," he said.

Think about where you want to end up. "You're not going to walk on as a key grip or a best boy or a dolly grip," Dagg said, but "you can start charting your course early on." For example, he said, if you want to be a dolly grip, be the first guy on the set in the morning laying and leveling tracks for the dolly.

CHAPTER 17

How to Work in Animation

When people in Hollywood work in animation, they aren't necessarily "animators." Animation is its own comprehensive industry with pre-production, production, and post-production processes that resemble live-action ones. But they have their own nuances.

Someone who works in animation pre-production could be a producer, responsible for identifying projects, hiring a director, finding financial backers, managing the budget, and shepherding the entire process from conception to distribution.

Producers can be independent freelancers working with the staff at a smaller independent studio (for example, Titmouse or Filmless). They could be creative executives at large animation companies that are often subsidiaries of live-action studios—for example, 20th Century Animation and Pixar are part of Disney, and Cartoon Network Studios is a subsidiary of Warner Bros.

In pre-production, there are also a number of development roles specific to animation. These include concept artists, who come up with the initial sketches and look of the project; storyboard artists, who create a full visual representation of how the story will play out; and sheet timers, who take every frame of film and break it down into timed sections for the animators.

The work of a writer in animation varies, depending on whether it's for a board-driven (referring to storyboards) or script-driven project. For board-driven TV shows such as *Ren & Stimpy*, *Adventure Time*, and *Steven Universe*, writers typically outline the story, leaving the storyboard artists to create the details, dialogue, and jokes. In script-driven shows, such as *The Simpsons*, *BoJack Horseman*, and *Bob's Burgers*, the foundation is set by the writer's room and the storyboard artists' job is to illustrate what's on the page.

Once a project reaches production, directors oversee the voice actors and guide artists on their vision for each scene. They work with character designers, colorists, prop designers, and background designers, as well as the layout artists who figure out how to put all the parts together into a cohesive picture.

In post-production, there are editors, composers, and sound designers. The role of an editor in animation is different from live action because everything needs to be preplanned. The editing is usually more straightforward and happens faster. Composers working on animation often deliver more whimsical and energetic scores because they're dealing with fantasy worlds and anthropomorphic characters.

Within animation, there are 2-D and 3-D productions. 3-D projects (Pixar films like *Toy Story* and *Inside Out*) are much more complex than 2-D projects (*The Simpsons* or Miyazaki films) and require more staff. There are animators who focus specifically on taking a character and rotating it. Other necessities unique to 3-D include modeling, which involves translating 2-D designs into models ready to be animated; rigging, or creating a skeleton for the 3-D model; texturing; and lighting.

How long a job in animation lasts depends on the project. If it's an animated sequence incorporated into a live-action TV show or film, the jobs are typically short-term gigs that last a matter of months. If it's an animated TV series, the jobs are generally seasonal, possibly running for eight months, with a two-month break before picking up again. Unlike live-action films, which are typically finished within a year or two, animated films are multiyear endeavors. The first *Moana* took five years, and the sequel took four. *Coco* took six years to make, and *The Lego Movie* took seven.

What Qualities Do You Find in People Who Are Successful in Animation?

"Introverts can win in animation," said animator and director Mike Milo (*Scooby-Doo and Guess Who?*, *Woody Woodpecker*), who interviewed over twelve hundred animation pros for his website, Animation Insider. "There are a lot of shy, introverted artists who sit in the corner, do great work, and don't bug anyone. And they thrive."

This is because animation is a skills-based industry. Networks and referrals are always helpful, but animation is the rare Hollywood field where talented people can get hired with no connections—based on the strength of their portfolio and how much their skill set matches the specific needs of the project.

Animation is also a team-based industry, which means it favors people who are good collaborators. You won't be drawing whatever you want to draw, and you won't always be drawing in your own personal style. You're drawing what a director or showrunner tells you to draw. Even directors and showrunners have limitations due to budget, time, and the capacity of their team. Save your ideas for your own personal side projects.

Finally, workers in animation must be able to handle pressure, albeit a different kind than in live-action productions. Because animated films take longer than live-action films and require more preparation, the work can feel more tedious. But animated projects are much more expensive and labor-intensive. If there are any changes needed in the later stages of the workflow, it's harder to cover up with a creative edit. You would have to go back to pre-production and start the process all over again—which could cost millions.

"It's not like live action, where you might not even know what your call time is the next day," said Kevin Noel, Sony Pictures Animation senior vice president and program chair of the CAPE Animation Directors Accelerator program. "Animation has a lot more fires to put out, but you can see them coming from a mile away."

How Do You Get Started?

Learn the twelve principles of animation, outlined by Frank Thomas and Ollie Johnston in the 1981 book *The Illusion of Life: Disney Animation*. Professionals consider Thomas and Johnston's teachings on these techniques—squash and stretch; anticipation; staging; straight-ahead action and pose-to-pose; follow through and overlapping action; slow in and slow out; arc; secondary action; timing; exaggeration; solid drawing; and appeal—to still be a good starting point, forty-five years later.

There are countless tutorials online and many of them are free. Take online courses from websites like Animationclub School, Skillshare, Udemy, and TipTut, whose lessons you can find on X and Instagram by searching for TipTutZone. Binge YouTube channels like AI Animation, Okay Samurai, and Cartoon Brew. Learn software programs for animation, compositing, and 3-D rendering such as Adobe After Effects, Adobe Animate, Procreate, SketchUp, Houdini, ZBrush, and Blender. Look up ScreenSkills' Careers in Animation job profile, where you can download a comprehensive illustrated PDF flowchart that describes all the different careers in the animation industry.

Watch highly regarded animated projects, such as *Spider-Man: Into the Spider-Verse*, *We Bare Bears*, *Bluey*, and *Avatar: The Last Airbender*. Pause the video at your favorite scenes, watch them frame by frame, and analyze the lines, depth, and movements.

Getting a degree in animation or going to art school can help you develop your skills and find a network, but it's not necessary. If you're going that route, in fact, some professionals recommend finding a program that is not too expensive, because a fancy school on your résumé won't necessarily get you the job (although it could help you build a network that boosts your career over the long haul).

The only surefire way to get hired as an artist is to have an impressive portfolio. You want your portfolio to showcase your technical skill and versatility and your ability to draw confidently, consistently, and solidly. Make sure that your portfolio demonstrates that you've mastered human anatomy, character turnarounds, and perspective.

Draw all the time. People who work in animation are always creating, so if you're going to work alongside them, you have to get your skills to a professional level. For many gigs, it's about not just drawing well but also drawing fast. Storyboard artists, for example, often need to quickly improvise to find creative solutions and fill any holes in the story line.

What Are the Career Paths?

There are two main pathways in animation. If you prefer to stay in a position that lets you focus on the artistic aspects of the job, you might start out as a general animator, storyboard artist, or modeler and work your way to art director, where you would be in charge of all the visuals of a project.

By contrast, if you want to be a director, showrunner, or creative executive at an animation studio, you'll need to develop managerial skills. You'll be in meetings all day, hearing what people above you expect and figuring out how to communicate that to the people below you. You'll have to be not just a visionary and a technician but also a leader for tens or hundreds of people.

A starting point for those sorts of jobs could be doing administrative work as a runner (an assistant in the production management department), production coordinator, or production manager—different productions use different job titles. You'll see firsthand how the process comes together, learn the vocabulary of the animation industry, and understand how best to communicate during production crises.

These paths are not mutually exclusive. It's common for people working in animation to jump back and forth between different roles from project to project. Throughout Milo's three-decade career, he continues to take jobs as an animator, director, storyboard artist, writer, producer, and screen timer (the person who breaks the scenes down into individual frames and manages the timing of the project).

Another way to think about career paths is assessing what type of animation you want to do. One option is animated educational children's programming like *StoryBots* and *Dora the Explorer* that teaches young kids reading or language skills. Another is programming designed to entertain adults, whether it's for mature audiences (such as Genndy Tartakovsky's *Primal*) or less mature ones (e.g., *Family Guy*). Anime used to be a niche genre from Japan, but there's increasing demand for anime-style animation in cartoons around the globe.

Animators can also have full careers outside of Hollywood by working on commercials, video games, and mobile apps.

How Do You Make Money? And What Kind of Money?

According to 2025 data from Glassdoor, the average annual salary for an animator is $72,160 a year and the average salary for an animation director is $136,701 a year.

IATSE Local 839, also known as The Animation Guild, sets minimum wages for productions covered by union contracts. To get into the union, you have to get hired on a union project, but this is generally easier to do in animation than in live action. Many animation studios that work on union productions regularly hire nonunion workers. The fee to join is equal to two weeks of union-scale wages in the job category in which you're first hired, plus a one-time processing charge of $100.

An extensive list of weekly minimums for 2026 is laid out in The Animation Guild's website. An animator, background artist, layout artist, or model designer must be paid a minimum of $2,449.20 a week, for example. An assistant director gets paid a minimum of $1,977.20 a week. The weekly minimum is $1,903.20 for an associate animation writer and $3,440.80 for a supervising animation writer. For CGI animators and modelers, the union sets rates with specific studios. A CGI animator and modeler's weekly rate for Disney is $2,449.20; for DreamWorks, it's $2,597.60. Generally, professionals say the pay for animation in feature films is better than for television and 3-D is a more lucrative career than 2-D.

But save your money. Be prepared for periods where you're inundated with work and others where no one is hiring. During the COVID-19 pandemic, animation was booming, while live-action shoots were shut down to avoid outbreaks. But by 2023 and 2024, Disney had cut back on projects, Netflix's animation unit had announced layoffs, and Warner Bros. Discovery's digital-first animation studio Rooster Teeth The Cartoon Network had shut down.

"This business is nothing but a roller coaster," said Bernie Petterson, supervising director of *Pete the Cat* and storyboard artist for *Phineas and Ferb*. "I've been through about four or five cycles now. It goes up hard, and it comes down hard."

A lot of artists in the industry don't rely solely on animation jobs. They may find a low-stress desk job or remote gig where they can either draw on their downtime or end their workdays with enough energy left to focus on their art. They may teach at a community college. They may distribute their work on YouTube, TikTok, and Instagram—or through comic books. Some business-savvy animation artists like Vivienne Medrano, known by her online alias VivziePop, have built up enough of a following to finance their own work. She crowdfunded her musical series *Hazbin Hotel* through Patreon and founded her own animation studio, SpindleHorse Toons.

How Is This Career Different from Ten or Twenty-Five Years Ago?

Technology has made processes faster, and anyone with access to the Internet can play around with animation tools and teach themselves professional skills. Younger animators are also well-versed in social media and aware of the need to design an impressive website, build their own brand, and attract followers.

As a result, the industry has become a lot more competitive. Decades ago, it was common for hiring managers to bring in a talented newbie, look over their portfolio, and have conversations to figure out where to best place them. But now hiring managers can be extremely specific. If they need someone to draw dogs, they can pick someone who happens to be adept at drawing the exact kind of dog they need. It's harder for younger animators to receive mentorship.

There's also a fear that more animation jobs will be outsourced to countries with cheaper labor. Many studios already send some animation work abroad. Industry folks also worry that advancements in AI will take away more animation jobs. In animation, AI can currently automate repetitive tasks, create realistic faces and backgrounds, generate 3-D models, animate 3-D objects, and more.

But that's the nature of technological change. Milo remembers in the nineties when veteran animators resisted going from paper and pencil to computers and styluses. Before Photoshop, animators couldn't layer images on top of one another, and the advancement of photo editing software resulted in less work for artists who were trained in hand drawing. AI will inherently disrupt the industry, but it may speed up production, reduce costs, increase the volume of animated projects, and create other kinds of jobs.

What's Some Good Advice?

Try multiple things to discover your best fit. When Ellen Su, an animation artist who worked as a recruiter for Titmouse, gives advice to students, she asks them: What is the kind of problem you can lose time trying to solve? She went to school for 3-D animation but realized it wasn't for her. She didn't enjoy struggling with the software. "What people in 3-D don't tell you is that you need to know math," she said. Once she realized she was happiest drawing pictures, she switched directions and focused on 2-D.

Start by drawing props. Many people want to be character artists, but it's a coveted slot, because there are a limited number of character artists needed for each team. Petterson started by drawing props—cell phones, kitchenware, and athletic equipment—and eventually got hired as a background designer, character designer, writer, and supervising director.

Take feedback gracefully. You can grow tremendously just by getting feedback. "It doesn't matter how old you are, I can still learn from a student," Milo said. "Animation and art in general is so subjective, everybody has an opinion, and everybody's opinion is valuable."

Don't be intimidated to talk to seasoned artists. "In L.A., we are taught to ignore celebrities. But in animation, nobody is known," Milo said. "Go ask them questions. Everyone loves talking about themselves and their work."

CHAPTER 18

How to Work in Visual Effects

A film or TV show is, at its heart, one long visual effect: a series of moving images that immerse viewers into a fictional reality, whether it be a village in Elizabethan England, a neighborhood in 1980s Brooklyn, or a postapocalyptic wasteland in Australia.

On a Hollywood production, though, VFX artists are the ones who do the reality-bending things that can't be accomplished by actors, set decorators, stunt performers, and pyrotechnics experts. Instead, they use computers, software, and creativity to bring the filmmakers' vision to the screen.

Often VFX work involves creating larger-than-life sci-fi creatures—as when Mr. X, a VFX studio in Toronto, earned its first Oscar nomination creating the giant HellCrab that threatened Queen Sand-Gobbler in Netflix's *Love and Monsters*. Sometimes VFX artists are brought in to make a bit of physical movie magic more convincing, harrowing, or exhilarating. For example, in *Star Wars: The Force Awakens*, Industrial Light & Magic's VFX artists enhanced real-life sets and handmade models to create the breathtaking Millennium Falcon backdrops. And frequently, filmmakers will use visual effects to enable human actors to do superhuman things. See, for example, the epic final battle scene in *Avengers: Infinity War*, where more than thirty-eight Marvel Cinematic Universe characters battled the population-destroying villain Thanos.

Visual effects are expensive, but effects-laden movies can be blockbusters. James Cameron's *Avatar: The Way of Water* famously cost about $460 million to make but earned $2.32 billion in the box office, and *Jurassic World* had a budget of around $200 million and made $1.7 billion in box-office receipts. Granted, dazzling visual effects are no guarantee of success—witness *Furiosa: A Mad Max Saga*, which in 2024 had the worst Memorial Day weekend in almost thirty years.

Notably, visual effects are used in more than just big-budget fantasy films. VFX artists are responsible for any work it takes to create computer-generated graphics and combine them with what's filmed on set. A lot of VFX work is subtle to the point of near invisibility. Driving scenes are usually done in front of a green screen with the background added later using visual effects. In a period show, the VFX team might remove any electrical wiring or skyscrapers in the distance. If a production is filmed in Toronto, but the story is set in New York, visual effects will go in and change all the street signs from blue to green. Large crowd scenes can be digitally augmented with visual effects.

Visual effects is often the biggest department in the list of credits at the end of the movie. Outsiders often assume that everyone who works in visual effects is an artist. But the VFX department is its own ecosystem, with work being done in pre-production, production, and post-production.

There are the artists, animators, designers (modelers who turn the 2-D images into 3-D); colorists, lighting artists, and compositors (who take all of these separate elements and put them together in a cohesive story). There are also coordinators who manage the workflow; producers who figure out how the work can be executed on time and under budget; on-set supervisors who capture what's being filmed so the designers have something to work from; and engineers and developers creating tools to make all these processes faster.

"Whatever you're into, there's probably some position that caters to that thing," said Chris White, a VFX supervisor at Wētā FX. For instance, there are people who specialize in furry creatures.

Maybe you're not even an artist, but you are a computer programmer who is fascinated with anatomy. VFX creature departments, which work on developing new characters, need programmers who understand the way muscles move and jiggle under the skin to help create the software the artists use to build these monsters and aliens.

There are VFX artists who specialize in background environments. Unlike in acting, where the background is meant to be ignored, the VFX environment artists in charge of building out cities, deserts, or galaxies are the ones who determine the entire look of the scene.

Google ScreenSkills' website and look up their Careers in Visual Effects job profile, where you can download an illustrated PDF flowchart that describes all the different careers in the VFX industry.

What Qualities Do You Find in a Successful VFX Worker?

All these roles require different skills, but one thing that people who work in visual effects have in common is that they love the intersection between art and technology.

Here's an example from Marcella Brown, a VFX senior effects technical director at Industrial Light & Magic who specializes in water. In addition to doing hyper-realistic work for such films as *Avatar: The Way of Water*, she helped animate the stylized, anime-inspired water in Pixar's *Elemental*, a rom-com between the fire element Ember and water element Wade.

For the pivotal *Elemental* scene where water breaks through a dam wall, flooding the streets and threatening to destroy Firetown, Brown's team not only had to design the look of the water but they also had to think about the physics: how big the splashes needed to be, how the sunlight would reflect off the waves, and how fast different pieces of debris would ride in the floodwaters.

The job also attracts people with big imaginations. For the *Suicide Squad* spin-off series *Peacemaker*, the VFX team created Eagly, Peacemaker's bald eagle sidekick. Though director James Gunn originally tried to use a real eagle for the shots, they opted to do a fully virtual version instead, giving the VFX team some unique challenges. One of the more memorable ones: How do they most realistically animate an eagle giving his best human friend a hug with his wings?

Swaybox Studios VFX compositor Brittany Piacente, who worked on Eagly, said her line of work is good for people who don't like doing the same thing over and over. "Some compositors tend to explain it like Photoshop on steroids with moving pictures," she said. There are so many programs to learn, and many different ways to achieve the same effects, so it's fun to keep up with the most updated technology and learn new tricks.

How Do You Get Started?

Often people begin by learning animation or other computer graphics. Jason Gottlieb, a VFX artist and supervisor, had aspired to be an animator since he was a kid. For his senior project at film school, he took things one step further and sought to combine different styles of animation—a feat he had to figure out how to pull off. Little did he know, he was teaching himself the basics of compositing.

Many VFX professionals go to a film or trade school to learn the craft. Schools that specialize in VFX training include the Gnomon School of Visual Effects, SCAD, Full Sail University, and the School of Visual Arts. There are also online schools, including CG Spectrum and Lost Boys. Look up the website for The Rookies, a community of digital artists, to find its latest annual rankings of schools, which are based on feedback from thousands of students, judges, and reviews. You can also scroll through the winners of their annual Rookie

Awards—targeted at students, hobbyists, and emerging artists—to get an idea of what students can produce.

Outside of film school, you can find instructions on the basics of visual effects through a number of different YouTube channels, including Entagma, Doxia Studio, Film Riot, Video Copilot, Shanks FX, and Comp Lair, and LinkedIn trainings on such fundamental software tools as After Effects and Blender, as well as broader skills such as VFX keying, 3-D modeling, and generative AI. Compositing academy.com offers free tutorials in the popular compositing program Nuke, as well as paid courses. These resources can also help you narrow down what you want to explore in the field.

It helps to learn some of the most commonly used software programs, platforms, and languages in the industry, including Maya, Houdini, Nuke, ZBrush, Mari, Unreal, and Python. Rebelway, an online training website, has a library of free VFX courses. The online learning site Udemy has many reasonably priced classes, ranging from about $20 to $100.

You can learn how several professionals in the industry got their start by listening to VFX-devoted podcasts. Brown hosts the *VFX Club* podcast, which has eight seasons of interviews with VFX professionals. The *CG Spectrum* podcast, hosted by VFX producer Maxine Schnepf and game development art manager Justin Mohlman, is also a helpful resource with advice for newcomers.

Mentorship organizations can help newbies start making connections in the industry. Once you sign up for a The Rookies account, at therookies.co, you'll be able to share your artwork with over ninety-eight thousand members, build a digital portfolio, get access to classes, interact with professionals, enter challenges—and ideally get hired. Women in Animation advocates for gender equity in the animation, VFX, and gaming industries. Female animators can go to WIA's website to find more information on tiers for membership that give access to the nonprofit's job board, Discord chat, and professional growth events. They also accept applications for two mentorship programs a year.

Learning skills and making connections are necessary steps, but not sufficient. To get that first gig as an intern or assistant at a VFX studio, you'll need a demo reel for prospective employers that shows examples of your work. A beginner reel is typically about a minute. Use Vimeo, make sure it's accessible to all (no password required), focus the reel on the type of job you're looking for, start with a unique shot that will capture people's attention within the first few seconds, and showcase only your best work.

To find an opening at a VFX studio, you can consult specialty sites such as VFXjobs.com and Animationandvfxjobs.com, entertainment-industry sites such as Mandy.com, and general employment sites such as Indeed.com and LinkedIn.com. You can search for entry-level positions or for openings that require specific skills that you possess, such as knowing how to use Blender.

The most entry-level positions at a VFX studio are interns and production assistants. (Some countries, including the UK, call production assistants runners.) Production assistants typically do errands and administrative work, such as getting coffee and organizing schedules. It's menial labor, but the benefit is the exposure you gain to the various aspects of studio work. In some companies, it'll put you on the path toward production management. You can also meet colleagues who may ask to see your portfolio and become your mentors.

What Are the Career Paths?

Generally, a VFX artist starts as a junior artist and gradually progresses to a mid-level/intermediate artist, then to senior artist, lead artist, and eventually a supervisor, who manages the entire team.

In the production or engineering teams, you'd start out as an entry-level assistant and work your way up. Schnepf started with an internship in a small VFX company in Toronto working on commercials. Her first job was in a tape room monitoring the rendering, but she eventually got the opportunity to shadow a producer and become the office manager.

Though she initially thought this would be a stepping-stone to work in VFX animation, she found it stressful to be creative on demand. She liked doing the logistical tasks, though, such as budgeting, scheduling, and handling expenses, so she became a production coordinator, then a production manager, and eventually a VFX producer.

There's also room to transfer to different departments within visual effects. Dylan Sisson started as an artist—doing computer graphics, painting, illustration, and toy design—but eventually became a product specialist at Pixar working with software. He then became the creator and designer of RenderMan, 3-D rendering software that has been used to create visual effects for Pixar, Disney, *Star Wars*, and *Lord of the Rings* films. He is now Pixar's marketing manager.

It is possible to get a job at a big studio and stay there for most of your career. Sisson has been at Pixar for twenty-five years. White entered Industrial Light & Magic (a division of Lucasfilm) as an intern, before he became a VFX supervisor at Wētā FX (*Lord of the Rings*, *Avatar*), where he's worked for over twenty years.

But most people work contract to contract with studios. Most big projects, like films and TV shows, are done by VFX studios. Professionals estimate that an average entry-level contract is about six months to a year. It's also common to be hired for a two-week contract—and for it to be extended if they like working with you.

Another thing to note is that a lot of VFX professionals move around. While some Hollywood industries have a handful of big-city hubs, such as Los Angeles and Atlanta, visual effects is an industry where you can work anywhere in the world. Many of the professionals we talked to work remotely, but their work has taken them to San Francisco, Los Angeles, Seattle, Atlanta, Montreal, Toronto, London,

Wellington, Sydney, and more. Studio Hog's website counts about 630 VFX studios globally and provides data on each one's size, location, and links.

And like most Hollywood career paths, there are a lot of ebbs and flows. But when work is plentiful, and once you've gotten a good reputation as a reliable worker, many professionals rely on connections to string together a consistent schedule of gigs.

How Do You Make Money? And What Kind of Money?

Glassdoor, Talent.com, and ZipRecruiter estimate the average salary for a VFX artist in the United States to be between $100,000 and $115,000 a year, according to 2025 data. The U.S. Bureau of Labor Statistics estimates that the median pay for special-effects artists and animators was $99,060 per year in 2023.

Professionals caution, though, that there is an extremely wide range of incomes. They can be paid hourly or daily rates. Others will have a yearly salary. It all varies from studio to studio, project to project, country to country. Faster turnarounds and higher-budget projects pay more.

Rebelway has a free seventy-page e-book about how to land a dream job in visual effects that includes a section on VFX industry salaries. It estimates that VFX internship salaries start at $11 to $17 an hour, junior VFX artists make an average of $51,552 a year, mid-level VFX artists make $67,724 a year, senior VFX artists earn $104,000 a year, and VFX supervisors make $160,000 a year.

Piacente said she started at $17 an hour and has had rates all over the map throughout her career, reaching up to $83 per hour. Her experience matches the results of a widely circulated survey of VFX salaries that has amassed over three thousand entries and shows annual salaries, before benefits, ranging from $60,000 to $200,000.

Most VFX jobs are nonunion, but after some high-profile media stories in 2022 exposing toxic working environments, VFX workers started organizing what would become VFX-IATSE, a wing of the International Alliance of Theatrical Stage Employees. In 2023, VFX-IATSE published survey results showing that 70 percent of VFX workers reported having worked uncompensated overtime and that the majority of VFX workers feel their work is not sustainable in the long term.

In 2023, Walt Disney Studios and Marvel VFX workers voted unanimously in favor of unionizing with IATSE. In 2024, *Avatar*, *Saturday Night Live*, and Apple Studios VFX workers followed. Professionals hope these efforts will improve working conditions and increase pay.

How Is This Career Different from Ten or Twenty-Five Years Ago?

As technology has advanced, the quality of VFX work has improved noticeably, even on low-budget films. Software like Blender (for 3-D computer graphics), DaVinci Resolve (for editing and visual effects), and Polycam (for 3-D scanning) can be used for free. Vast backgrounds that used to be difficult to film can now be created quickly digitally. Projects that used to take five or six hours to render can now be done in minutes. These technological advancements have expanded the career options and specializations within the VFX industry.

And it helps that filmmakers now have a better understanding of how to use visual effects most efficiently. In the 1990s and 2000s, productions would constantly ask VFX teams to fix shots in post-production without understanding how difficult, time-consuming, or expensive it would be. It also created a division between the "digital" artists in post-production and the "analog" artists in pre-production and production, who worried that their work would be drastically altered in the final stages.

Now there are more efforts to work together and bring VFX professionals into the discussions earlier. There's also a better understanding of what parts of filmmaking work better digitally, what's better to shoot on camera, and how to integrate those two pieces.

What's Some Good Advice?

Pay attention to your environment. "It's very important as artists to just observe the world around you," Brown said. "Because that's going to be your leading reference for what's real, especially if you're an animator. Pay attention to how the clouds move. Pay attention to how people walk. I know it's boring, but sometimes I'll just watch the rain."

Keep track of where you apply and the people you interview with. "Though the industry may seem big because of the reach of studios across the world, it's actually pretty small," said Piacente. It's common to interview with the same HR people who may work for different companies over their career.

Focus on what you do best. White said a common mistake he sees is applicants' not gearing their portfolio toward the position they want. "They'll say they're a digital artist, send it off, and leave it to someone in recruiting to figure out where to put them," he said. "It's better to say, 'I'm an animator,' 'a lighter,' or 'a modeler.'" It might be helpful to be a jack-of-all-trades, to understand how different departments work together. Because there are so many different roles within visual effects, however, you should focus on what you love. When you're really good at a certain skill, that's how you get job security.

Be generous with information. Technology is always changing. "What helped me throughout my career was I was always sharing the technology or software or things that I had created," White said. "Getting my work out there and trying to help other people do their work—that helped propel me up the chain."

Let new technology excite you. There's a lot of fear about AI and other technologies taking over Hollywood jobs, and sometimes the fear is misdirected at the VFX industry. During a publicity tour for

Oppenheimer, director Christopher Nolan spoke to the media about how there were no "CGI shots" in the film. This comment led many to think he was declaring there were no visual effects in the film. Later, the film's VFX supervisor, Andrew Jackson, clarified that this wasn't true.

VFX artists can find these misunderstandings frustrating because they oversimplify and undervalue VFX work that is already often invisible. While AI will undoubtedly disrupt Hollywood, VFX artists have already been using some of this technology for decades—and much of it can make their jobs quicker, easier, and safer.

White suggests that those who are worried about visual effects taking over their analog positions should bring their skills into the visual effects artists' virtual playground. He points to *Black Panther* and *Avatar*, where costume designers used fashion software to build the characters' clothes, "even though they never existed outside the virtual world."

"Back in the day, they thought television was going to kill film," he said. "And these arts still exist, even as the new ones come in."

CHAPTER 19

How to Become a Special-Effects Artist

When George Lucas released his first *Star Wars* space epic in 1977, he set out to dazzle audiences with visual effects more advanced than anything ever seen. Mission accomplished. But not all the movie magic in *Star Wars* came from computer-driven effects; some of it was conjured by physical objects crew members built and manipulated. That includes the spaceships that battled in the movie's climactic scene, when rebel forces tried to thread missiles into the bowels of the planet-sized Death Star.

The rebel X-Wings and TIE Fighters racing through a Death Star trench weren't made of pixels; they were custom-crafted models roughly the size of a crew member's torso. The trench, meanwhile, was a sixty-foot mock-up in a parking lot. For the scenes featuring the ships' pilots, Lucas shot close-ups of costumed actors sitting on wooden platforms that were hoisted, rocked, or shaken by crew members, giving the illusion of their ships hovering, zooming through space, or veering to avoid enemy fire.

Today, filmmakers continue to rely on special effects (or "practical effects") like these, even though advances in technology have enabled them to do considerably more through purely digital means than they could in 1977. Special-effects artists are still getting hired not just because digital effects are expensive but also because filming with actual objects can be easier for the cast and crew.

Actors need to respond to and interact with things, and having real objects in the scene simplifies the camerawork. Besides, "it's a very difficult thing to make something digitally that will fool the human brain into thinking it's absolutely real," said Brian Poor (*Aquaman*, *The Predator*). "We know something isn't quite right when we see it."

Poor is an expert in animatronics, or the art of making inanimate objects move in an engaging way. Often the object needs to look like a real animal, but it might also be a creature or robot sprung from the filmmaker's imagination. Or it could be a body part doing something that body parts are not supposed to do.

A primary focus for special-effects artists is manipulating the environment in front of the camera, such as by simulating smoke, fog, rain, or snow. And by the way, making it look like it's raining is harder than just turning on some sprinklers. "To get it to appear on camera, it has to be tremendously heavy, just to make it look like regular rain," said Tobey Bays, business agent for IATSE Local 44. "It's always twice as much as you think you're going to need."

Special-effects pros also start controlled fires, blow things up, and make things move—for example, using hydraulics to help a superhero shove cars aside, or inverting a set with a giant gimbal to make it seem as if a character is walking on the ceiling. They create the breakaway furniture that crumbles safely under actors in fight scenes, the glass that they smash through, and the vases broken over their heads.

The field of special effects also involves makeup artists who create prosthetics—for example, to show a human transforming into a werewolf or being decapitated. But that's a separate group from the pros who specialize in environmental effects and model building, and we'll address that work in the chapter on makeup artists.

What Qualities Do You Find in a Successful Special-Effects Artist?

It almost goes without saying that people in this field are extremely creative. But as with other positions that support the principal filmmakers and actors, being good at special effects requires a problem-solving, results-oriented mentality. That's because you're often asked to do something that's never been done before. Above all, special-effects artists are highly adaptable, with the ability to switch gears quickly and be flexible. On any given day, it's safe to expect a monkey wrench to be thrown into your plans.

The best special-effects artists are the ones with the most diverse skill sets and who can be relied on to complete any task thrown at them. That's why it's helpful to have well-rounded mechanical knowledge and some skill working with your hands—or, as Maggie Anne Goll (*Bill & Ted Face the Music*, *The Forever Purge*) put it, "being able to get dirty."

Bays said the people who become special-effects workers in his union have a wide-ranging aptitude for science, as their duties may require some knowledge of chemistry, physics, math, engineering, or hydraulics. "They're also skilled welders, and just have a good general knowledge of materials and processes," he said.

Poor suggested that the field attracts people who are "visual thinkers"—those who need to see something to figure it out, rather than having it explained to them. "I can look at a mechanical system and understand how it works," he said. "As soon as somebody wants me to figure out something with math, we're in trouble."

Poor's epiphany about special effects came when he saw a movie with a creature whose skin had been completely removed. An art student at the time, he knew right away that he wanted to do work like that.

"I didn't want to necessarily be a fine artist, but I wanted to do something creative," he said. "And I wanted to get paid to make things. Which is a drawback of being an artist."

Big egos and negativity have no place in special-effects departments, where teams of talented people spend hours on end together—often late into the evening and early morning—all in pursuit of a singular vision.

How Do You Get Started?

You don't have to move to Los Angeles to work in special effects; you just have to be in a place where movies, TV shows, commercials, or plays are produced.

For example, Fon Davis got his start in carpentry in San Francisco, working first at scenery shops—where various pieces of a film set are fabricated—before signing on as a set builder at Colossal Pictures, the animation and live-action company best known for its unconventional mash-ups of visual styles. Colossal was the first place he'd ever worked at that had a model shop, which exposed him to the craft of model building for film and television. From set building he expanded into props, miniatures, and other special-effects work. And from there, he wound up with a job on *The Nightmare Before Christmas*.

He spent more than three decades in special effects, building robots, spaceships, and other miniature marvels for such blockbuster projects as *The Matrix* and *The Mandalorian*. Now he runs his own L.A. production company, Fonco Studios, a full-service company that (among many other things) fabricates props, models, creatures, and other special effects.

Many of the jobs in special effects are found at specialty studios. To land one of those gigs, you'll need to show your future employer something that demonstrates what you can do.

That means assembling a portfolio that speaks to your aptitude for the kind of work involved in special effects, as well as the ability to carry something through and finish it, even if it's not the most polished example of your work, Poor said. It could be a haunted house you helped stage, he said. Another artist he worked with recently made a version of a robot from *Star Wars* with 3-D-printed parts that he could control electronically.

So, how do you get those basic skills?

One option is to study crafts related to practical effects at a school, such as Los Angeles Trade-Technical College, the Otis College of Art and Design, the Gnomon School of Visual Effects, Games & Animation, the Michael Vincent Academy, and the Stan Winston School. Universities with film programs, such as USC, are also possibilities, albeit expensive ones.

A background in engineering—whether through a degree or work experience—can translate well to a career in special effects. Goll, for example, was raised by two chemical engineers.

Working as an intern or apprentice in carpentry or another special-effects-related discipline is a great way to hone your skill set and build a portfolio. Experience in a machine shop can be good too. Pro tip: Welding is often in high demand, if you're not sure which craft to explore.

Some effects experts got their feet wet in the industry as production assistants. While shouldering much of the heavy lifting on set, production assistants have an opportunity to learn key tools of the trade and form meaningful connections with special-effects coordinators with hiring power. To find a job as a production assistant, it helps to know a producer—or someone who can introduce you to one. Failing that, PA jobs are often advertised on online job boards that are industry-centric, such as Mandy and Backstage, or local, such as Craigslist. But don't forget to look on LinkedIn, Indeed, and ZipRecruiter.

What Are the Career Paths?

Most newcomers are initially hired as prop makers, tasked with fabricating and assembling various items for a production and expanding their repertoires in the process. Once admitted to Local 44, the union that represents most special-effects workers (along with prop makers and other crew members) in California, they then must log twelve hundred hours' worth of specific kinds of work, including building models, manipulating various materials, and using machine tools, to move up to the Prop Shop level.

After at least four years at the Prop Shop level, they can apply for designation as a special-effects worker. They'll have to pass written and oral exams that test their knowledge of the tools and techniques used by special-effects artists along with their budgeting and organizational skills.

Once you've passed both the written and oral assessments, Goll said, "you can lead a show. You can be the big dog on top" as a special-effects coordinator. Among other things, the coordinator decides which sorts of effects will be used and who will provide them.

How Do You Make Money? And What Kind of Money?

Like many jobs in the entertainment industry, special-effects work isn't necessarily a steady job. Instead, pros frequently jump from gig to gig, some of which pay more than others. Being a special-effects artist can be kind of a nomadic existence, said Davis, whose employment history includes stints with Disney, Lucasfilm, and Paramount. It's rare that you work in the same place for long stretches of time.

"It's not for the faint of heart," he added. "If you're like me, and you love variety and you love challenges and you love the way you feel at the end of every project because it was hard, then you're cut out for this. But if you're looking for stability, if you're looking for predictability, you go work for the government. You don't work in entertainment."

Many of the best-paying gigs in film and television are available only to members of a union. Union scale starts at roughly $54 to $58 an hour for special-effects artists in Local 44. The union also provides health and retirement benefits to members in good standing.

On low-budget films and TV shows covered by union contracts, prop makers can expect to make anywhere from $26 to $45 an hour, plus overtime, although the production may bargain for lower rates.

To get into Local 44, you have to spend at least thirty days working on a union project, which you can't do unless you get a permit from the union—something that's supposed to be available only when no union members can do the work. Alternatively, you can work thirty days on one or more nonunion projects that "flip," meaning that the crew votes to organize and the producers agree to a contract with IATSE.

For those not in the union, one option is to get hired at an independent, nonunion effects shop. These outlets have taken on a lot of work that used to be done by union members at the studios, which is "kind of a sore point for us," Bays said.

Generally, yearly income for special-effects artists ranges from about $40,000 to more than $100,000—depending on the quantity and type of jobs completed.

Those looking to make some cash on the side might choose to offer "effects packages" full of professional equipment to various productions for lease or rental, or to sell things they craft independently, using the creative skills they hone on the job.

How Is This Career Different from Ten or Twenty-Five Years Ago?

In this competitive world, special effects that take a miracle to pull off today soon will be expected to be done routinely. The landscape of the industry has transformed radically and consistently over the years.

"We're always evolving to change with whatever technology there is," Davis said. "It's like you're a student for your entire career. You have to constantly be studying and learning . . . about the newest, latest, greatest technology."

Of course, one of the most significant areas of technological advancement over the last few decades has been computer-generated imagery (CGI), which has dramatically expanded the realm of possibility for the VFX and special-effects departments.

A standard explosion rigged by special-effects technicians, for example, can now be augmented via computer-generated imagery in post-production to appear grander or closer to the camera. A miniature model designed and built by special-effects artists can be scanned into a computer and enlarged on-screen by the visual-effects team after filming—no camera tricks necessary.

Multiple special-effects experts emphasized the recent importance of developing a level of proficiency in the virtual sphere as well as the practical one to account for the increasing hybridization of the two disciplines.

"To really understand the broad art of film effects, you really need to have an understanding of computer graphics and visual effects and camera—all the post-production side of it—as well as the production side of it," said Todd Masters (*True Blood, Legion*). "You need to be able to manage a lot of different skill sets and speak a lot of different ways to different artists and filmmakers."

As digital tools become more powerful and less expensive, however, the risk grows that virtual effects will take the place of more physical ones—leaving fewer jobs for the makers of models, explosions, creatures, and artificial weather.

What's Some Good Advice?

Look at other artists' work. "Find out what the current state of the art is, how these shots are being done, and find out how they used to be done," Poor said. "There's some fatigue with the digital stuff. So find out what's going on. Pay attention to the credits at the end of that newly released movie and find out who is doing what. Then you can start asking questions. It doesn't hurt to ask."

Too often, creative folks can become so fixated on their own methods, they fail to consider that "there are so many ways to do something right, and it never hurts to learn a new way," Goll said. When they're starting out, "far too many people talk . . . rather than listen," J. D. Streett (*Men in Black*, *Entourage*) added. "It's a learning period."

Join a special-effects group on Facebook. There are multiple groups on Facebook for people working in special effects. Aside from a large public group for the special-effects community, these are private groups, so you'll need to pass muster with the administrators to join. But they all offer sounding boards and guidance.

Fail in private. Don't be afraid of failure, Davis said, but you can avoid failing in public by tinkering with new technologies and materials in the privacy of your own home. That way, by the time you arrive on set, no one's going to see you make the mistakes, because you've already made them.

If you're a woman, don't be intimidated. Goll estimates that she's one of about six younger women coming up in the special-effects industry right now. But it doesn't have to be that way. "There really aren't many of us," she said. "I still get asked who my dad is, and . . . I want to laugh and say back, 'Well, who's yours?' Because I worked my butt off to get here. . . . You just gotta keep kicking ass, and you have to have the passion for it."

PART 7

DESIGN

CHAPTER 20

How to Become a Production Designer

The production designer is the leader of the art department who oversees the visual look of a project. Another way to put it: The production designer is in charge of everything on-screen that appears behind the actors.

Reflecting the position's influence, the production designer is one of the first people hired in the pre-production process to help the director and cinematographer create the story's world. The first step is to analyze the script and figure out what colors, textures, lighting, shapes, and iconography can help convey the arc of the story. Production designers will often create a giant timeline of images that express the look of the film from beginning to end. They may also accompany the location scout to look for the best places to shoot.

After a location is chosen, it's the production designer's responsibility to prepare it for the camera, according to the script's needs. Sometimes that means bringing in a lot of props. Sometimes it means constructing an extra door or replacing all the furniture. Other times, it makes more sense to build an entire set from scratch.

These decisions are usually predicated on the budget, which the production designer is responsible for managing. The designer is also often managing the biggest crew, which includes the design team (art director, set decorators and dressers, props, graphic designers, and more) and the construction team (which can include landscaping, transportation, and ventilation).

The project's other design departments also coordinate heavily with the production designer. For example, the costume designers and the production designer need to be on the same page so that the colors and textures of the clothing don't clash with (or too closely match) the background.

Sometimes the environment becomes a character in the film. For example, production designers on Wes Anderson films are working with a specific aesthetic: bold colors, vintage style, and attention to symmetry. Production designer James Connelly's sets for *The Voice*, *Top Chef*, and *The Masked Singer* are loud, breathtaking, and whimsical—and they help create the shows' brands.

But most of the time, the work of the production designer is almost invisible. In the opening scene of *Everything Everywhere All at Once*, Evelyn Wang is sitting in her apartment's dining room organizing receipts. On the wall behind her is a shelf cluttered with knickknacks and laundry bags. The dining room table is filled with endless piles of paper. Jason Kisvarday, the film's production designer, gave his set decorator, Kelsi Ephraim, fifty reference photos of messy apartments to use as inspiration. The project's art director, Amelia Brooke, chose the paint colors of the apartment and worked with the carpenters to build it.

But it doesn't look like an entire team of professionals created it. It feels like Evelyn's apartment has been like that for a very long time.

What Qualities Do You Find in a Successful Production Designer?

Production designers are usually good artists or architects who think visually. But it's not just about being able to draw or create blueprints. They need to have a clear sense of taste and make a lot of quick, efficient decisions about colors, textures, objects, and locations.

The job is different from that of an interior designer, who needs to make sure a space is both beautiful and functional. Production designers are guided by the script. They don't have the creative freedom to make choices based solely on aesthetics, so they must love the process of telling a story.

But their designs don't need to last—they just have to make it to the end of the shoot. "In Hollywood, we do a lot of printing," Connelly said. "A lot of the textures that you'll see on sets, they're really just prints—a graphic printer just shoots it out—so we can fake lots of different scenes with faux finishes and molding shadows, just with graphic design."

A production designer also has to be an adept and resourceful problem solver. A common challenge for production designers in Hollywood is that the director or showrunner needs something that's not funded in the budget. A production designer's job is to create illusions to help the story achieve a desired look (and, just as important, make an emotional connection) in other ways. The nature of set work is that there are often last-minute changes, so it's not uncommon for production designers to have to go out in the middle of the night to fix something on set so the crew can still shoot the next morning. They have to be the type of person who can handle that kind of stress.

At the same time, they have to be very collaborative, because they work with a lot of people with different personalities. That means doing a lot of negotiating to figure out how to get the best work out of the team.

Production designers tend to like learning about other cultures, because they never know if they're going to be prepping a shoot at a temple in the Himalayas or making a house in the suburbs look like it's from the 1950s.

And lastly, a career as a production designer requires good organizational skills. It doesn't matter if you design the most beautiful set. If you go over budget, you'll never get hired again.

How Do You Get Started?

You can start with a degree in art, design, or architecture. But having a specific degree in architecture or fine arts isn't a requirement. Kisvarday earned a bachelor's degree in business at Loyola Marymount University and learned everything about the film industry on the job. He started at an effects shop called New Deal Studios in Santa Monica that specialized in miniatures. He became a production assistant in the art department and worked with props.

Many designers start out as production assistants somewhere on set and make their way into the art department. Others have internships or assist on Broadway shows. If you have a specific skill—perhaps a specialization in wallpaper, upholstery, and drapery—use your expertise as a way to get your foot in the door and move up.

The Art Directors Guild has a Production Design Initiative program that provides mentorship, supervision, and on-the-job training for future production designers and art directors. Applications are typically due in March and they take about twenty people a year, based on applicants' portfolio of sketches, digital illustrations, spatial models, floor plans, and more. To apply, go to the guild's website at Adg.org.

United Scenic Artists (IATSE Local 829) also has an Equity Through Design Mentorship program that educates college, high-school, and junior-high-school students about opportunities in this field. To apply, go to Etdmentorship.org. Local 829 also has three-year Scenic Artist Apprenticeship training programs—one based in New York, the other based in St. Louis. To learn more, go to Usa829.org.

Anytime you can design an environment for a low-budget film, a student film, or another project, do it. Production designer Tom Lisowski recommends starting with music videos.

"You start the job on Friday and need to be ready to shoot it on Monday," he said. "It's trial by fire. But music videos have the advantage of not being dependent on continuity, so you can often mix and match styles—and make use of whatever you can get your hands on."

These skills will come in handy later in film and episodic work, he said.

Lisowski is the author of *Art Stars: Legends of Production Design*, an extensive compilation of interviews from production designers, including Academy Award winners Hannah Beachler (*Black Panther*) and Dante Ferretti (*The Aviator*), that is a useful read for newbies. Other helpful resources for aspiring production designers include Jane Barnwell's *Production Design for Screen: Visual Storytelling in Film and Television*, *The Art Direction Handbook for Film & Television* by Michael Rizzo, and *Designing for Screen: Production Design and Art Direction Explained* by Georgina Shorter.

Join production design networks such as Production Designers Collective and Production Hub, where you can create a profile and find job postings. Keep an eye out for art department openings on Entertainmentcareers.net, Mandy, Indeed, and LinkedIn.

What Are the Career Paths?

There are two main pathways. You can start doing production design on small projects and gradually move to bigger and bigger projects. Or you can start at the bottom of the art department and slowly make your way up.

If you start as a production assistant in the art department, one common pathway is through set design. You'd likely start out as an assistant set dresser (who arranges all the decor and props on the set before the shoot), work your way to the lead dresser, or become a buyer, the person who helps find and purchase the materials. You could eventually become a set decorator, who is the person who helps the set designer take a script and create a list of items—for example, furniture, lighting, and artwork—for each environment that will be filmed.

Or you could help with the project management tasks. You typically start as a coordinator or administrative assistant and eventually work your way up to an art director.

The relationship between a production designer and an art director is like a marriage, said David Morong, an Emmy-nominated art director (*Carnivàle*, *Big Love*) who teaches production design at San Diego State University and the American Film Institute. The production designer typically has to manage the leaders above them, making sure the director, producer, and showrunner are happy. The art director manages the workers below them in the hierarchy. Sometimes these needs clash and the production manager and art director need to find a resolution that advances everyone's interests. Because art directors deal with every aspect of bringing the filmmakers' vision to fruition, it's good to know how to art direct a project before becoming a production designer.

It's also worth noting that many people don't want to be the head of the department and shoulder all the administrative responsibilities that come with it. Becoming an art director or set designer is a career goal too, and professionals can also go back and forth between being a production designer, set designer, and art director, depending on their skill sets.

How Do You Make Money? And What Kind of Money?

The Art Directors Guild, represented by IATSE Local 800, has contracts with studios and production houses that set minimum rates for its members' services on film and TV projects. As of 2026, art directors make a minimum of $50.80 an hour, assistant art directors make a minimum of $44.10 an hour, set designers make a minimum of $39.30 an hour, and art department assistants make a minimum of $18.80 an hour.

Production designers' salaries are negotiable. The minimums provide a benchmark for their market value, and it's possible to negotiate for at least as much or more outside of the union as well.

According to 2023 U.S. Bureau of Labor Statistics estimates, the annual mean wage of set and exhibit designers for the Hollywood motion picture and video industries is $80,960. Most jobs are in California and New York, with some hubs in Georgia, Utah, and Florida.

Estimates of a production designer's earnings that include industries outside of Hollywood are lower. The Economic Research Institute's SalaryExpert database estimates the mean annual salary of a production designer to be $49,548. According to 2024 ZipRecruiter data, the average salary for a production designer in the United States is $73,691 a year. According to 2022 data in *Backstage* magazine, entry-level jobs started at $34,000 annually.

Professionals say it takes years to book consistent jobs. In the beginning, you're likely making a couple hundred dollars a day in the rare weeks you're employed. And even when you are successful, you'll rarely have continuous employment. Morong said over the course of his career he never had a job that went more than eight months. "If you can string together thirty weeks of employment over the course of fifty-two weeks, that's the sweet spot," he said. "Forty weeks is a really good year."

How Is This Career Different from Ten or Twenty-Five Years Ago?

Production designers used to have to physically construct all of a film's sets. But as VFX technology has advanced, environments can now be created or enhanced in post-production. For example, the art department might have to build only the part of the wall that's behind the actors and the rest can be added digitally.

There isn't yet a standard guideline for where the job of the production designer ends and the work of post-production visual effects begins. Traditionally, production designers would be done as soon as the film wrapped production, and they'd move on to their next project. But in recent years, there has been more collaboration between the production team and the VFX artists, and the production designers may stick around longer to help the VFX team bring the director's vision to the screen.

What's Some Good Advice?

Rewatch your favorite movies. Since you already know what happens in these films, ignore the story and pay attention to the background. That'll give you a sense of how each specific environment is put together. Think about the decisions that must have been made to create that story.

Learn basic lighting principles. Lisowski recalled one of his early projects, where he designed an underground cellar with a single hanging lightbulb that would have been too dark to shoot. Reviewing the initial sketches, the cinematographer asked, "How am I going to light this?"

Because a production designer is hired so early in the process, you might be designing sets before a cinematographer is on board to help advise on how they will be shot.

It's best to understand lighting and make it a major part of your design, so you can predict what things are going to look like through the camera lens. Lisowski and the cinematographer were able to find a solution by adding high cellar windows and fluorescent practical lights.

Take your physical health seriously. Production designers say that when you're on a project it takes over your life. You're there at 6 a.m., and you don't come home until night. You're probably traveling to multiple places, on your feet all day, and not getting enough sleep. Adopt physical and mental practices to build up your endurance and stamina.

Make friends with directors. A partnership with a successful director can be long and fruitful. Nathan Crowley has been Christopher Nolan's go-to production designer on many of his films. Rick Carter has worked on many of Steven Spielberg's films. Grant Major, the production designer on *The Lord of the Rings: The Return of the King*, first worked with Peter Jackson on one of his first features, *Heavenly Creatures*.

CHAPTER 21

How to Become a Costume Designer

The costumes in film and television aren't just fashion statements. The clothes are integral to an actor's preparation, because oftentimes the fitting room is the first time the actors see themselves as that character. The costumes also help form the audience's first impression of a character on-screen, before any dialogue is even spoken.

Costume designers, who serve as the head of a production's wardrobe department, start by breaking down the script and working with directors, producers, actors, and the rest of the crew to figure out how to visually express the characters. This involves taking into consideration things such as the time period, location, personalities, and mood.

For many contemporary shows, the costume team will search thrift stores, designer boutiques, malls, pop-up markets, costume shops, or ethnic enclaves to find the best fits. There are also projects—usually fantasy, sci-fi, and period stories—called build shows, because you can't purchase any of the costumes. The costume team has to create and illustrate them from scratch and hire artisans to build them.

Whitney Anne Adams started her movie career as a costume design assistant on Baz Luhrmann's *The Great Gatsby*. As it was a big-budget film that placed a high priority on the period clothing, *Gatsby*'s costume department included assistants, buyers, tailors, dressers, illustrators, cutters, costumers, stylists, textile artists, jewelry makers, coordinators, consultants, supervisors—all headed by costume designer Catherine Martin.

Adams's duties as an assistant included going through F. Scott Fitzgerald's novel and making a spreadsheet of every visual reference. She and the costume team then researched period clothes from photographs, articles, and illustrations and found dresses from vintage stores for reference. To dress the hundreds of background actors for the party scene, she collected thousands of swatches from fabric stores all over New York. She organized them into binders by type: cotton, sequins, lace, glitter, and more.

The team modernized the historical looks—"skirts were shorter, heels were higher." All of Leonardo DiCaprio's suits needed to be tailored perfectly. They designed, sewed, and did beadwork for the showstoppers like Carey Mulligan's chandelier dress but also stitched together unique clothing—spiderweb dresses, mermaid costumes, and a butterfly-winged outfit—for background characters in the lavish party scenes.

There can certainly be glamorous moments working in costume design. But the work requires a lot of physical labor. People in the wardrobe department are often on their feet all day, transporting bags, steaming clothes, or running from fitting to fitting. They have to deal with soiled clothing.

"A lot of people think costumes are smoke and mirrors, and clothes just appear," Adams said. "A lot of folks just don't know how truly difficult it is to make every single costume happen."

Adams remembers bawling on the *Gatsby* set on the day of the shoot. Her team spent months making hundreds of costumes, and it was the first time she saw them all together.

What Qualities Do You Find in a Successful Costume Designer?

An interest in costume design often starts with an interest in fashion. But one main difference is that in the fashion industry the clothing is the star, whereas in costume design the clothing is there to enhance a story, not distract from it.

Hollywood costume designers need to be very meticulous. It helps if you like spreadsheets, because there's a lot to keep track of. Costume designers dress not only the principal cast but also guest stars and background characters. Because scenes are often shot out of order, designers need to plan accordingly. If a scene takes several days to film, the outfit has to be managed so it appears the same way for continuity.

Costume designers also need to remember whether an actor likes a particular undergarment or panty hose, and if anyone wants armpit shields. They have to make sure the stunt doubles' costumes are exactly the same as the corresponding actors', except for being one size larger to accommodate the padding and with gussets sewn in so that their pants don't rip mid-kick.

And on top of all that, costumes in film and television will be captured on camera in both close-up shots and wide shots. So costume designers simultaneously plan for the minute details and the bigger picture.

Lastly, professionals agree that it helps to be a quick problem solver. "Can you MacGyver under pressure?" said Janelle Carothers, the costume designer for *Unstoppable* and *All Rise*. "I love that you might know what Prada's latest season looks like, but if we're rolling, can you take a piece of bubble gum and fix a hem if you only have ten seconds to do it?"

Costume designer Mona May, who broke into the industry with her iconic work on *Clueless*, remembered one time when her team realized it was missing a priest costume. "We ended up using a tablecloth, kind of cutting a hole in the head, draping it, and making some kind of a shawl."

How Do You Get Started?

While it's not necessary to go to school, it helps to have a technical skill. Salvador Perez, most known for his work on *The Mindy Project* and *Never Have I Ever*, took four years of sewing in high school, and by the time he graduated he was proficient.

"Everybody wants to go to school to be a costume designer, but very few want to go to school to be an ager/dyer, a cutter/fitter, or a seamstress," he said. "There are whole careers in costumes that have nothing to do with design, and having the technical skills is a good way to break into the business."

One of costume designer Natalie Bronfman's favorite parts about working on *The Handmaid's Tale* was the variety of artisans hired for the production. "I even had shoemakers," she said. "When do you have that?"

Cutters and fitters are responsible for making patterns and tailoring the clothes. Agers and dyers are the artists who take new clothes and make them look like they've been worn. Especially in action films, where characters get into fights, the clothing has to be adjusted for all levels of breakdown. The ripped pants and the faintness of the bloodstains help tell the story.

Buy low-cost clothing from a thrift store or ask for donations from friends and family and practice tailoring. Work at a fabric store, costume rental shop, boutique, or department store. Volunteer to help with theater productions at your local school or community center.

Google "costume assistant jobs" or "wardrobe assistant jobs" to find entry-level positions at such sites as EntertainmentCareers.net, Indeed, and ZipRecruiter. Another common way into the industry is to start as a production assistant in the costume department. Production assistants aren't allowed to handle the clothes, so they mostly run errands, but it's a great place to learn how the industry works, meet people, understand the pressures of the job, and figure out the timeline needed to get a costume ready for the camera.

What Are the Career Paths?

To work your way up to assistant costume designer—and eventually costume designer—you can take the set or office route.

Those who go on a film or TV set to help actors get into their clothing—after the costume designer and assistant costume designer have come up with the vision for the costumes—are called costumers. There's a key costumer who supervises the wardrobe department's on-set duties; a truck costumer who manages the clothes in the trailer; set costumers who make sure that the actors are comfortable and that the costumes fit exactly the way the costume designer wants them to; and costumers dedicated to the background actors.

The people who prefer the office route will oversee operations, which includes buying or building the costumes. Duties vary, but in general, costume coordinators handle the receipts and work with the shoppers, who go out to purchase the clothing or fabrics needed after the designer comes up with the plan. They report to the costume supervisors (also called wardrobe supervisors), who handle a lot of the logistics, including hiring the crew and managing the budget.

Once you understand how costumes work on set, you should try to get a job as an assistant costume designer. It can take years, but that's where you'll start to learn the political aspects of managing a department.

It's also helpful to get experience working on different types of sets. In an indie film, the wardrobe department could be just a handful of people, whereas Bronfman's *The Handmaid's Tale* team had fifty-seven people and May's team for Disney's *Enchanted* had about one hundred.

It's not a straightforward pathway, so don't let your ego get in the way of taking smaller jobs that might help you in the long run. After working on commercials and a small feature film, Susanna Song, costume designer of *Minari*, got a costume designer job on a big-budget film that allowed her to travel to Russia, Romania, and Greece. While that was a glamorous job, when she returned she didn't have another gig lined up.

But she had an opportunity to be a production assistant for a day on a Universal project to cover for someone. There was a part of her that didn't want to go back to assisting. But she took it and ended up making some important relationships there. "In a way, I had to take two to three steps back in order to take a big step forward in my career," she said.

How Do You Make Money? And What Kind of Money?

Costume designers are part of the International Alliance of Theatrical and Stage Employees. Within the union, there are two costume guilds: Local 892, the Costume Designers Guild, which includes costume designers, assistant costume designers, and illustrators, and Local 705, Motion Picture Costumers, which includes the folks who are on set, as well as anyone who creates costumes or maintains the clothes.

The goal is to get into a union, designers said, because its members get paid at higher rates and receive health insurance and a pension. (Production assistants are not part of the union, so they'll often make minimum wage for a ten- to twelve-hour day with no benefits.)

The pay difference is another reason Perez recommends newcomers enter the industry through a craft, as opposed to a wardrobe PA gig. According to the 2026 rates negotiated by IATSE, dressers earn a minimum of $30.15 an hour, while stitchers are paid $33.80 an hour. Set supervisors, costumers, and those who work in costume breakdown (the job of taking an outfit and making it look like it's worn down, bloodied, torn apart, or whatever is needed for the script) earn a minimum of $35.80 an hour. Assistant costume designers, coordinators, and set supervisors earn a minimum of $40.15 an hour. Many of these jobs require sixty hours a week.

Though the union doesn't set minimum rates for costume designers, the Costume Designers Guild's Pay Equity Committee launched the 2022 campaign #NakedWithoutUs that included data from IATSE showing that costume designers on average make $3,131.89 for a sixty-hour workweek—less than the average cinematographer, makeup department head, hair department head, and production designer. According to 2025 data from the Economic Research Institute's SalaryExpert database, the average annual gross salary in the United States for a costume designer is $45,087.

How Is This Career Different from Ten or Twenty-Five Years Ago?

Instagram has become a powerful tool for aspiring costume designers to showcase their creative personas. May said that when she hires people she definitely looks at their social media. Perez encourages costume designers to build a brand, because then they can leverage their name recognition for higher pay.

Schools are offering more relevant instruction today as well. There were design programs for fashion twenty years ago, May said, but fewer of them catered specifically to costume design for film and television. Now many of the top film and fashion schools—from USC and UCLA to NYU and SCAD—include costume design programs.

Costume design explainers are also much more readily available online, with fashion media outlets like *Vanity Fair* and *Vogue* regularly asking actors and costume designers to show the process of creating iconic Hollywood looks. Adams hosts an interview podcast, *Tales from a Costume Designer*, where she interviews costume designers, costume department members, and filmmakers. *The Art of Costume Podcast*, hosted by Elizabeth Joy Glass and Spencer Williams, has been highlighting the latest in Hollywood costume design since 2021.

What's Some Good Advice?

Be confident that your unique background is an asset. Song's research on how South Korean immigrants dressed in the United States in the 1980s helped when she was hired as costume designer of *Minari*, but she also drew on her instincts and family history. She understood that a low-income Korean family would still want to dress well and that the kids' clothing would be more Americanized. She pushed for a light blue polyester blouse with a polka-dot skirt for Monica, the immigrant mother, because it reminded her of an outfit her mom kept in her dresser for a long time. "I remember as a little kid, yanking on that skirt," she said.

Make your actors feel confident. "Actors are balls of insecurity, so your job is to make them feel their best," Perez said. "It's about being able to communicate and listen. What do they need to feel better? Is it having a darker color or fitting the sleeves?" It's best when you're not forcing anyone into your design but you're collaborating with them into your design.

CHAPTER 22

How to Become a Choreographer

There are many roles for choreographers in the entertainment industry. They are featured on reality-TV shows like *Dancing with the Stars*. They are behind musicals like *Moulin Rouge*, *The Marvelous Mrs. Maisel*, and *Crazy Ex-Girlfriend*, where dance is an integral part of the storytelling.

But choreographers aren't needed just for showstopping musical dance numbers. They're hired whenever any type of coordinated movement is going to be filmed. In club scenes, choreographers are there to hype up the crowd and suggest moves. They also often help with long takes called oners, where everything happening on-screen needs to be tightly executed.

There are lots of gigs where choreographers are hired short-term to help with specific scenes: *The Office* coworkers parading down the aisle at Jim and Pam's wedding or Elena's good-bye for Nina Dobrev's final episode of *The Vampire Diaries*.

In these situations, the choreographer must come prepared with the material they're going to teach the actors, along with multiple backup plans in case the actor can't pick up the moves or the director prefers something else.

It's not uncommon for a choreographer to have fifteen minutes to coach an actor between takes, because actors tend to have very tight schedules. It's also normal to contend with last-minute changes because there was a script or song change. Choreographers have to be able to handle these moments without stressing the actor, who likely was already nervous about having to dance on camera.

Unlike choreographers hired for concert tours or music videos, film and TV choreographers are often working with nondancers. *La La Land* featured many eye-catching dance performances, but stars Emma Stone and Ryan Gosling aren't professional dancers.

"My job is not to train them to be professional dancers," said the film's choreographer, Mandy Moore (not to be confused with the singer and *This Is Us* actor). "It's to coach them to a point where they can do what they need to do for their characters in the story."

What Qualities Do You Find in a Successful Choreographer?

Usually, choreographers are professional dancers who have been dancing since they were kids. It's also common for martial artists who can do tricks and flips to transition into a dance career.

There are choreographers like Sonya Tayeh (Broadway's *Moulin Rouge*) who aren't as comfortable performing but enjoy composing dances and figuring out how you can evoke emotions through movement.

The job is about not just creating the moves but also coaching and guiding people so they can execute the moves on set. It's a fun profession that's challenging and competitive at the same time. "You need a sense of relentlessness and drive," Tayeh said. Though she considers herself a shy and nervous person, she knows how to walk into a room with confidence and advocate for her vision.

There's not a lot of stability in this career path. You'll have to say yes to most projects that come your way to eke out a living, and when you get a job, it takes over your life for that amount of time.

"This is one of those jobs where it's not a job," said choreographer Alison Faulk (*Magic Mike*). "It's your passion, your heart, your love—something you *have* to do."

How Do You Get Started?

Choreographers create a story nonverbally, and that specialized skill requires a lot of knowledge.

"When they say they want Fosse, do they mean they want dark, moody lighting?" said Kathryn Burns, two-time Emmy-winning choreographer (*Crazy Ex-Girlfriend*) and president of the Choreographers Guild. "Do they want it to be sexy and burlesque? Do they want it to be campy? When someone says hip-hop, do they want nineties, funk, popping, locking?"

So it's important to learn as many genres of dance as possible. This will help you get more jobs as a dancer and make you more versatile as a choreographer.

There are many well-known studios in dance hubs like New York and Hollywood. Many New York studios, including Broadway Dance Center and Steps on Broadway, focus on training for Broadway, whereas L.A. studios, including Millennium Dance Complex, EDGE Performing Arts Center, Debbie Allen Dance Academy, and Movement Lifestyle, often train you to perform for a camera, even if it's just for your Instagram page.

But there are great programs all around the nation. Oklahoma City University has a specific degree track for dance performance in the entertainment business. Center Stage Performing Arts Studio in Utah is known for training many *Dancing with the Stars* professionals, including Julianne and Derek Hough.

Find the choreographers you admire and take their classes. Most choreographers teach at multiple studios. Classes are also where you can find your community, so you can hear about gigs, network, and practice together.

Once your skills have advanced, you can also apply for dance instructor jobs. Keep tabs on sites such as Dancingopportunities.com, Danceusa.org, and Danceteacherfinder.com for job listings.

If anyone needs an assistant, offer your help. Take any job that can help you learn how the set works. When you are able to gather enough material for an impressive reel, look for an agent or manager who will advocate for you. You can also submit your work to the Choreographer's Carnival, an open showcase for choreographers' routines that takes place in Los Angeles, New York, Chicago, Las Vegas, and Ranica, Italy. Go to Choreographerscarnival.com for rules on how to submit, as well as information on classes taught by the judges.

The Choreographers Guild is also a helpful resource for education and networking. The labor organization was formed in 2022 to advocate for choreographers for film, television, concert tours, award shows, and music videos. Once you've completed one choreographer credit in a project covered by SAG-AFTRA, Actors' Equity Association, AGMA, AGVA, or SDC—or the equivalent body of professional work that can be submitted for approval by the guild's membership committee—you can apply for membership at Choreographersguild.org.

What Are the Career Paths?

The common route is to first get a job as a dancer. Then you get the attention of a choreographer, who could eventually hire you as an assistant choreographer. You do that to learn the ropes until someone gives you a shot at being the associate choreographer. Then you work your way up to choreographer.

Dancers generally don't have any direct input on the choreography. Their job is to go to rehearsal, learn the routine, and nail the moves during the shoot. Assistant choreographers help teach the dancers the routines. They might be taking notes, helping to fine-tune the choreography, or making sure there is continuity, but they usually come into the project when the choreography has already been designed. The associate choreographer is part of the collaborative process with the choreographer. They can suggest concepts, logistics, and specific moves.

Choreographers are in charge. They decide what dance moves to use; their job is not just a creative one but also a managerial one. They meet with the director to understand what the dance needs to accomplish for the story. They talk to the costume designer because gussets are needed in the pants so they don't rip when the dancers do flips. They talk to the producer if they need to advocate for extra days of shooting. They talk to the casting director to help assess which dancers or actors will be able to handle the film's choreography. They meet with the music department.

The job is so all-encompassing that choreographers can learn enough skills to eventually become directors.

How Do You Make Money? And What Kind of Money?

When you're starting out as a choreographer, the rates are likely to be very low. You're taking the jobs to try to impress people who could hire you in the future.

According to 2025 data from the Economic Research Institute's SalaryExpert database, the average choreographer's gross salary in the United States is $64,071, with an equivalent hourly rate of $31. It predicts that the salary potential will increase 12 percent in five years.

There's no standard day rate for choreographers. "Some people might get five hundred dollars a day, which is on the low end, and then someone might get paid five thousand dollars or more if there's a large budget and you're in demand," Faulk said of choreographers in the entertainment industry.

The Choreographers Guild helps its members negotiate not only for wages but also for residuals, royalties, and credits. Burns said these are common problems: She was once left out of the credits of an Oscar-nominated film she worked on.

To qualify for membership, applicants need to have at least one choreography credit in a SAG-AFTRA, Actors' Equity Association, American Guild of Musical Artists, American Guild of Variety Artists, or Stage Directors and Choreographers Society production. Alternatively, an applicant can submit a body of work for potential approval from the membership committee.

Choreographers who work on camera as dancers can join SAG-AFTRA, which is one way to gain health and pension benefits. The 2026 minimum pay rates for dancers set by SAG-AFTRA are broken down into daily and weekly rates, and there are three levels of payment based on whether dancers are doing a solo/duo performance ($1,246 a day / $4,010 a week), performing with three to eight dancers ($1,092 a day / $3,676 a week), or performing with nine or more dancers ($953 a day / $3,342 a week).

How Is This Career Different from Ten or Twenty-Five Years Ago?

When Moore first moved to Los Angeles in the early nineties, it seemed like people had tired of the dance music videos of the eighties and dance had disappeared. But it started coming back with the return of the boy bands.

Around the mid-2000s, Tayeh started seeing a movement toward showcasing dance not only for music artists but also in commercials (for iPods, Gap, and Old Navy), runway fashion, dance films, and reality competitions.

Emilio Dosal—associate choreographer for *Wicked* and *In The Heights* who won an Emmy for choreographing Disney's *Sneakerella*—started getting attention for his moves during the rise of YouTube in the late 2000s. "If you had a camera and a tripod, you'd set that up in front of a mirror, record a dance class, and throw it up on YouTube," he said. "And regardless of whether it went viral or not, it was a way of showcasing the work and embracing each other as part of a movement."

Now it's all about TikTok, Instagram, and other social media platforms—which can send a newcomer's career skyrocketing. Posting your videos is a good way to showcase your unique style and skill set.

What's Some Good Advice?

Don't look down on the gigs that don't require complicated moves. Moore made a lot of money in her early career doing commercials that most would never think even had choreography. For one gig, her job for the day was to help a model sit down in a chair for the camera. "I've trained my whole life to do kicks and turns and jumps and leaps, but my knowledge of how to explain to somebody how to sit correctly on the right count is also part of the skill set you need as a choreographer," she said.

Familiarize yourself with camerawork and editing. This is an important skill to have because sometimes directors will ask choreographers for advice on how to shoot the dance. Other times, you might adjust the choreography depending on how they plan to shoot. The newer generation of choreographers have an advantage because they're comfortable filming themselves and they can quickly understand how to look at dance through the lens of a camera phone.

Look into being a movement coach. Austin Butler used a movement coach to learn how to embody the physicality of Elvis. Veteran movement coach Jean-Louis Rodrigue worked with Margot Robbie to embody Barbie and helped Ke Huy Quan keep track of all the Waymond characters in the *Everything Everywhere All at Once* multiverse. Choreographers can often use their skills to help actors practice getting into the physicality of a character or help directors map out an intimate scene, she said.

Maximize your own potential. Dosal said when he started auditioning he noticed he was usually the shortest person in the room. So he'd push his arms out farther during the dances. He'd put more vigor into his flips. "What ended up happening is, I'm in the air, and casting directors end up turning in my direction," he said. "And they're like, 'Oh, this kid's flying. This tiny kid is bigger than the rest of them right now.'"

CHAPTER 23

How to Become a Makeup Artist

Hollywood makeup can be broken into two categories: beauty makeup—sometimes called straight makeup—and special-effects makeup.

"Beauty makeup" refers to the work it takes to make anyone on camera look like they fit into the world that's being created on-screen. This could include making a rom-com star look radiant in a pivotal dance club scene. It could mean making a background actor in a sixties period film look so natural that they don't distract from the story.

Special-effects makeup, on the other hand, significantly alters a person's look. Examples include creating unique characters like Beetlejuice, Edward Scissorhands, Mrs. Doubtfire, and *Pirates of the Caribbean*'s Jack Sparrow (all helmed by Ve Neill); transforming Gary Oldman into Winston Churchill in *Darkest Hour* (which won Kazu Hiro an Oscar); or turning a crowd of background actors into zombies in *The Walking Dead*. You might be creating burn scars or other wounds and injuries.

Out of the almost one hundred credits that Hollywood makeup artist Jennifer "JQ" Quinteros has accumulated over the last fifteen years, the one she's asked most about is her first: 2011's *X-Men: First Class*. The Marvel film was such a large-scale production that each mutant had a dedicated makeup team.

Quinteros was a makeup assistant on the team led by makeup department head Lufeng Qu that transformed Jennifer Lawrence into Mystique, the iconic blue-reptile-skinned shapeshifter.

All Lawrence had on were the silicone prosthetics that were applied on her entire body, and the process took almost eight hours a day. Eight women worked on her simultaneously.

Quinteros would mix silicones in the morning and make sure everyone had the correct tone of blue paints. She'd accompany Qu to production meetings and help answer emails. Most valuable, she said, was learning the hair and makeup trailer etiquette. When is it OK to open a door? How do you touch someone without making them uncomfortable?

"To me, there's nothing more magical than when you are painting someone's face and you slowly watch the character show up in your chair," Quinteros said. "You can see people's bodies change as you do that. You can see their eyes change."

Makeup artists also accompany the actor on set and apply touch-ups in between takes to keep the makeup fresh. At the end of the day, makeup artists also help actors get out of character, which can be just as important as creating them. "Some roles are excruciating," she said. "So you want to help the actors wash that character away."

What Qualities Do You Find in a Successful Makeup Artist?

Makeup artists who choose the entertainment industry have to love collaborating with teams to help create characters and tell stories. They need to have the stamina to work long hours on sets for weeks or months at a time. Makeup artists are often on their feet most of the day, and it's not uncommon for some jobs with quick turnarounds to require twenty-hour days.

Quinteros recalls being on a shoot in Malaysia for a plane crash scene, where she had to keep paddleboarding to and from the actors in the open water to do fake blood touch-ups. Another time at a shoot in

Colorado, she had to help one of her actors dressed in period clothing climb up the side of a cliff. She also has memories of being in a tent in the middle of nowhere in 107-degree weather, trying to keep her actor's makeup perfect through the sweat. "People think I'm just putting blush on," she said. "But it's a very adventurous lifestyle."

Hollywood makeup artists not only need to be creative but they should also be able to create safe spaces for actors. The hair and makeup trailer is the first place actors go in the morning and the last place they go before they leave for the day.

Lastly, it helps to be detail oriented. Part of the job of a Hollywood makeup artist is to re-create a character's look precisely for multiple days straight.

How Do You Get Started?

Like many other roles in Hollywood, becoming a successful makeup artist requires not just talent but also a willingness to invest time and money into your craft.

There's the DIY option.

Social media is flooded with makeup tutorials. You can binge YouTube videos to learn about color theory and classic Hollywood glam makeup. You can follow the lead of makeup influencers, including Nikki La Rose, Hindash, and Lisa Eldridge, who experiment with different beauty looks on themselves. Madeyewlook, Pinkstylist, dope2111, Glam&Gore, and Ellimacs SFX are some examples of popular YouTube channels that focus on special-effects makeup.

There are books—including Dick Smith's *Do-It-Yourself Monster Makeup Handbook*, Tom Savini's *Grande Illusions: The Art and Techniques of Special Make-Up Effects*, and *Stage Makeup* by Richard Corson—that teach the basics of special-effects makeup.

But many professionals recommend formal training at a beauty or cosmetology school to learn a wider range of techniques—including airbrushing; latex and silicone application; aging and deaging; blood effects; mask making; oral prosthetics; and lifecasting—creating a three-dimensional copy of a living human body through molding and casting.

There are makeup schools like Cinema Makeup School, Michael Vincent Academy, Make-up Designory, L Makeup Institute, Vocational Academy of Makeup and Prosthetics, and Savini's Special Make-Up Effects Program. Neill cofounded her own makeup school, Legends Makeup Academy. Film makeup courses can be found at some programs for aspiring below-the-line workers, such as Stockade Works in the Hudson Valley, New York. You can also get a degree in theater, and many of those programs have classes and specializations in makeup.

Once you've gotten the basic skills, you can look for a job at a salon, or you can start as a freelance makeup artist and build up your client list. But eventually, you need experience on a set. Volunteer for student films. Reach out to professional makeup artists you admire and let them know you're available if they need an extra assistant.

Associations to join for networking purposes include the International Makeup Association, the American Association of Cosmetology Schools, the Professional Beauty Association, and the Aesthetics International Association.

Learn skin care and other beauty skills as well. Knowing how to do hair, styling, and costuming can set you apart from other applicants—and allow you the most flexibility to jump from gig to gig as you work your way up.

What Are the Career Paths?

As you begin to build your portfolio, you can progress from assistant to makeup artist to makeup department head. The department head's job includes hiring and supervising members of the team, finding the right materials needed for each set, lining up a lab to fabricate prosthetics and special effects, if needed, and applying makeup.

The size of the makeup department on set varies, depending on what the makeup requires, how many actors are involved, how many times an actor goes through makeup, and how much time the sessions require.

Each person on set is assigned actors, and actors of a certain caliber can often request their own makeup artist. So, another way to increase work is if an actor requests you not only on set but also for magazine shoots, press tours, or red-carpet appearances.

How Do You Make Money? And What Kind of Money?

Becoming a makeup artist is an up-front investment with a slow return. It can cost up to $30,000 for comprehensive education, including tuition, lab fees, and a starter kit. Most early-career makeup artists have to take any job that comes their way, and as with so many jobs in Hollywood, it may be hard to make a living.

A makeup artist job on a nonunion production can pay your bills, but you often earn less than union counterparts. Professionals recommend joining the Make-Up Artists and Hair Stylists Guild—Local 706 of IATSE, the union that represents many of the crew members on film productions—as soon as you can.

There are two ways to get union membership. One is referred to as "60-60-60." You need to show proof that you've worked 60 days on sets (which can include nonunion work) in each of three years within a five-year period in Los Angeles County. Or you can qualify for membership through an "off-roster hire" by completing 30 days worked (from first day of hire) on a union set in Los Angeles County within a period of 365 days. You have to make at least minimum wage in order for the union to count the work toward the number of hours needed to join Local 706.

The IATSE union sets a wage scale for its members. As of 2026, a third assistant makeup artist earned a minimum of $23.76 an hour; a second assistant makeup artist earned a minimum of $35.04 an hour; a first assistant makeup artist earned a minimum of $38.24 an hour; and a makeup department head earned a minimum of $42.76 an hour. Special makeup effects artists don't have a minimum and are able to negotiate themselves.

Being in the union won't necessarily guarantee you more jobs, but it will open the door to more opportunities. Being a part of an agency that contracts out makeup artists can also help increase your chances of getting hired.

According to the Bureau of Labor Statistics, getting a full-time job as a makeup artist for film or television can be lucrative—the bureau estimated the average annual salary was $119,940 in 2023. But that estimate doesn't account for self-employed artists, who comprise most of the field, and high earners skew the average, professionals say. According to 2025 data from the Economic Research Institute's SalaryExpert database, the average special-effects makeup artist gross salary in the United States is $92,717.

How Is This Career Different from Ten or Twenty-Five Years Ago?

Now a fifty-year veteran of the industry, Neill is known as a pioneer in special-effects makeup. Back in the seventies, she was using foam latex instead of the new skin-like prosthetics. "It definitely wasn't perfect, and you could definitely tell that it wasn't skin, but film cameras had a way of kissing the edges," she said. This helped in hiding the imperfections that would normally be captured by today's digital cameras.

The rise of makeup influencers has also created a potential pathway into the industry. But it's important to understand that making content online is different from working on a film or TV set.

"I have had some influencers come onto my sets as additional or day players for the very first time, and they're on their phone because their job is social media," Quinteros said. "And it's like, 'No, no. Your job today is this makeup artist on set. In fact, they need you off of your phone, and you're not allowed to record this or post it. Actually the opposite, you might get sued if you record this person.'"

What's Some Good Advice?

Seek a mentor. When Quinteros got the *X-Men* job, she was a twenty-four-year-old recent graduate, and it was her Cinema Makeup School mentor, Leonard Engelman (*Rocky*, *Ghostbusters*, *The Princess Diaries*), who recommended her to Qu.

Learn the business side of the industry early on. To get jobs, you'll have to learn how to market and brand yourself. You'll need to learn about contracts.

Venture outside Hollywood to help pay the bills. The skills of Hollywood makeup can also be applied outside of filmmaking. Makeup artists are needed for print shoots, commercials, theater, and broadcast journalism. You can work retail at makeup counters. Makeup artists can also land jobs at amusement parks and toy manufacturers. Mold makers are needed in multiple industries. Dental labs need people skilled at crafting fake teeth.

Have your portfolio on hand when you go to events. Take samples of your work to conventions and other events, and don't skimp on the quality of the photos, said Jerry Gergely, technical director for Tom Savini's Special Make-Up Effects Program at the Douglas Education Center in Pittsburgh. "You can get hired from one photo if it shows the basic skills," he said.

CHAPTER 24

How to Become a Hairstylist

Hairstylists in Hollywood work with a project's creative team—including directors, showrunners, producers, actors, makeup artists, and costume designers—to establish a character's look. Hair can be a visual signal for a character's evolution. For example, when the normally uptight and put-together rom-com lead's hair becomes frizzier after a brutal breakup once she stops taking care of herself.

It can represent culture. Camille Friend's *Black Panther* team relied heavily on consultants to create looks that rang true to ancient African and Mayan cultures. For the Amazon series *With Love*, Anissa Salazar designed an elaborate floral headpiece for Emeraude Toubia's character, Lily, in the "Día De Los Muertos" episode. She wanted it to resemble the costumes she grew up watching in the Day of the Dead parades—it had marigolds, roses, and butterflies—and she was also inspired by her sister's big, curly hair.

Sometimes stylists are most satisfied when they're able to make the wigs, extensions, and other enhancements appear clean and seamless—especially in close-ups—because they know how hard it can be to make them look natural.

Salazar was tasked with coming up with more than twenty hairstyles in the multiverse-exploring film *Everything Everywhere All at Once*—at least one hairstyle per universe for each of the key characters. She put Stephanie Hsu in a wavy, shoulder-length pink wig for her grand entrance as the villainous Jobu Tupaki. In the celestial "everything bagel" universe, Hsu donned a big, braided donut sticking up straight on top of her head (representing a black hole), and the braided strands of the donut crisscrossed down over her forehead into thin, long pigtails that fell to her waist. As much fun as she had with Hsu's more iconic looks, Salazar is equally proud of the main wig that Michelle Yeoh wore to embody Evelyn, the ordinary, exhausted middle-aged Laundromat owner.

"It looks disheveled for a reason, with the grays and the blotchy black on the left side," she said. "It felt very familiar. I wanted to show the audience Evelyn's hair was authentic and chaotic at the same time."

What Qualities Do You Find in a Successful Hollywood Hairstylist?

Most of the professionals didn't realize that working in Hollywood as a hairstylist was a career option for them when they were growing up. But they all had been doing hair for fun since they were young, whether they grew up in a family member's salon or practiced on their friends.

Many Hollywood hairstylists are drawn to the entertainment industry because they love combining their passion for hair with storytelling. They enjoy researching different styles of different periods.

It also helps for hairstylists on set to be welcoming and even-tempered. The hair and makeup trailer is often the first stop in the actors' long day of shooting. It's important to help actors feel comfortable so they can get into the right headspace and do their best work.

Aspiring Hollywood hairstylists should have a lot of stamina, because it's a physically demanding job. Eighteen-hour days are common. Hairstylists are often the first ones on set and among the last ones to leave. You have to be able to handle stress and adapt quickly to unpredictability. If the director wants one thing and the actor wants another, a hairstylist needs to be versatile enough to come up with a compromise that keeps the peace and merges the two visions.

How Do You Get Started?

Start with beauty school. This is crucial not only because you need a cosmetology license to get into the union but also because you need a solid foundation. Friend's Hair Scholars and Susan Lipson's On Set provide mentorship for newcomers interested in learning the basics of the industry. There are also courses available at Behindthechair.com and Sharon Blain—and from training centers run by Vidal Sassoon, Paul Mitchell, Goldwell, and the Aveda Institute.

Practice curling and flatironing hair. It's important for hairstylists to educate themselves so they know how to work on different hair textures.

Learn how wigs work—how to design, style, and attach the wig to the actor's hair, as well as how to distribute different types of hair underneath a wrap in order for the wig to fit perfectly. Hairstylists in Hollywood often work with wigs if the production can afford it, because it's less of a challenge to achieve continuity from shoot to shoot and many actors prefer not to have their own hair worked on for hours and possibly damaged.

Take classes after beauty school for wig making and other techniques specific to doing hair for the camera. You can also start by assisting on student films.

Once you're ready to work, you can find jobs on Staff Me Up and Crewvie. Many aspiring hairstylists work at salons—or one-on-one with clients—while they slowly book Hollywood jobs.

Hairstylists also start by getting jobs doing hair for background actors, who are on-screen in nonspeaking roles. One of Friend's early jobs was working on background for *Pirates of the Caribbean.* If it's a big movie, people who work on background talent can be working every day.

"I always tell people, 'Don't throw your nose up to that. That's a great place to learn,'" she said. "You meet so many artists when you're working background, and it raises your skill level because you get to learn how to do things really quickly."

What Are the Career Paths?

In a hair trailer, there's usually a department head, one or two assistant department heads (called keys), another hairstylist, and a barber. Friend said on big days, when there are many background actors, she can have up to twenty-five hairstylists and multiple teams when scenes are being shot simultaneously.

The hair department head manages the team. That person oversees hiring people, meeting with the other creatives, designing the looks, and managing budgets. But once the pre-production is done and everyone is on set, every hairstylist has actors they're assigned to every day.

Though there are various tracks in the union—including film, television, commercials, theater, and amusement parks—hairstylists can work on a variety of projects, jumping from gig to gig. It's best to diversify your résumé, mixing it up with comedy, drama, period, and sci-fi projects.

There is also crossover between hairstylists who work with celebrities for red-carpet appearances or photo shoots and those who work on film and TV projects. Often stars will get permission to bring a personal hairstylist onto the set.

How Do You Make Money? And What Kind of Money?

The goal is to work enough hours to qualify for the Make-Up Artists & Hair Stylists Guild, also known as IATSE Local 706, where there are minimum pay rates. You can join through the "60-60-60" strategy, which requires you to log sixty days of work per year—on network television, videos, or nonunion film or TV production—three times over a five-year period. Or you can qualify if you complete thirty days of work on a production covered by a union contract, which a nonunion member can do only if hired "off-roster."

Though these films might not pay well, they could be the projects that help you acquire enough hours to get into the union. Once you're in the union, it's easier to get jobs, because you're included on one of the rosters the union maintains. Money isn't the only reason to take a job. If you make connections with directors or producers, you might get hired for their next projects.

The IATSE union sets a wage scale for its members. As of 2026, a second assistant hairstylist earned a minimum of $35.04 an hour, an assistant hairstylist earned a minimum of $38.24 an hour, and a hair department head earned a minimum of $42.76 an hour.

For hairstylists who do not want to work full-time, they can make money "day playing," where they work fewer than sixteen days on a project. Others might prefer to work in commercials, where you can make a bigger chunk of money in a shorter amount of time.

How Is This Career Different from Ten or Twenty-Five Years Ago?

As the industry adapts to more diversity in front of the camera, Hollywood hairstylists must become proficient at multicultural hair techniques, from braids, locs, twists, and knots to flower-adorned updos and hijab-friendly styles.

The entertainment industry has adopted more inclusive hiring practices. If the hair is essential to world-building—whether it's introducing viewers to the mythical Wakandan tribes or placing the story in the shogun period of Japanese history—productions often hire specialists or consultants to create looks that are authentic to characters' cultural backgrounds.

Advances in digital technology have also changed the job of a Hollywood hairstylist. High-definition cameras also made details like flyaways or not-so-hidden pins more noticeable, requiring hairstylists to maintain a higher standard of perfection.

On higher-budget projects, hairstylists will often select a wig or design a hairstyle that acts as a foundation for any computer-generated enhancements. The hairstylists also help the VFX artists maintain continuity so that the physical and digital elements work together seamlessly.

What's Some Good Advice?

Be comfortable doing basic makeup when starting out. Once you get into Local 706, the union requires you to choose between hair and makeup, but often low-budget union jobs hire one person to do both hair and makeup, said Guyla Wilkerson, the hair department head of *The Holiday Proposal Plan* who has worked as a hair stylist on *No Good Deed* and *Never Have I Ever*.

Don't fake it till you make it. "If I give you something to do, and you don't know how to do it, tell me," Friend said. "And I'll be so happy to explain it to you and show you exactly how it should be done. Instead of [you] not knowing how to do it, and I give you a ten-thousand-dollar wig and you ruin it."

Be willing to experiment. Friend recalls an underwater scene in *Black Panther: Wakanda Forever* where actors had to shoot in water tanks for eight or ten hours a day. They soon realized the hair product left a murky cloud in the water, making it difficult to film. They needed another way to secure the wigs. Friend mixed spirit gum—the adhesive used for wigs—with alcohol to turn it into hairspray that wouldn't cloud the water. They coated the wigs with the mixture and sewed the wigs tighter on to the actors' hair so they wouldn't come off.

"So much of it is trial and error," Friend said. "And experience. You take what you learn from one project and then you have a new tool for the next one." Her experience with underwater hair helped her when she got the job for the *Little Mermaid* remake.

PART 8

POST-PRODUCTION

CHAPTER 25

How to Become an Editor

Most workers on a film crew are defined by what they add to the production—lights, camera, acting, that sort of thing. The editor's job is to find what to leave out.

Think of the editor's cuts like a sculptor's work to reveal a figure within a block of granite, or a mosaic artist's choices of tiles to put in a mural. Typically, editors start with the footage from the previous day's shoot, which usually includes several takes for each scene and shots from more than one camera angle. They then whittle the mass of media down and grab the best bits to form a draft of those scenes.

But the process involves much more than just tossing out the less appealing takes. "You think an editor only cuts? No, we actually build worlds," said Julio C. Perez IV (*It Follows*, *Euphoria*). "Cutting is a fundamental element of many elements. We do a lot more fusing, fusing ideas and rhythms."

On a granular level, that translates into deciding how much of a good shot to use—how long to let a moment linger, how hard to push the pace. Those choices depend in part on the type of story being told.

Stephanie Filo (*We Grown Now*, *A Black Lady Sketch Show*) said a comedy might require a snappy tempo, but in a hard-hitting documentary an editor might want to let the camera linger on an interview subject or verité scene so you can see more nuanced expressions or pieces of an interaction. In a horror movie, an editor might want to create a pattern with their cuts that, when broken, creates a jump scare.

Editors also have to pay attention to the flow of viewpoints provided by the different camera angles, as well as the consistency of the actors' interpretations of their characters. The best actors will give you a lot of range in their performances, and editors can't have the characters veering wildly from cut to cut.

The goal is to give each scene the look and feel that the director (or the showrunner, if it's a TV series) intended while also conveying the tone of the script—and keeping the project to a certain running time.

As the first one to watch the footage, the editor also will suggest scenes that need to be reshot or footage that needs to be added. For example, a camera angle may not have worked as expected, or a scene may need a reaction shot from an actor.

The work is repetitive and tedious, as editors spend hours at a computer looking at the same scene over and over, then making a digital record of the changes they're proposing. Few, if any, editors cut and splice lengths of film by hand anymore; all the editing is done through software, usually by Avid or Adobe. They often work in tandem with a team of editorial assistants, who prepare the footage for editing and can give second opinions on scenes.

Although editors have a lot of power over how the story is told, it's not their story. That's why the work often starts long before the cameras roll, as editors familiarize themselves with the director's vision.

Tyler Nelson (*The Batman*, *Creed III*) said he reads the script three or four times before he starts his work. Then when it's time to cut the footage for a scene, he'll reread the scenes before and after that one (and look at any relevant footage already cut) to know where the emotional focus needs to be.

Once the principal photography is finished, the editor spends several days putting all the previously edited footage into the right sequence—rather than being shot from beginning to end, films are usually shot in an order dictated by the budget and the availability of locations, actors, and equipment. The result is an editor's cut or, as some editors prefer to call it, an editor's assembly.

Then the editor and the director will spend about a week (for a scripted TV show) to ten weeks (for a feature film) painstakingly going over each scene, looking at all the available footage, shaping sequences, trimming moments that aren't essential, and refining the rhythm of the film, to help realize and refine the director's vision, said Carsten Kurpanek (*Jolt, Rambo: Last Blood*). This "director's cut" is then presented to the producers and studio executives, who offer notes about the changes they'd like to see; these are the folks who control the final cut in most cases, so the editor has to address their concerns.

"Your job is to kind of find a way to honor the note while still protecting the director's intent," Kurpanek said.

The filmmakers may also hold test screenings to see how well a movie works with viewers, resulting in more requests for changes before the film is considered finished. "Editing is the last rewrite of the script, as the saying goes," Kurpanek said.

Nevertheless, the audience shouldn't be able to see the editor's hand in the final product. As Jenni McCormick of the American Cinema Editors put it, "It's meant to be an invisible art."

What Qualities Do You Find in a Successful Film or TV Editor?

Editing is blue-collar work, the pros say—no college degree is required to be successful at it.

There are technical skills involved, but they can be taught. "Being a good editor is like being a good musician," said Ri-Karlo Handy, an editor and producer whose Handy Foundation trains would-be professionals. "Some people may be born with some actual talents, but for the most part, you take a piano lesson, a guitar lesson, whatever, and you get better over time."

So it's important to be a willing learner and a quick study. Another mark of a successful editor is the initiative to hear ideas and expand on them, rather than doing exactly what the director or showrunner asks and nothing more.

Being personable is important, because editors and their assistants spend long hours working together in the same venue. So is being able to read the emotions of the room you're in, which reflects one's ability to read the emotions in a scene. Collaboration is a huge part of the job as well. That often means anticipating what the rest of the filmmaking team wants in a scene.

"You're almost a mind reader," Filo said. "You have to know what the director wants, or what the producer wants, or what the studio might want."

Another important attribute is the ability to concentrate on something for hours on end. That's because editors may sit at their screens and work on a single task for twelve or fifteen hours straight. It's a job that requires not only patience but also stamina.

As with many members of a film crew, editors need to be capable of navigating around problems to get the job done. You may be well suited for this field, Handy said, if you're really good at solving puzzles and looking at the world from different perspectives.

During the industry's early days, film editors were most often women, cutting some of Hollywood's most renowned epics, like *The Wizard of Oz* and *Lawrence of Arabia*. Film historians say that's because film editing was seen as less glamorous work that was more technical than creative. But as the job grew in perceived importance, it was increasingly filled by men; according to a 2021 survey by the Motion Picture Editors Guild, only about 29 percent of its members identified as female. Nearly 70 percent were white males. More recently, a study by Martha M. Lauzen of San Diego State University found that only 21 percent of the editors on the 250 top-grossing films in 2023 were women. That same study offered an explanation for the imbalance: Most of the films were directed by men, and men hired male editors far more often than female ones.

How Do You Get Started?

The pros agreed that there are many ways to get started, but to advance, you'll need to learn the skills and make connections within the filmmaking community.

One way to do both is to go to film school, where you'll learn not just how to cut scenes on film but also the various other aspects of filmmaking. Understanding the different facets of production helps you to be a good editor and, more fundamentally, helps you decide what to do in the industry.

The Handy Foundation's training program for assistant editors gets deeper into the nitty-gritty of how to get started in the industry than film schools do. In addition to teaching how to use digital editing software, the program trains students about the workflows specific to unscripted television, where there is a strong demand for editing help. It also connects students to a network that can lead to jobs, including roughly two hundred Handy Foundation graduates who have ties across the industry.

Not that film or trade school is a prerequisite. "I've heard dozens of stories where people didn't go to film school, are self-taught all the way, and are really successful editors," McCormick said.

Filo, for example, was a journalism and political science major in college before moving to Los Angeles to try to get into the film and TV business. She landed a job as a night assistant editor, helping to organize footage for a French documentary, which proved to be a life-changing gig. From there she worked as an online editor (the person who adds the finished sound, effects, and color correction to an edited film) and an assistant editor until she eventually got a chance to cut footage—first on a TV documentary, then on a succession of scripted TV series, reality-TV shows, and feature films.

There are various resources to help novices learn how to use the tools of the trade, including YouTube videos, Linda.com, and Avid, which offers tutorials and a free version of its Media Composer editing software. But there's only so much you can learn in a lecture or from a book or a video—you have to use the software and practice the craft, making mistakes and learning from them to improve your skills.

Happily, the field offers multiple mentorships, apprenticeships, and other opportunities to learn from the pros. In addition to the American Cinema Editors' training program, which Kurpanek and Nelson lead, the major studios, the Television Academy Foundation, and many production companies have internships.

Nelson said the American Cinema Editors' internship program consists of a one-week lecture series, then four weeks of visits to editing and production facilities for feature films, scripted television, and unscripted television, including those involved in sound, visual effects, and other aspects of post-production. The program, which focuses on the work of assistant editors, also includes networking opportunities to help interns make connections with potential employers.

Kurpanek advised that the goal when you start your career should be to get into the union by working enough days within a year as an assistant editor to qualify for membership. (That would be the Motion Picture Editors Guild, also known as IATSE Local 700.) You do that by helping out on nonunion shows, which may be documentaries, reality-TV shows, independent features, or movie trailers.

Regardless of the starting point, a fledgling editor will probably spend several years working in jobs that don't involve much actual editing. "That's what the hustle is—being able to grab on to any small scrap," Perez said. "Make that money so you can stay in the city where your serendipitous meetings and bumping into people can eventually pay off. But it can take a while."

Ideally, you'll meet editors who become mentors, giving you opportunities to cut scenes on the side and explaining the decisions they're making about footage.

The lack of diversity among editors remains a hurdle for women and people of color, though. "I think I was editing for about ten years before I met another Black editor," Filo said. "I thought I was the only one for a very long time."

The disparity persists in part because many editors find work on the strength of whom they know and whom they've worked with. That's a problem for a lot of women and people of color, because they haven't had the chance to make those connections, Filo said. The industry is trying to diversify the editing ranks through more outreach from the studios and producers to editors from underrepresented communities. There are also self-help efforts like the Handy Foundation's programs and the social media groups that support editors who are women, nonbinary, or people of color.

Virtually all editors work as freelancers, making their living from job to job, so earning the trust of other filmmakers is crucial to carving out a foothold in the business. Good word of mouth is often the connective tissue between jobs. But the opposite is true too. "It's a small industry," said Sam Levy (*The Starling Girl*, *Griffin in Summer*). "If you do something crazy on your first film, it might be tough to find your next one."

The growth in unscripted television has boosted the demand for editors, as has the increase generally in the amount of original film and TV content being produced. The U.S. Bureau of Labor Statistics projects the market for film and video editors and camera operators will grow 7 percent by 2032, which is faster than the average field.

What Are the Career Paths?

The most common route to an editor's chair travels from internship or apprentice to assistant to editor on a TV show or film. Along the way, fledgling editors are likely to hone their skills by working on short films and music videos.

Assistants handle the grunt work, freeing editors to focus on cutting scenes. A big part of the assistants' job is managing the footage—logging it into the editing software, storing it, then matching the footage to the edits made on computer. They also serve as the contact points for other post-production workers, coordinating with the camera, sound, and effects departments.

You can spend years in lower-level jobs before you get the chance to edit, which may leave you demoralized or burned-out. But in retrospect, Levy said, you'll see that you've gained a wealth of information about the filmmaking process as an assistant. "What you're really learning," he said, "is how to run a professional feature film from the first day of shooting . . . to the day of delivery."

The higher you rise in the editing hierarchy, Kurpanek said, the more time you spend delegating tasks and managing the sometimes conflicting desires of the director, the producer, and other key filmmakers. "The actual aspect of editing becomes a smaller part of your skill set," he said. "You're a politician, you're a therapist, you really have to juggle a lot of management skills as well."

How Do You Make Money? And What Kind of Money?

The route you choose at the start of your career can determine how long it will take you to make a living as an editor.

If you decide to go to film school, then work for free on your friends' films to develop your editing chops, it might take a long time before you get hired on a project with a substantial budget. But if you go the internship–assistant editor route, you could be joining the union much faster.

Filo said editors sometimes do side gigs for less money or for free to broaden their experience, so as not to be pigeonholed in one type of work. Jumping between different genres is a way to develop your editing muscles, she said, adding that the techniques she learns in one can prove valuable in another.

Being pigeonholed is a real hazard. Perez said he had to turn down dozens of horror scripts after editing *It Follows* to avoid being typed as an editor just for that genre. Then, when he was editing seasons of *Euphoria*, he kept getting offers to edit teen dramas.

To join the guild as an assistant editor, you need to have worked as an assistant for 100 days over the previous two years on projects in the United States or Puerto Rico covered by guild contracts. To join as an editor, you need to have logged 175 days as an editor on such projects over the previous three years. Those hours are harder to amass than it may seem; the guild contract requires these positions to be offered to union members, if any are available, before hiring nonunion pros.

The contract sets a minimum pay level that is higher for major studio productions than for independent projects. Even on the lowest-budget indie films, though, a union editor is guaranteed almost $2,670 a week in wages for on-call work in 2026, and more than $1,600 for being an assistant editor. On a major studio motion picture, the minimum weekly pay in 2026 for an editor on call was more than $4,450.

How Is This Career Different from Ten or Twenty-Five Years Ago?

The profession changed dramatically after software was introduced in the late 1980s and early 1990s that allowed editors to choose and cut footage on a computer, instead of having to do it by hand. Now editors have to learn the ins and outs of various programs that evolve over time, although much of the work with those systems is done by assistants.

More recently, the pandemic drove many editing jobs out of the office and into the home, a change that has lingered long after the face masks and home test kits were sidelined. That means less contact between assistant editors and other filmmakers, a change that has had troubling implications, Filo said. In particular, she worries that it will be harder for assistants to find mentors and the pathway into an editor's seat.

The proliferation of unscripted TV series has created more opportunities for editors, but the pace is faster and the deadlines tighter. A series like *Law & Order* might have one person editing an episode, but *The Voice* may have twenty editors, fifteen assistants, and fifteen producers, Handy said.

In addition to having more team-oriented editing, unscripted television also has more diverse groups of editors. "You're telling culturally relevant stories, and you need their opinions," Handy said. The drive to include creative people from diverse backgrounds is intentional, Handy said, and has spilled over into scripted television.

What's Some Good Advice?

Don't be afraid to cold-call someone. A properly crafted cold call or email can take you very far in connecting with the right people, the pros say. So, too, can networking in person to meet the types of post-production professionals you'd like to work with. Said Levy, "You just have to be brave in putting yourself out there. It really is a foot-in-the-door industry."

Hone your organizational skills. One of the most important parts of getting ready to edit a movie is having a good system for organizing the footage. In fact, that system can help tell the story the way the filmmakers want it told.

Watch a lot of film and television. "Develop your aesthetic compass, because ultimately that's what is going to get you hired—your taste and your ability to implement it," Perez said. Find editors whose work you admire and learn how to emulate it.

Recognize the difference between investing in your career and being exploited. Early on, Kurpanek said, performing some work for free might be a good thing. But it depends on the context—for example, he said, don't waive your right to overtime pay, and don't stay in an unpaid internship with someone who doesn't offer a contract after six months.

Earn the trust of other filmmakers. Once you've earned the trust of a producer or a director, that person will call on you time and again. "It's like finding your family," Nelson said. "I worked for the same team for fifteen years with, like, two very short breaks between movies or TV shows."

Know that you can't fix everything in post-production. Many directors have a shooting style that requires a particular kind of editing, taking the usual tricks and tools off the table. For example, Handy said, a director who likes to do scenes in one long take has to get that shot right, because an editor can't cut in snippets from different camera angles to show things the audience needs to see or hide things the audience doesn't.

Have interests outside of editing. Nelson said it's important to do things that will separate you from the stress of the job. The things you see and learn in your free time can make you a better editor, he said, by helping you spot things in footage that don't jibe with reality. "You will be surprised how often those little nuggets . . . can work their way back into your professional life," he said.

Understand the demands of the genre you want to work in. Not all editing jobs are the same. If you want to edit reality TV, talk to people who work in reality TV, and likewise for film or documentary categories, Handy said.

Don't take every job that's offered. Levy and Perez said it's important to focus on the work you really want to do. Rather than doing everything that comes your way, Perez said, try to learn to be very selective, and to notice when a more promising opportunity comes along.

CHAPTER 26

How to Become a Sound Designer

We call filmmakers visionary when they bring wondrous, strange, or frightening worlds to life. But vision is just half the equation. To be truly immersive and transporting, a film or TV show needs to have sound that matches its imagery and advances its story.

Some of those sounds are recorded when the scenes were shot on set (production sound); many others are crafted by audio specialists after the filming wraps up (post-production sound). That may include the words the characters speak, the noises they make as they move and interact in a scene, and the sounds of the world around them—whether it be as routine as doors closing and floorboards creaking, or as unusual as stars exploding and buildings collapsing.

The top person in a project's sound department is the supervising sound editor, who oversees everything that's spoken or heard (other than music, which is the purview of the composer). Just underneath this person on the organizational chart—and it's often the same person doing both jobs—is the sound designer, who assembles the sonic palette of sound effects that the filmmakers want for each scene.

The sound designer's work begins after the filmmakers go through a rough cut of the film or TV show to determine which scenes need sound effects—either instead of or in addition to the production sound—and what they should sound like. It could be something simple, such as bringing out the footsteps of an approaching character, or something not so simple, such as inventing the sound of a magical weapon firing.

Depending on how big the production's budget is, a sound designer may be assisted by a dozen or more people working on post-production sound effects, including Foley artists who create sounds by performing in sync with the film footage and sound effects editors who draw from a library of recordings.

One challenge for the sound designer is understanding exactly what the director is looking for, given how hard it can be to describe something never heard before. Getting on the same page as the director is key, and part of that is understanding the tone the filmmakers want for the film or show.

For example, a director may want a completely realistic-sounding rocket liftoff. But when the rocket explodes, the director may want some extra tension in that moment beyond the raw sound of a projectile blowing up. Maybe that means burying the sound of a sputtering engine in there or adding an animal's screech or whine or roar to the mix.

When it comes to designing sounds, as David Acord of Skywalker Sound (*Guardians of the Galaxy Volume 3*, *Andor*) put it, 60 percent of the work is done by your imagination, 40 percent by your ears.

Sound designers have to make dozens of creative decisions about a sound before they play it for a director for the first time. Ultimately, the choice comes down to finding the sound that's going to serve the emotional needs of that scene—what are the characters trying to convey, where is the director trying to take the audience, and what can the sounds do on top of the dialogue, the visuals, and the music?

Increasingly, the opportunities for sound designers are coming from technology and video-game companies, not just filmmakers. That's one reason the demand for sound professionals is growing, industry analysts say. Which is not to say that you should abandon your dream of crafting medieval battle sounds for the big screen and aim instead to design the warning tone your car makes when you leave the lights on after parking. It's just to note that the world of sound effects and sound design is evolving.

What Qualities Do You Find in a Successful Sound Designer?

Simply put, it's someone who wants to tell stories through sound. A common feature is a background in music, with or without formal training—Acord, for example, was in bar bands, as was James Lucero (*Star Trek: Lower Decks*, *The Legend of Vox Machina*) of Margarita Mix in Hollywood. Harry Cohen (*Mufasa: The Lion King*, *The Piano Lesson*) got his start as a professional keyboardist. Percussionist David Van Tieghem has been the sound designer for multiple Broadway productions.

"When you're playing music, you are honing your ears. You're listening to all the different instruments; you're listening to the notes played so you can play along," Lucero said. "Everything in sound is ear training in the end."

It almost goes without saying that the job requires an ear for detail, an ability to peel apart the layers of a complex sound. That's something you can develop with practice and experience, the pros say. But good sound design requires more than just the ability to re-create the creak of a door hinge or the bustle and clatter of a lunch counter. It's also finding a way to elicit the emotional response that a scene demands.

One of the first things you have to teach yourself as a sound designer is to not think literally. For example, when you're being asked by the director to create the sound for a gangster's car, the most important information is not what kind of car it is. It's who the gangster is, what kind of person he is, and how he wants to be perceived.

So if the car is a souped-up Ford Mustang, you could certainly start with a recording of an actual souped-up Mustang. A good sound designer then asks what can be credibly layered into that sound that also conveys the essence of the character—say, that he's wild and out of control. That might mean layering in the sound of roaring animals or heavy surf. That's why sound designers tend to be creative, imaginative people, not just technicians.

At the same time, there is a technical side to the job. Successful designers have a solid grounding in how sound is generated and shaped, the frequency ranges that different sounds occupy, and other fundamentals of the science.

They also tend to be technologically adept. It's de rigueur to be familiar with, if not an expert at, the digital audio workstation software the industry uses—examples include Pro Tools, Logic Pro, and Ableton Live, for which you can find an endless variety of tutorials online—as well as the virtual instruments and effects that plug into these programs. And not only is the technology continually evolving, but the software used for Hollywood productions (where Avid's Pro Tools rules) is different from the programs used for video games, the theater, and other applications.

One paradoxical thing about sound designers is that they like to spend hours perfecting a single sound by their lonesome, yet they're also team players. That's because they're supporting someone else's vision—typically, the director's—and not their own. You have to be able to throw your prized creation away and go in a different direction when the director doesn't like a sound.

Sound designers aren't magicians or endowed with extra powers. They pay special attention to sounds and the way they relate to one another, how they can be used to reinforce or create emotional responses or tell stories—and these are things anyone can learn.

How Do You Get Started?

The career path depends on the type of sound design you want to do, whether it be for film and television, for theater, for video games, or for tech companies. Although the skills involved are similar, each requires a different knowledge base and connections.

For film or television, try to land a job helping out with sound on a set, as Acord did, which will familiarize you with many aspects of the filmmaking process. Or ask sound professionals to let you watch them work for a day. You'll be surprised by how many pros will let you shadow and learn from them.

There are a number of places to find sound designers to shadow, starting with IMDb.com—an IMDbPro account will provide contact information, but it carries a subscription fee. There's also the trade association that represents film and TV sound professionals, Motion Picture Sound Editors—its quarterly magazine, which is available free online, is a potentially rich source of names. And then there's the Facebook Sound Design group, which is open to the public and has roughly thirty thousand members.

Even better is getting an apprenticeship, which used to be a standard way to launch a career in sound design but is not as common today. The experience apprenticeships offer dealing with real-world film and TV issues is invaluable. Some post-production companies will advertise apprenticeships online; you can also search the audio jobs section of Soundlister.com for opportunities. If all else fails, try to visit all the audio post-production studios in your area and introduce yourself to the folks in charge.

Two common prerequisites when starting out are perseverance and serendipity.

"Nobody likes to hear this, but it's a lot of luck," Acord said. He was raised in rural Delaware with no industry connections, and his break came when he landed an unpaid internship in Philadelphia in the art department of the movie *12 Monkeys*. He parlayed that into a series of paying gigs on the set, striking up a friendship with the members of the production sound team. They took him on as the utility guy on their next job, helping to set up and maintain the recording equipment. That led to seven years of work in production sound.

"Luck can certainly help get that foot in the door," Acord added, "but it's your skill that keeps you there."

After moving to San Francisco with his wife in 1999, Acord decided to shift into post-production and had to make connections all over again. That bore fruit in 2001 when an acquaintance tipped him off about an apprenticeship at Skywalker Sound on *Star Wars: Episode II—Attack of the Clones.* He's worked in post-production sound ever since.

It's easier to make connections now in the era of social media, although getting established in post-production sound still can be a challenge. Take Vanessa Flores (*Our Father, Legends of the Hidden Temple*) of Banana Post in Burbank, for instance. After earning an associate degree in film studies from Riverside Community College in 2015 and a certificate in audio engineering with post-production audio from Musicians Institute in Hollywood in 2016, she was left asking, "Now what? Where's the jobs?" She eventually took a weekend shift at a warehouse to support herself while she did freelance work editing recordings and designing sounds, reaching out to and networking with as many filmmakers as she could.

Today, social networks offer great opportunities to connect with filmmakers from the comfort of your home, although you'll need to use a different approach on each platform. On Facebook, just type your city and "film group" into the search field and you'll get a long list of related groups to sort through and join (or request to join, if it's a private group). On Instagram, Flores suggested starting with a film-related community such as @learnfilmmaking, or searching by hashtag (e.g., #BRoll) to find people whose work you'd like to contribute to. TikTok and LinkedIn can be searched by hashtag too. You can't just jump into a group on Discord—you have to be invited—but sites like Disboard.org let you search for Discord groups and ask for invites.

In a field dominated by white men, Flores said, "I knew I had to stand out from the pack." That meant mastering the technical side of the job to "not give anybody a reason to doubt what I could bring to the table."

She got leads and tips from mentoring sites such as SoundGirls .org and People of Color in Audio, and as she did more work on low-budget independent projects, she built up her presence on Instagram and other social media networks by posting frequently and sharing tips. "I got so many referrals because I was out there," Flores said.

Within a few years, she landed a full-time job as a sound editor at Banana Post in Burbank, which handles the post-production sound for several unscripted TV shows. Flores credits her boss, Chad Mumford, with giving opportunities to people like her who are underrepresented in the field. Now she posts job openings, discusses techniques, and shares interviews with other pros on her Instagram feed.

Increasingly, people train for a career in post-production sound at a film school, community college, or trade school, all of which can be found by searching online. But training is just the table stakes. You'll still need to develop a body of work to show prospective employers and clients, possibly by tracking down student filmmakers and volunteering to do sound for them. Another way to find opportunities is to scour the postings at sites such as Staff Me Up, Mandy, and even Craigslist.

Happily, the technology for recording and shaping sound is far cheaper and more accessible than it used to be. Although the tools used by established pros can be expensive, you can try out demo versions of digital audio workstations like Pro Tools (the film and TV industry's most widely used software for recording and editing) or Nuendo, or use Reaper, which is free.

Flores said you'll need a good pair of headphones and at least one other piece of software: a manager for your library of sound effects (she suggested SoundQ, from Pro Sound Effects, and Soundly, both of which include sound effects with their monthly subscription fees). The workstations come with built-in ("stock") effects for treating audio, but you may want to invest in plug-in programs to convert conventional recordings to multichannel Dolby ones and to remove background noise, especially if you're working with dialogue.

There are many free or inexpensive plug-ins from such sources as the Plugin Alliance and Brainworx.

What Are the Career Paths?

There's no one route to becoming a sound designer. Oftentimes, people will start by handling multiple other sound jobs on smaller productions.

For example, Lucero had just started working at a post-production studio in New York when he was hired to do the sound for a new animated series for children, *Dora the Explorer*. Over the course of thirty-four episodes, Lucero says, he worked not only on sound effects but also on dialogue and music editing, which involves such things as removing unwanted noise and adjusting the volume and tone.

The skills involved are different, though; editing dialogue is nothing like performing as a Foley artist or mixing sound. So on productions with larger budgets, the tasks tend to be split among people who focus on each of those specialties. Still, some sound designers say that it's good to get experience in all of these jobs. As a practical matter, the more sound tasks you know how to do, the greater your chances are of finding work.

You don't have to work in film or television to have a career in sound design—there are many opportunities in theater, video games, apps, and podcasts.

Once you've shown your ability to manage all the tasks of a sound designer and developed relationships with filmmakers and showrunners, you could move up to be a supervising sound editor, where you oversee all aspects of the project's sound (sometimes in tandem with a second supervising sound editor who specializes in dialogue).

That position connects more directly with the filmmakers and is more actively involved in deciding which scenes need what types of sounds. On many projects with two supervising sound editors, one of them will also handle the sound design duties.

How Do You Make Money? And What Kind of Money?

There are post-production studios that offer full-time jobs to sound designers, but the work typically is project based. If the project is a film or TV show, chances are that the jobs will be done by union labor—sound workers are represented by IATSE Local 700, the Motion Picture Editors Guild—at union rates. Depending on the production's budget and location, the weekly rates for sound editors can top $3,600.

On nonunion work, the rates are up for negotiation. Fledgling sound designers are in a tough spot: They need to do as much work as they can to establish their reputation and hone their skills, but they also have to pay the rent. Flores recommends the freelance rate calculator from Sheetlist, a free Google spreadsheet that helps you figure out how much you need to charge for the different jobs you're performing in order to stay afloat.

How Is This Career Different from Ten or Twenty-Five Years Ago?

The biggest change in post-production sound happened when digital technology replaced analog tape and tube-based equipment, a process that was in full swing by the late 1980s and early 1990s. That made the tools for creating, recording, editing, and mixing sounds far more accessible, affordable, and powerful.

These changes, though, have brought many more aspiring sound designers into the field. So to be able to make this a full-time job, it's not enough just to be technically adept—you need to also bring creativity, professionalism, and strong communications skills.

The most dramatic difference in the career nowadays is on the demand side. Video-game studios have become a major new source of work for sound designers and, increasingly, other tech companies have as well.

For a glimpse of the variety of jobs available for audio professionals, go to Soundlister.com.

The clouds on the horizon are the sound design services being pushed by generative AI companies. In theory, AI-powered tools could help sound designers work faster and put more options at their fingertips. The risk, though, is that the tools will help filmmakers fill the sonic needs of their projects without a sound designer's help.

What's Some Good Advice?

Listen to the world around you. Acord said he carries a recorder with him just about everywhere. "Sometimes I'll just hear in the wild a particular sound and think, 'I need to grab that.' I don't know what I'm going to use it for, or when I'm going to use it." The point, he said, is to recognize the potential in the sounds you stumble across, and "build this creative palette that you're going to lean on."

Examine the work of other sound designers. Lucero said that when he was just starting out, he would deconstruct other people's work during off-hours, looking at their techniques and the sounds they used. "It was a tremendous amount of practicing."

Have a presence online in the spaces where your prospective clients are. For example, Flores said, if you want to work on commercials, you have to find where the directors or producers who are making commercials live on social media and build relationships with them there.

Pay attention to the business side of your craft. This is particularly important if you do sound design as a freelancer. You'll need to understand how to get the word out about yourself, how to send invoices and pay taxes, and how to make ends meet when jobs are temporary and payment is delayed.

Keep in mind that sound design isn't a technical job. It's mostly an aesthetic job. In fact, one reason top supervising sound editors started calling themselves sound designers in the 1970s was to push back against the notion that they were just technicians who spent their days dumping other people's work onto the cutting-room floor.

CHAPTER 27

How to Become a Composer

For moviegoers of a certain age, there is one musical snippet even more famous than the four opening notes of Beethoven's Fifth Symphony: the deep, bowed strings that announce the arrival of Bruce, the great white shark in *Jaws*.

Nothing demonstrates the power of a movie or TV show's original music better than composer John Williams's theme, which cranks up the audience's anxiety long before the aquatic killing machine breaks the surface. It also shows how directors and composers work together to engage and move audiences on an emotional level.

Most of the time, a score isn't as palpable a trigger as it is in *Jaws*. It may be working in the background to help set or subtly shift the mood; it may hint that trouble is coming or that problems have, at last, been resolved. The signals the music sends, though, all reflect deliberate choices made by the composer and the rest of the creative team.

The process starts with the creation of what Genevieve Vincent (*The Broken Hearts Gallery*, *Fantasy Island*) calls "a special musical language for the film or TV show with which to articulate the tone." That language may have to evoke the time and place of the action, as well as the personality traits of the characters. Composers develop a toolbox of sorts over time, filled with specific chords or instruments that map well to certain cinematic moments.

Another important part of the process is figuring out which scenes require the composer's touch. The composer typically joins a "spotting session" with the filmmaker, producers, music supervisor, and sound designer to decide where the score should come in for each scene and how prominent it should be. Often the film will have a temporary score put together by a music editor, which the composer might use as a starting point for discerning what the director wants.

For each scene that requires original music, the composer has to present a short composition—called a cue—that passes muster with the director (or, in a TV series, the showrunner) and other key people on the production. "Even the studio heads will come and listen to the score," said composer Chanda Dancy (*Blink Twice*, *Lawmen: Bass Reeves*). "Everyone listens, and everyone has an opinion."

Although the music a composer crafts is unique to the project, the work is nothing like writing a symphony, a piano sonata, or even a pop song. Instead, it's more like building furniture to fit a specific space and specific tastes. That's because a composer for film and television is writing cues to match what the filmmakers hear for a scene.

The composer has administrative duties too. As the head of the department responsible for the "underscore"—the original music that plays throughout, often in the background—the composer has to hire musicians, book studio time, and oversee the recording of the final version of the cues approved for the project.

So if you're a musician who loves to help other people tell their stories, and if you're fluent in both music technology and project management, composing for film or television may be the job for you. As with seemingly every other job in the entertainment industry, though, it takes years of work to get to the point where you can be a full-time composer.

What Qualities Do You Find in a Successful Composer for Film and Television?

It almost goes without saying, but it's hard to be a composer if you haven't had any musical training. That doesn't have to be a degree from Juilliard, however—it can just be years spent learning to play an instrument (especially if it's the piano) or performing music onstage.

Not having training in an instrument, composer Michael Yezerski (*The Deb*, *Blindspotting*) said, "sets you back a long way." But given the advances in music software, he added, "it's very clear that a laptop or an iPad or even a phone is an instrument. As long as you have a few years under your belt mastering that, you're probably on your way to being a composer."

More than just being good at playing music, a composer needs to be musically inventive and adaptable, capable of writing in multiple different styles. When a director wants a score that fits Paris in the Jazz Age or Oklahoma in the Dust Bowl, you'll need an ear that can recognize what distinguishes the music of those times and places.

It will help if you enjoy tinkering with sounds and are curious about instruments and music technology. And it's a really good thing if you enjoy developing new skills, because the job involves a lot of that.

You also need to be able to produce on demand, not just when inspiration strikes. As composer Leo Birenberg (*Cobra Kai*, *Bottoms*) put it, good film composers "have trained their creative skills to work like a faucet." But most of the work you'll do as a composer won't involve composing. You'll have to manage the team responsible for the original music and its budget, which involves such things as lining up studio time, hiring session musicians and negotiating their rates, and finding someone to write out the sheet music for the demos you recorded. That requires the ability to stay organized and manage the workflow.

And like many, many hired hands in Hollywood, a composer needs to be extremely collaborative and team oriented.

"I'm in a service industry," Vincent said. "I'm in the arts, but I'm making something for someone else."

Communication skills are vital, particularly the ability to understand what a director or showrunner is asking for in a scene. "We often say, 'What's the note behind the note?' What is it that they're really asking for?" Yezerski said.

A director may single out a particular chord or instrument as problematic, but in reality the whole cue isn't working. To get the score to the right place faster, sometimes the composer needs to read between the lines. It also helps to have thick skin, because you'll get a lot of criticism. But it's never personal, Dancy said. "It's literally all about the project."

How Do You Get Started?

Typically, would-be composers make many incremental moves to gain connections, experience, and credits.

A common path is to work as an assistant to an in-demand composer, learning every aspect of the workflow. Even then, though, you'll need to pursue opportunities to write music for smaller projects in your free time. For example, Birenberg and his frequent collaborator, Zach Robinson, both worked for Christophe Beck, the composer on *Frozen* and a dizzying variety of other film and TV projects. Working for any composer who does projects of that magnitude, Robinson said, is the best kind of master class.

You can study composing at a film or music school, but you probably won't learn much there about the logistics of doing music for film or television. Unless you watch someone writing music to picture again and again, Birenberg said, "you'd really be extremely clueless."

But that's not the only way in. Dancy, for example, said she decided not to become a composer's assistant because "it was a lot more of a boys' club than it is now." And not just a boys' club—a white boys' club. So for about ten years, she wrote music for her friends' student films and short films, then their first features. Her career built up from there—but it took a long, long time. To make ends meet, she held jobs at Activision ("I played video games on the late shift, and I composed music during the day"), at a friend's sound design company, and at an agency that checked for glitches in movie DVDs caused by the conversion from analog to digital.

Many of the pros said that friends and fellow students from their college networks provided key opportunities to compose scores. It's something you'll hear a lot in the film business: People form a peer group as students or neophytes who rise together, giving one another a hand along the way. Working on friends' and fellow students' films helps composers address a Catch-22: It's hard to get hired without film credits, but you can't get credits if you haven't worked on anything.

There's also the DIY route.

Stephen Letnes, who is legally blind, taught himself the tools of the trade by listening to film composers' YouTube videos. Then he tapped into the network of friends he'd made in college to line up jobs as a composer, beginning with young students' films and gradually working his way up to commercial film and TV gigs.

If you're looking to follow Letnes's learn-at-home lead, Ian Hultquist (*Quiet On Set: The Dark Side of Kids' TV, Dickinson*) pointed to the YouTube videos by Spitfire Audio, a company that sells sound libraries, and Dutch composer Tom Holkenborg (also known as Junkie XL) as good sources. "All that stuff was not quite there when I started," Hultquist said, "but now, literally, you can learn a ton from YouTube."

A handful of organizations have launched programs to help composers find their footing in the industry. At least two of the three major performing rights organizations offer or contribute to fellowships: Broadcast Music, Inc., has four and SESAC (originally the Society of European Stage Actors and Composers, but now just SESAC) supports New Music USA's Reel Change Film Fund, a grant program that helps composers on low-budget productions polish their work. NBC Universal also runs a two-year program called the Universal Composers Initiative (universalgtdi.com/composers) for composers from diverse, global backgrounds.

There's also a group that helps promote and develop female film and TV composers: the Alliance for Women Film Composers (theawfc.com). For the cost of an annual membership fee ($30 for students, $50 for professionals, in 2025), women gain a listing in the organization's directory and "access to events, workshops, newsletters, festival brunches at Sundance and Tribeca, and networking opportunities," according to its website.

For composers of color, there's the Composers Diversity Collective, founded by Michael Abels, the African American composer whose work includes the scores for Jordan Peele's three horror films. Among other efforts to support its members, the group has been holding virtual mixers with studio executives and periodic get-togethers to connect new composers with senior mentors.

Composers with disabilities can also join Recording Artists and Music Professionals with Disabilities (rampd.org), an organization launched by the mononymous singer/composer Lachi to advocate for inclusion and accessibility in the music industry. Roughly twice a month, RAMPD holds "Water Cooler" sessions on Discord for members to interact and share performances.

What Are the Career Paths?

Besides a composer's assistant, there are many rungs on the ladder leading up to the composer's perch.

Orchestrators translate a composer's demo into parts for the various instruments to play. Copyists convert the orchestration into sheet music that session musicians can easily read and perform. Music coordinators may help organize and assist recording sessions for the score. Those sessions can also involve a conductor, engineers, a producer, and a mixer, among others. Composers may also bring in contractors, such as Joy Music House, which has a staff that can provide a full range of help, from writing music to hiring an orchestra. There are also jobs at agencies where composers can write music for commercials.

Once you've established yourself as a composer for film and television, other doors open. Composers have gone on to earn credits as producers, executive producers, and even directors.

"Now that you're really part of the industry, you can diversify, essentially," Dancy said. "And I think it's important to do that because I think it makes you a better artist and it expands your network."

How Do You Make Money? And What Kind of Money?

Unlike most other filmmaking pros, composers are not unionized (but not for lack of trying). There is no union pay scale to provide a wage floor on productions with union contracts. Nor are there standard fees, but instead a wide range of payments. The fee for a project is negotiated with the studio or the producers, and it may be an "all-in" amount that has to cover the cost of the session musicians, the recording studio, and anything else involved in delivering the finished score.

Amie Doherty (*She-Hulk: Attorney at Law*, *Spirit Untamed*) spent her first few years in the business barely making minimum wage. "I always thought it was an investment in myself."

Hultquist said that on a lot of his early films he'd be paid $10,000, but at least half of that would go to expenses and much of the rest he'd spend upgrading his studio. "Then it might be another two or three months" before another job came in. The last few years have been considerably better, he said, but added, "I still have scary days."

Making matters worse, the budget for music is often set after every other aspect of the production takes its share. Composers have little room to negotiate; as Birenberg put it, "By the time you get the call, all the money's been spent."

It typically takes five to ten years of writing scores before a composer is earning enough to make a living, the pros said. Having a lot of savings or another job, or both, is crucial.

Ultimately, you need an experienced agent. "There's no way I can roll in and say to these big studio heads, 'I should be paid this,'" Dancy said.

One thing that can help make up for a low fee is the royalties that composers may collect each time their film or TV show is aired publicly, when the soundtrack plays on streaming services, and when soundtrack CDs are sold. But if you take a job as a composer on a work-for-hire basis, you won't get any royalties, because the studio or producers will claim the royalties for themselves.

Although streaming services have increased the demand for composers' services, they have eroded royalty checks. That's because the royalties for compositions on a streamed show are nowhere near parity with network TV, Robinson said.

How Is This Career Different from Ten or Twenty-Five Years Ago?

The biggest change in the field has been the advent of increasingly powerful and affordable software programs and other digital tools to create and record music. For just a few thousand dollars, a composer can set up a home studio and record demos for filmmakers—a change that has lowered the barrier to entry into the field.

Many composers still record their cues with human musicians playing in professional studios, despite the improvement in digital instruments. But if they don't have the budget to hire session musicians? Yezerski says it's possible now to create a high-quality film or TV score on a computer without live instruments.

One other noteworthy change is the willingness by filmmakers to hire a broader range of composing talent. "There's a hunger and desire for composers of all backgrounds to share not only their experiences but also their lived musical identities with the world," Yezerski said.

It's also much easier for composers to share their compositions with potential employers and draw attention to their work, thanks to music streaming services such as Spotify. Dancy said she used to hand out CDs of her recordings, which wasn't very effective because "nobody listens to CDs." But now Spotify's algorithms will put her work next to well-known composers' scores, and that proximity has paid off. "Literally, I got a call from a huge producer who was listening to my music on Spotify," she said.

There's a wider range of works today that need original music, including video and computer games, apps, and conferences. For example, Lachi said she's been hired to write "walk-on music" for conference speakers—little jingles that play as they make their way onstage.

Also new: AI-powered programs that can compose music. With songwriters and music publishers claiming that generative AI violates their copyrights, however, the risk of lawsuits may deter filmmakers from replacing human composers with digital ones.

What's Some Good Advice?

Get a formal music education. Understanding music history and how styles have evolved is a prerequisite for this job, given the huge variety of styles you're often required to write in. And while there's a place for scores built on guitars, synthesizers, and other non-orchestral instruments, the pros say it's still crucial for a composer to understand the full range of what an orchestra can sound like, and how to make one sound like that.

Learn how films are made. "As a composer, it's easy to stay in your composing cave," Dancy said. "But it's really important to get out there and be part of the filmmaking process itself."

Take jobs that will help you network. "Try to put yourself in professional situations that are in the circle of film music," Birenberg said. That proximity will eventually give you opportunities to show your skills. "At some point or another," he said, "you're all musicians and you have a lot in common, and things need to get done."

Get familiar with digital audio workstations, the computer programs that serve as digital recording studios. Hultquist said you should know any one of them inside and out while being familiar with the other major brands.

Don't try to impress people with a demo that sounds like John Williams. "John Williams exists," Robinson said. "I'm more interested in hearing what you can do with no budget," especially the music you can create from found sounds. "Go deep on your own style," Vincent said. "Spend as much time writing music for yourself as you can so you know what your musical language and your style is."

Be willing to work for free, but only if the circumstances are right. Sometimes it's worth helping someone who can't afford to pay for your services in order to develop the relationship. "If they don't have the money, maybe they will on their next project," Vincent said. However, that doesn't mean working for free on a studio project or a film with a decent budget. Nor should you take a job that underpays just for the sake of the exposure, Lachi said. "Exposure is not something you can write on your rent check and hand to your landlord. . . . It will never do what you think it will do."

Don't give up. "It can be really, really hard at times, especially if you don't have a big financial pad to fall back on, like I didn't," Vincent said. "You have to grow accustomed to being uncomfortable. If you're very risk averse, maybe this isn't the job for you."

Live a well-rounded life. Robinson said that he doesn't subscribe to the notion that "you have to grind it out every day, no weekends, no time with friends." To keep the creative juices flowing, he said, "you need the time to recharge your brain." Dancy agrees. "People like people who are human. You're not just the music-composing robot. You have your own story and your own perspective and your own life lens. So live it."

CHAPTER 28

How to Become a Music Supervisor

No one says a word in the opening sequence of *The Sopranos*, but you'd never think to watch it with the sound off.

It's not that the vistas of industrial and working-class New Jersey are particularly evocative. It's the song that plays as mobster Tony Soprano drives through them—Alabama 3's "Woke Up This Morning," a propulsive, bluesy number about loss and unfulfilled promise—that transforms the sequence into something tense and menacing, hinting at the violence that will eventually erupt on-screen.

The crew member who's responsible for the music that helps tell the story is the music supervisor. That includes advising the filmmakers on whom to hire for other key parts of the music team, such as the composer who writes original music for the production. The music supervisor and the composer also suggest which scenes will have recorded songs, original music, or both. Ultimately, the filmmakers decide which song to use in a scene, and it's not always the supervisor's first choice.

Regardless of who picks the tunes, it is the supervisor's job to obtain permission to use every piece of music heard in the production, whether it's a full song or just a snippet playing in the background when a character walks through a room. To do so, a supervisor first has to figure out who holds the copyrights to the song, the recording of the song, and any samples in it, all of which have to be licensed.

It's a challenging process that involves research, negotiation, and, if necessary, a shift to alternative choices that better fit the budget. For help on that front, supervisors can draw on the expertise of sync agents who represent large groups of copyright holders.

Supervisors also have to be adept at negotiating contracts, because they have only so much money to spend on licensing. Copyright owners don't need a good reason to say no to a license—they can say no because it's not enough money, because they don't like the story being told, or because they don't want to be associated with the director or star.

There are many different ways a song can be used in a project, and there's no price list. "It's all negotiable," said Gary Calamar, whose credits include *3 Body Problem* and *Titans*. Generally, though, the bigger the artist and the more prominent the use, the higher the fee will be, leaving less money for other licensing needs.

The time you're most likely to notice the supervisor's work is when a song plays over the end credits of a movie—maybe it's the perfect summation of the emotion (the Beach Boys' "Feel Flows" in *Almost Famous*; Rihanna's "Lift Me Up" in *Wakanda Forever*), maybe it's just a great joke (Sid Vicious covering "My Way" in *Goodfellas*, the Beatles' "Baby You're a Rich Man" in *The Social Network*).

You'll feel it too, subconsciously, at least, in the songs that characters hear on a car radio and other background moments—they help establish the era and the characters' milieu. Witness, for example, the cool late-twentieth-century hip-hop exuberance of *Teenage Mutant Ninja Turtles: Mutant Mayhem*, a vibe that sets the tone for the young heroes' adventures in New York City.

Still, being a supervisor is not about your particular musical tastes or what you like to listen to at home. "It's having a knowledge of what works in a scene and why and understanding what it is the director is trying to say, what you want the audience to feel," said Robin Urdang, whose credits include *The Marvelous Mrs. Maisel* and *Call Me by Your Name*.

"Is it something specific? Do you want to lead them, do you not want to lead them?"

Music supervisors also must contend with last-minute changes and tough deadlines. Oh, and yes, they'll have to try to please the multiple people—producers, showrunners, directors, editors, writers—who have ideas for which songs should play when. Everybody has an opinion about what the music should be, because everyone has a visceral reaction to music.

What Qualities Do You Find in a Successful Music Supervisor?

One thing that many pros have in common is a history in or around the music industry. That reflects a common, deep-seated love of music.

George Drakoulias, whose credits include the film *Barbie* and the TV series *Severance*, still produces records. Thomas Golubić (*Breaking Bad*, *Poker Face*), Calamar, and Morgan Rhodes (*Space Jam: A New Legacy*, *Dear White People*) are current or former DJs at influential Southern California radio stations. Jen Malone (*John Wick: Chapter 4*, *Euphoria*) was a publicist for garage rock bands in Boston. Urdang was a business representative for the vocal group Manhattan Transfer.

But when asked what interests or skills make a person a good fit for this job, the pros rattle off a number of more practical qualities.

You should be highly organized, detail oriented, and capable of managing the flow of a lot of information, because you may be working on multiple projects at the same time.

You should be diplomatic, skilled at reading a room and adept at forming consensus, because the songs have to work not for you, but for the people in charge of the storytelling. Half joking, Urdang put it this way: "You have to have a minor or a major in psychology, because it's so political. You have to be able to . . . deal with a lot of personalities."

Remember, a music supervisor can't just dictate a show's soundtrack as if it were a Spotify playlist. The job isn't to pick every single song in a film or TV show—it's to help fulfill the director's or showrunner's vision for the music in the project. They'll say they need a song for such-and-such scene, the music supervisor will come back with five suggestions, and they'll often say they'd like more choices.

The process can be kind of heartbreaking, Calamar said. "Sometimes I will come in with a song that I think is so perfect, and I can't believe I've nailed it. And they'll say, 'That's pretty good. What else you got?'"

You should love to do research, because you're called on to suggest songs from across the landscape of times, genres, and regions. You may also like being ahead of the curve and unearthing little-known gems. For some supervisors, looking for the song can be more fun than finding it.

A supervisor has to be resourceful and slow to give up. For example, you may have a tiny music budget for an indie film, but the director really wants to use a Rolling Stones song. So you have to think creatively about what you can offer as compensation. That could be offering the band a share of the project's profits in lieu of their customary gigantic fee.

Supervisors are also good at translating musical ideas into words. "Sometimes directors need someone to help them explain what they're hearing or not hearing," Drakoulias said. "If someone says, 'I want it more purple,' you have to be able to figure out what that means."

Finally, you should be able to stay calm under the pressure of production deadlines, because songs can fall through at the last minute and the supervisor has to scramble to replace them.

Having good taste in music matters, the pros said, but taste is subjective. More important is knowing many different types of music, being familiar with labels and music publishers, and keeping an open mind.

How Do You Get Started?

The good news is that there are so many hours of TV shows and films being made these days that the demand for music supervision is enormous.

To develop the necessary skills, you have several options. Some colleges, film schools, and online programs offer classes in music supervision taught by people who are active in the field (Malone, for instance, took a class from Golubić at UCLA Extension). That's a way to learn key aspects of the job and make connections. The easiest way to find this instruction is by searching Google for "music supervision course" or "music supervision class."

If you take the school route, befriend the filmmakers in your class and offer to work on their movies. Student films present a great opportunity to teach yourself about copyrights and music licensing.

Another path is to intern for a music supervisor or for a studio or label executive who works with supervisors. Some internships are available through college film programs, where you'll earn credits toward a degree but possibly no pay. Others are offered by freelance supervisors who want to train the next generation and could use the help.

"When people work for me, it's hands-on. They're seeing and learning everything," Urdang said. "I want them to learn. I want the next group of music supervisors to succeed."

You can find internships on EntertainmentCareers.net or on general-interest job sites, such as Indeed.com and ZipRecruiter, although using a site that's not focused on the entertainment industry will mean sorting through a lot of unrelated openings. Another way to hear about internships is to join or volunteer at the Guild of Music Supervisors. Golubić, Calamar, and Urdang helped establish the organization to raise the profession's profile, improve collaboration, honor exceptional work, and put out a ladder of opportunity. The guild offers DIY training materials and networking opportunities, which is a good way to find supervisors looking for help.

The guild is also trying to help the profession diversify; among other steps, it has been holding events in East Los Angeles and South Los Angeles to promote the profession to people who didn't know it was an option.

This being the entertainment industry, the relationships you make will be the keys that open doors for you. Most supervisors you talk to will cite the mentors who taught them how to clear songs, manage budgets, and navigate a production's egos.

For example, Malone decided to take a wild stab at music supervision after being inspired by the musical choices in the movie *Iron Man*. "I knew nothing about making television or movies, what an editor did, music clearance, publishing—nothing," she said. "But it didn't matter. This is what I wanted to do."

So she moved to Los Angeles with just her car and her clothes and threw herself into networking, starting with the people she knew from her time in public relations. She also researched music supervisors and what shows they worked on, what they said publicly about their work, and who their agents were. A good source for much of that information is IMDb.com, although you'll need to pay for an IMDbPro account ($20 a month or $150 a year) to find contact information and agents' names.

Malone heard about a free event called Hunnypot Live, a biweekly talent showcase and live podcast recording session in Los Angeles frequented by industry professionals. She went and just happened to meet Dave Jordan, the music supervisor on *Iron Man* (and many other Marvel Studios projects since then). "We just hit it off. I told him I wanted to intern for him." He told her to start working for him the following week.

After a summer stint with Jordan, Malone took an internship at

MTV (which required her to be enrolled in college, which she, umm, finessed) that led almost immediately to a job as a music coordinator at VH1. The skills and insights she gained there helped Malone capitalize when a friend from Boston asked her to clear a song for the cable TV show *Baskets*, for which she soon assumed the music supervisor's role. The same friend was producing *Atlanta* and helped her become music supervisor for that series too.

"And then the phone started ringing for more scripted projects," Malone said. She eventually started her own, all-female music supervision company, Black & White Music. It's a good idea to follow Malone's LinkedIn feed—she often posts job openings around the industry for music supervisors and related professionals.

Building a public profile as a radio DJ helps, especially if you work at a station in the heart of the film industry. Rhodes said her break came when an indie filmmaker taking a movie to the Sundance Film Festival called her to come on as music supervisor because of her work as a DJ at KCRW in Santa Monica. That was Ava DuVernay, and the film was *Middle of Nowhere*. Happily, Rhodes had relationships with a lot of artists and labels that she could draw on because she had to learn how to clear songs on the fly.

What Are the Career Paths?

There are two rungs on the ladder below music supervisor—assistant music supervisor and music coordinator—on larger-budget productions. An assistant music supervisor is an entry-level worker who handles simpler tasks at the boss's direction while gaining experience and familiarity with the job. One step above that is a music coordinator, who can perform many of the supervisor's functions but isn't ready to lead the conversations about the choices being made.

Then there are the jobs that focus on just a portion of the music supervisor's work. There are music consultants who specialize in the creative aspects of the job—for example, helping filmmakers make their music choices historically accurate. And there are people who specialize in obtaining licenses to the songs.

Beyond that, some supervisors opt to leave the freelance world in favor of a job at a Hollywood studio, working with producers and directors to hire supervisors and overseeing music budgets for their productions, among other duties. Or they join a record label or a sync agency, working to get songs placed in films. Or they take a music supervising post at a company that produces trailers for movies and TV series. Some shift into film or TV production.

How Do You Make Money? And What Kind of Money?

There is no hourly or weekly pay scale, because there is no union, although some guild members have discussed trying to form one. Nor do supervisors earn residuals or royalties. Instead, they receive a flat fee per episode or per film. If you're on a show for a year, the pros said, the fee amounts to a couple of hundred dollars a week.

Rates are typically a factor of the production budget, which is set by the studio or the producers. Budgets will vary according to the size and scope of the project, along with the expected market for the film or TV show. Regardless, the pros say, the pay isn't commensurate with the amount of work required. As a result, many of the people who get into the field don't stay long.

"If you want to make a living at this," Calamar said, "you have to have multiple projects going at the same time, which can make you a little bit crazy." People just starting out should have a backup plan and some side hustles to carry them through the inevitable downtimes.

Urdang agreed. "I'm used to it and I can handle five projects at a time or six, but if you've just started out, you can't."

How Is This Career Different from Ten or Twenty-Five Years Ago?

The flip side of the explosion in content and opportunities caused by the rise in streaming video is that there are far more music supervisors competing for work. "I often say it's harder to get the job than to do the job," Calamar said. "Even though I've had some success over the years, I'm still hustling."

Meanwhile, streaming music services have vastly simplified the task of researching songs. In the old days, a supervisor would have to track down physical copies of the records put out by the artists who might be appropriate for a project. Now, Golubić said, "I can do an Internet search . . . and potentially find some interesting options, and potentially find the people who can license them to me, in half an hour."

Music publishers are far easier to find too. In pre-Internet days, you'd have to get the publisher information from ASCAP and BMI, the two largest performance rights organizations, whose phones were always busy. And when you finally got through, you could ask for only three songs at a time.

What's Some Good Advice?

Learn the intricacies of copyrights and licensing. Speaking for many of her colleagues, Rhodes advised would-be supervisors, "Learning the ins and outs of clearance and licensing, and also learning about performing rights organizations and royalties, is a really good start." To familiarize yourself with the basics, consult the licensing information offered online by ASCAP or one of the other performing rights organizations and by filmmaking organizations (e.g., documentary.org). When in doubt, do an Internet search for "sync licensing basics." There is also a wealth of material on YouTube, as well as online courses from music supervisors, aimed at bringing filmmakers up to speed on how to clear songs for their projects.

Spend as much as your budget provides. Urdang tells the cautionary tale of how she spent less than her budget during the first season of *Burn Notice*, only to have her budget cut for Season 2. "Do not come in under budget," she said. "It does not do any good for anybody."

Take "no" for an answer. "'Be dogged and persistent' is, to me, a terrible piece of advice," Golubić said. He drew a bright line between going to great lengths to find rights holders and badgering them if they decline to license their tracks. "A polite no," he said, "is a clear no."

Be realistic about licensing fees. Sometimes a new producer, showrunner, or director will contend that rights holders will license their songs for peanuts because the exposure will help the artist more than money. That is just outdated thinking.

On one film, Calamar said, the director's husband was a well-known tattoo artist. "She thought it would be reasonable to trade her husband's tattoos for licenses." Calamar eventually obtained the rights to the songs with dollars, not body art. "I knew I would never offer that, nor would any record company or publisher entertain that in exchange for a license."

Make sure you love this work before committing to it. "You're never going to make it if you're not passionate about it," Urdang warned. "Because it's a lot of hard work. And it's a lot of politics. You have to please a lot of people. . . . You have to be open. You can't take things personally. You can't have an ego."

Keep your reach within your grasp. Drakoulias offered one last pro tip: Don't promise you can get a song by the Beatles.

CHAPTER 29

How to Become a Foley Artist

Back when silent movies gave way to talkies, filmmakers found that the microphones on their sets captured little more than the actors' dialogue. Without additional sound recordings, their films would depict an eerily quiet world with stealthy figures heard only when they opened their mouths to speak.

The solution advanced by Jack Foley, a writer and director at Universal Studios, was to project the film on a screen and create a soundtrack of the noises he made as he mimicked the actors' movements and actions. For example, he'd capture the patter of footsteps while walking in time with the actors, covering the floor with whatever material made the right noise. Similarly, he'd record the jingle of keys being drawn from a pocket, the smack of doors opening and closing, and the whoosh of a chair cushion compressing under the weight of an actor sitting down.

His techniques were so influential, the entertainment industry named the practice after him.

Foley artists can now be found pretty much wherever movies, TV shows, or video games are made. That's true despite the vast improvement in microphone technology since the first time Foley mimicked an actor strolling down a sidewalk. And unlike the man himself, the names of modern Foleys typically show up in the credits for the projects they enhance.

In a live-action film, much of the sound comes from the recordings made on set as the cameras roll. But a portion of the audio is added in post-production by Foley artists, who give the filmmakers something that they didn't get from the set—more distinctive footsteps, perhaps, or a punch that sounds like it's cracking a bone. Unlike sound effects specialists, who use recordings from a vast sonic library, Foley artists create unique sounds for each film by performing in sync with the footage.

For animated or computer-generated images, there's no sound—all of it has to be done from scratch, whether by voice actors, sound effects specialists, or Foley artists.

The whole point of Foley is to ground the picture in reality, said longtime Foley artist Ellen Heuer (*Immaculate*, *12 Years a Slave*). For example, she pointed to her work on the film *The Perfect Storm*, where the challenge was to create a realistic sound to accompany the footage of a fishing vessel fighting through titanic waves. Much of the footage was silent, computer-generated imagery.

It's no simple matter to fake the sound of an entire ocean, Heuer said. So the sound editor set up a huge aboveground pool at a Warner Bros. sound stage and hung sheets of metal that reached from the ceiling down to the water. She stood in the pool and held the metal sheets stable while her partner was on the other side, blasting her with a fire hose. "It was an extremely ambitious attempt," she said—far more so than, say, placing a cup into a saucer in front of a microphone in time with an actor putting down her tea on-screen.

Foley artists don't just make noise. In fact, that's the least important part of the work, because anyone can do that. Rather, making noise is "one of the things that you do as a result of all the other things you put into being an artist," said veteran Foley artist Peter Burgis (*Gladiator II*, *Harry Potter and the Deathly Hallows*). Foley is about being an artist—seeing a character on-screen, then embodying that character's movements and actions. Maybe it's the gait of a man carrying the weight of the world on his shoulders. Maybe it's the exhaustion conveyed by the grocery bags dumped onto the kitchen counter.

And sometimes Foley artists are asked to imagine the sound of something you wouldn't find in nature.

For example, Heuer was asked by *Lost Highway* director David Lynch to record the sound of someone's head cracking from the inside out. At first, she had no idea what to do. After sleeping on it for a night, she went into the studio, put a small microphone in her ear, then recorded the sound of her chomping on a piece of celery while simultaneously recording the sound of her cracking a second piece of celery next to another mic.

"These are the things a Foley artist activates by having a rich imagination," Heuer said.

A stalk of celery (a Foley artist's most beloved prop) could be used for bones breaking, a wet chamois could be a rich bowl of spaghetti, and frying bacon could easily replicate the sound of rain.

What Qualities Do You Find in a Successful Foley Artist?

It's worth noting up front that there aren't a lot of working Foley artists out there, although the field is much bigger than it was a few decades ago. A popular Facebook group about Foley lists more than seven thousand members internationally, but the number of people actually making a living solely as a Foley artist is much smaller.

Vanessa Theme Ament (*Die Hard*, *Edward Scissorhands*) guesses that there are forty to fifty established "top-notch" Foley artists in the United States and at least one or two hundred people who are dabbling or just getting started in the field.

"It's a bit like professional tap dancers or professional harpists," said Burgis, a U.K.-based Foley artist. "Not that many of them."

Although Foley artists often are converted actors, dancers, or musicians, the field has attracted people with a wide variety of backstories. Ament, who has spent years teaching the art at Ball State University in Indiana and other places, said her students have included people trained in architecture, engineering, and the visual arts.

The various disciplines inform Foley artists in different ways. Those who've been dancers say it helps them mimic the movements of characters on-screen, as well as memorize lengthy sequences of actions. A background in music or dance provides a sense of rhythm that's important to a Foley artist's ability to "catch sync"—to time a performance to precisely match the actions on-screen. Those who were actors say it helps them understand the emotions they need to convey through sound, a vital aspect of the work.

Experience as an athlete can help with balance and coordination. The work of Foley artists can be extremely physical—"it has an uncelebrated athleticism all its own," Heuer said.

"I played softball, basketball, and swam, and I think a lot of those helped me with my coordination and breathing that was years of practice for being a Foley artist," said Katie Waters (*Another Happy Day*, *American Underdog*). "So if anyone wants or is thinking of becoming a Foley artist, it may be good to try a sport like tennis or baseball or softball or Ping-Pong—something to help with that hand-eye coordination."

How Do You Get Started?

This being the entertainment industry, professionals in the field say having connections to a working Foley artist is crucial. To do so, look for opportunities to work at post-production sound houses, which is where many Foley artists practice their craft.

In addition to general-interest job sites such as Indeed, ZipRecruiter, and LinkedIn, you can find openings in post-production audio by perusing entertainment-focused sites such as Soundlister.com,

Showbizjobs.com, the Hey Audio Student public Facebook group, or the SoundGirls private Facebook group (if you're female).

Ament said she was auditioning for a dialogue-dubbing gig when, helped by a Foley artist acquaintance, she landed a spot doing Foley at Gomillion Studios, a post-production house. She thought the Foley work would just help fill in the gaps between her acting and singing gigs. She did well enough, however, that she soon had steady work on TV shows and feature films, working both as a freelancer and in-house for post-production sound companies.

Alternatively, a number of film and trade schools offer classes in Foley as part of a broader movie- or sound-related program. It's not a prerequisite for working as a Foley artist, nor is it a guarantee of a career in the field. But it is a way to learn some of the skills and to make connections with filmmakers who could give you your first opportunities to do Foley work.

Waters grew up with a love of acting, music, and filmmaking, which culminated in her studying post-production sound work at Columbia College Chicago. Among her courses was one on the art and craft of Foley taught by Ament, author of *The Foley Grail: The Art of Performing Sound for Film, Games, and Animation.*

Yet it took Waters years to find steady work. An internship at Noisefloor Sound Solutions in Chicago helped her make connections, and she did Foley on a couple of films there as a freelancer before the company hired her as office manager, the only position that was open. She eventually moved up to become the company's producer, doing Foley when there was a demand for it. She's now the in-house Foley artist at Noisefloor.

Waters advises people studying the craft to meet as many filmmakers in school as possible, do as much Foley work as possible, and then stay connected with those people. "The more you do it, the more people will find out that you do it, and then you'll get more work."

Burgis had gone from a TV hosting gig at the BBC to a job as an assistant at a sound studio when he got the chance to perform footsteps with an established Foley artist, who told him he was a natural. That was around 1991, and with the country mired in a deep recession, he had to make a choice: "I could carry on being a mediocre assistant or I could be an unemployed Foley artist. So I became an unemployed Foley artist."

He spent about five years doing Foley for commercials and other small-budget projects before he landed his first feature film. It takes a long time, Burgis said, to develop a good library of sounds in your head and the knowledge required to recognize the sound demanded by a scene. He spent days listening to people at the seafront and in the subway, focusing not on what they said but on the sounds they made as they moved and how that was affected by the things they carried.

"Because it takes so long, you have to be totally dedicated to it," he said. "Because you can't really get work until you can do it, you have to be really gutsy, you have to stick with it, you have to keep banging on doors."

What Are the Career Paths?

There are a slew of jobs associated with the Foley process, which is itself just a portion of the work done on the sound of a film, TV series, or video game. But the skills needed to be, say, a Foley mixer or editor are very different from those required of a Foley artist.

Mixers and editors are adept with recording equipment; Foley artists are performers. In other words, doing well as a Foley artist doesn't naturally lead you to becoming a sound designer or sound editor. But it does help you make the connections needed to attract more work and, potentially, launch your own Foley studio.

How Do You Make Money? And What Kind of Money?

Foley artists work either on a freelance basis or as an employee of a studio, a post-production sound company, or, increasingly, video-game developers. The pay scale in the United States is shaped by IATSE Local 700 (aka the Motion Picture Editors Guild), whose contracts set different minimum wage levels for major and independent studios. For Foley work on a major motion picture, the hourly rate in 2026 ranged from $67 to $92.

Those wages apply only to jobs done with union labor, and it's worth remembering that for people new to the field, the work can be intermittent. The advent of streaming video has increased the volume of programs produced, but it also means fewer episodes per show and tighter production budgets.

At the same time, work for Foley artists on features filming in Los Angeles has waned, Heuer said. "It's all TV; it's all Netflix," she said. "Their budgets aren't the same, so the money's not the same. It's still decent, but it's sure not what it used to be."

The gaps between jobs can make it hard to earn a living, especially for those relatively new to the field. Andreína Gomez Casanova (*No Fathers in Kashmir*, *Cowboy Poets*), a Foley artist since 2017, said she sometimes waits two to three months for the next assignment. "I would encourage people to actively explore other areas within the field of sound" in addition to Foley gigs, she said. "In sound editing, there are more consistent job opportunities."

How Is This Career Different from Ten or Twenty-Five Years Ago?

One of the main changes has been the emergence of new opportunities—both in the films and TV shows made for streaming services and in other forms of entertainment. One example is video games, which are increasingly cinematic and, like other animation-based videos, rely on manufactured sound.

Granted, creating realistic sound for animated people can be a challenge for Foley artists. "Sometimes, really rough renditions of animation are incredibly difficult, because they are not human, they do not move in ways you can predict," Heuer said.

Nonhumans are a whole other issue. On *Who Framed Roger Rabbit*, Heuer said, her team spent hours trying to work out how to make the title character's body sound funny. They found that a fuzzy bunny wasn't a funny bunny, but an elastic one was. So they used pieces of rubber to make the sound when Roger Rabbit's ears twisted on-screen. "You have to develop the part of your brain that uses your imagination in such a way that you're entertaining people with sound," Heuer said.

Another emerging source of work for Foley artists is audio dramas and fiction podcasts. The medium is entirely audio, so Foley artists are often called on to help make the narratives more evocative for listeners.

One other big change has been the shift from analog to digital audio. Waters said there are sound effect libraries available now that include recordings of such things as people walking (with variations for different types of shoes), keys jingling, and clothes rustling. For some filmmakers, those recordings are an acceptable substitute for hiring a Foley artist.

But pasting in snippets of sound synchronized to the video is not just inefficient and less cost-effective; it lacks the all-important performance aspect of Foley. Heuer recalled the time she was doing the footsteps for Meryl Streep's ailing character in the film *Ironweed* and one of the sound editors, Kay Rose, had her do it again and again, saying, "I can't hear the pain, Ellen."

"Being in sync is one thing," Heuer said, "but emotions and the ability to 'act' the part is of equal value."

It remains to be seen whether a Foley artist's performance skills will protect them from obsolescence in an industry that embraces AI. AI tools are designed to learn from human models; Heuer thinks it's just a matter of time before the technology learns to replicate the performance of a Foley artist well enough to fool audiences.

What's Some Good Advice?

Take acting classes. Gomez said she did and "it really helped me to understand what the character is feeling and their place in space."

Find a way into the private Foley artist group on Facebook. Members include some of the top people working in the field. "That group is amazing, and I think it will help people interested in the field of Foley," Gomez said.

Not having a job in Foley doesn't stop you from working on the craft. "Practice, practice, practice, practice, practice. It doesn't matter where," Burgis said, adding, "Practice walking in time with people." Gomez suggested, "Just take one video, mute it, and record your own Foley. Don't wait to have a project to practice."

Learn more about filmmaking. "You really need a good understanding of the whole filmmaking process in order to find your place in it," Burgis said. For one thing, he said, it's important to recognize the points in a film when it's better off without your contribution.

Don't get attached to the sounds you create. You need to be willing to accept it when an editor tells you that the sounds you've produced don't work in a particular scene. "Your job is to provide, rather than to decide," Burgis said. "The humility comes when people say, 'No, I don't like that. Let's do something else.' You can't have an ego."

GLOSSARY

Above the line / Below the line: These phrases refer to the hierarchy of crew. You can imagine the "line" on a budget sheet that divides workers into "Above the line," those who lead the creative direction of the film (directors, producers, screenwriters, principal actors, and casting) and "Below the line" (everyone else).

Actors: The people who perform the lines of the script in front of the camera. There are live-action actors and voice actors. Actors can get jobs in theater, film, television, commercials, music videos, gaming, and more.

AD: The AD is the first assistant director, who is responsible for helping the director coordinate the cast and crew and keeping everyone on schedule.

ADR: Short for automated dialogue replacement. Done in post-production, this is where actors will rerecord their lines to address issues identified by the filmmakers (e.g., muffled sound), or where new dialogue is dubbed in (e.g., in a different language).

Agent: A representative who books jobs and negotiates deals on behalf of clients, who may be actors, directors, writers, or other top creative people.

AI: Short for artificial intelligence. Also known as machine learning.

AMPTP: The Alliance of Motion Picture and Television Producers that represents film and TV production company members.

APA: Agency for the Performing Arts, a large talent agency.

Audition reader: The person who reads the other lines in the scene during an actor's audition.

Avail: Short for availability, used by casting directors to put actors on "first avail." This means that they want to offer the part, but they're still awaiting more approvals. The production is asking you to be available on the shooting day, but because it's not a guarantee for work, you can respond as available for multiple projects.

GLOSSARY

Back-end: The compensation and profit sharing that happens among stakeholders after the project breaks even.

Background: Background actors, formally known as extras.

Best boy: Top assistant to the head of the electrical department or the key grip, handles administrative duties (e.g., payroll and inventory).

Boom operator: The sound person who is responsible for holding the boom microphone, which is the one on a long stick used to capture audio from a distance.

CAA: Creative Artists Agency, a large entertainment, sports, and media talent agency.

Call sheet: A daily filming schedule given to all cast and crew members before shooting.

Call time: The time you're expected to arrive to work on set.

Casting director: The person who finds, auditions, and makes deals with the actors who are ultimately cast for the project.

CGI: Short for computer-generated imagery. These digitally created visuals can be used to make entire animated films or enhance the live-action visuals captured through video cameras.

Choreographer: The person who designs any type of planned movement or dance necessary for the project.

Cinematographer: Also known as the director of photography, this is the person in charge of the camera department. The cinematographer's main job is to capture the images that convey the story the director is trying to tell.

Composer: The person responsible for writing the original music for a project, including the "underscore"—the mood-enhancing music that plays in the background for much of the film or TV show.

Costume designer: The person in charge of all the clothing in a project. Some projects require extensive shopping to find the right outfits, while others require the costume team to build clothing from scratch.

Coverage: Refers to script coverage, which is the review and analysis of a script, meant to help a person or company determine whether to consider it.

Craft services: The department on set that provides the cast and crew with food and drinks.

Crowdfunding: Raising money through an Internet campaign. It's an alternate way of financing a project outside established studios and streaming services.

DGA: Directors Guild of America, the entertainment guild that represents film and TV directors in Hollywood.

Director: The head of the set. In film, the director is also the visionary of the project. In television, directors work on individual episodes to help execute the vision of the showrunner.

Dolly grip: The person responsible for moving the cameras to capture the shots sought by the director and cinematographer.

Editor: The person who blends the multiple different takes and camera angles for a scene into a single coherent one, then combines the various scenes into a movie or TV show.

Foley artist: Someone who creates sounds in post-production to enhance or replace those recorded on set, typically by performing them in time with the footage shot for a scene.

Gaffer: The chief electrician on a project, responsible for supplying power and lighting for each scene.

Gersh: A large talent and literary agency.

Green light: When a project receives the "green light"—or is "green-lit"—this means it has received official approval to move forward into production.

Grip: One of the crew members who set up and take down much of the equipment used during production.

Hairstylist: The person who works on hair and wigs for a project.

IATSE: The International Alliance of Theatrical Stage Employees, one of the largest film and TV unions that represent technicians, artists, and craftspersons across the entertainment industry.

ICM: International Creative Management, a large talent and literary agency.

Key grip: Head of the grips, consulted by gaffer and cinematographer/director of photography on how the set will be rigged and shot.

Location manager: The person who scouts possible locations for filming various scenes in a project and takes care of all the logistics to get the location ready for the shoot.

Logline: A one-sentence description of a script, used to tease the story.

Makeup artist: A person who does beauty makeup, which enhances an actor's natural looks, or special-effects makeup, which can age actors drastically, add wounds, or turn them into supernatural characters.

Manager: A representative who focuses on developing the careers of writers, actors, and other top creatives. Typically works with fewer clients than an agent does.

Music supervisor: The person who helps choose and obtain the rights for the songs played during a movie or TV show.

One-sheet: A single page that summarizes your project, for marketing purposes.

PA: Short for production assistant. An entry-level worker who performs basic tasks, including errands and clerical work.

Paradigm: A large talent agency.

Perms: The large, permanently installed beams in the rafters of a sound stage, used for hanging lights, platforms, and other equipment.

Pilot: The first episode of a TV series that is used to sell the show.

Post: Short for post-production. This is where effects are applied, voices and sounds are rerecorded, music is added, and final edits are made.

Previz (or previs): Short for pre-visualization, this is the process of creating a plan for a scene—for example, a stunt, animation, or VFX sequence—before it's shot.

Producer: The person ultimately responsible for a film or TV show, the one who guides a project from idea into reality. An "executive producer" has a more limited role, typically in raising money for a project. Similarly, a "line producer" is someone who creates and oversees a project's budget.

Production designer: The head of the art department who is responsible for budgeting and coordinating all the visual elements of the film.

Publicist: The person who helps promote a client or project by pitching them to the media and securing other forms of attention and exposure.

Rep: Short for representative, usually refers to an agent or manager.

SAG-AFTRA: The performers' labor union formed by a merger of the Screen Actors Guild and the American Federation of Television and Radio Artists.

Second unit: A separate team of filmmakers working on a sequence distinct from the main production; for example, action sequences, crowd scenes, or exterior shots.

Showrunner: The head of the writers' room on a TV show. While directors are the visionaries on film, the showrunner is the leader of a TV show.

Sound designer: The person in charge of the sound effects in a project, overseeing the Foley artists (who create sounds through performances) and the sound effects editors (who use recorded sounds).

Spec script: Also known as a "speculative screenplay," this is a script that hasn't been commissioned. Though there is neither payment nor guarantee it'll be made, specs are written to showcase a writer's work.

Special effects: The simulations accomplished by physical means, such as setting controlled fires, building model spaceships, or blowing fake snow onto a scene.

Stunt performer: The person who performs the riskier physical movements on camera so the actors don't get injured. This could include tripping, falling, driving, horseback riding, swimming, or flying through the air on wires.

Table read: An organized reading and rehearsal of the script before it's performed.

Talent: Usually refers to actors, on-camera talent, but could also refer to any key person attached to a project in hopes of selling it.

Teamsters: The union that represents drivers, location managers, and casting directors. It's also referred to as Local 399.

Tentpole: A large project that a studio or network hopes will make a lot of money to support the smaller projects.

UTA: A large talent agency that represents artists, athletes, storytellers, and brands.

Visual effects: The simulations accomplished digitally, such as computer-generated images of a building being destroyed.

Voice actor: An actor who records dialogue off-camera, such as reading the part of a narrator, an animated figure, an anthropomorphized animal, a video-game character, or an enchanted object. Voice actors also work as narrators on audiobooks, commercials, and educational media.

WGA: Writers Guild of America. Generally referred to as the guild for writers, but it's composed of two unions that represent film and TV writers: Writers Guild of America East, based in New York City, and Writers Guild of America West, based in Los Angeles.

WME: William Morris Endeavor, a large entertainment, sports, and fashion talent agency.

Wrap: "It's a wrap" means the project is done!

Writer: The person who writes the script that is the blueprint for the project.

ACKNOWLEDGMENTS

The authors would like to thank the many people who contributed to the production of this book. Scott Kraft, a senior *Los Angeles Times* editor in charge of special projects, was the one who suggested writing it and who shepherded it to completion. Gail Ross, the *Los Angeles Times'* agent, helped the paper get the contract with Simon & Schuster. Mindy Marques was our editor there, and Johanna Li guided us through the production. Former *Times* editor Millie Quan, who edited the first draft, provided invaluable guidance on the book's style and contents. Matt Ballinger, former leader of the *Times'* Utility Journalism Team, and Julia Turner, former deputy managing editor for entertainment and strategy, helped launch the newspaper series on which the book is based. Many of the chapters were informed by the work of other current and former staffers for the *Times*, including Richard Verrier, Mark Potts, Judy Pryor, Faith Stafford, Juliette Toma, Michelle Rohn, Jessica Roy, Anousha Sakoui, Wendy Lee, Jessica Chen, Matt Brennan, Justin Ray, Karen Garcia, Christi Carras, Madalyn Amato, Betty Hallock, Salma Loum, Michael Ordoña, Ruth Samuel, Boris Kachka, Frank Wofford, Cody Long, Yadira Flores, Erik Himmelsbach-Weinstein, Maggie Beidelman, Care Dorghalli, Cesar Rojas Angel, Calvin Alagot, Dania Maxwell, Andrew Jackson, and Sean Grado. The *Times'* fabulous columnist Mary McNamara stepped up to write the introduction. Many thanks also to *Times* president Chris Argentieri, former *Times* executive editor Kevin Merida, assistant managing editor John Canalis, and General Counsel Jeff Glasser.

We are particularly indebted to the many Hollywood professionals who painstakingly explained what they do and how they got to where they are today. Although not all of them are named in the book, they all made extremely valuable contributions to our understanding of the industry. Industry professionals who generously provided guidance or participated in listening sessions with the *Times* include Brian Hu, Randall Park, Michael Golamco, Lacy Lew Nguyen Wright, Agnes Constante, Danielle Fox, Nelson Jimenez, Carolyn Michelle Smith, Behzad Dabu, Michael Svoboda, Ben Lopez, Julie Vu, Jeff Jablon, Erica Wernick, Andrea Apuy, Pamala Buzick Kim, and Chloe Coover.

Our heartfelt thanks go to our many interviewees, including managers Susan Ferris of Bohemia Group, Chris Giovanni of CGEM Talent, Craig Rogalski of CK Talent Management, David Neumann of Newmation, and Stephanie Moy of M88; music supervisors Thomas Golubić, Robin Urdang, George Drakoulias, Gary Calamar, Morgan Rhodes, and Jen Malone; Dan Koplowitz of Friendly Fire Licensing; sound designers and supervising sound editors James Lucero, Randy Thom, David Acord, Vanessa Flores, Cory Choy, Maddie Bautista, and Michele Darling; composers Genevieve Vincent, Zach Robinson, Leo Birenberg, Amie Doherty, Chanda Dancy, Ian Hultquist, Lachi, Stephen Letnes, and Michael Yezerski; producers Midge Sanford, Clay Epstein, Kara Durrett, Jon Kamen, Frank Scherma, Kibi Anderson, Phillip B. Goldfine, Carla Singer, Carol Baum, Lisa Demberg, and Mallory Schwartz; Dave Fraunces of The MBS Group; Michelle Satter and Shira Rockowitz of the Sundance Institute; Peter Broderick of Paradigm Consulting; current and former grips Chris Trillo, Gary Dagg, King W. Lanaux II, and Charley Gilleran; Thomas Davis, Chaim Kantor, and Tobey Bays of IATSE; gaffers David Goodman, Andy Day, Eric Fahy, and Tom Guiney; publicists Annalee Paulo of 42West, Erika Tucker of AM PR Group, and David Magdael of David Magdael & Associates, Inc.; special-effects artists Sandy Stewart, Todd Masters, Maggie Anne Goll, Brian Poor, J. D. Streett, and Fon Davis; costume designers Mona May, Natalie Bronfman, Susanna Song, Janelle Carothers, and Whitney Anne Adams; casting professionals Josh Ropiequet, Kim Williams, Billy DaMota, Dea Vise, Tanya Giang, and Jessica Daniels; choreographers Mandy Moore, Emilio Dosal, Sonya Tayeh, Alison Faulk, Luke Broadlick, Mimi Karsh, Chuck Maldonado, Kathryn Burns, and Steve Sidawi; agents Julie McDonald of McDonald Selznick Associates, Chris Noriega of the Verve Talent & Literary Agency, Erica Ling and Daniela Federman of WME, Tracy Christian of the TCA MGMT agency, Jen Rudin of Independent Artist Group, Yasmine Pearl of WME, and Ugonna "Ugo" Obioha of United Talent Agency; Amos Newman of Fifth Season; editors Julio C. Perez IV, Stephanie Filo, Sam Levy, Yvette M. Amirian, Tyler Nelson, Carsten Kurpanek, and Ri-Karlo Handy; Jenni McCormick of American Cinema Editors; location managers Lori Balton, Alison Taylor, Gregory Alpert, and Whitney Breite; actors Stephanie Beatriz, Nik Dodani, Vinny Chhibber, Adam Faison, Annie Gonzalez, Amy Hill, Anna LaMadrid, Behzad Dabu, Ben Whitehair, Carolyn Michelle Smith, DaJuan Johnson, Shannon Sturges, Brent Bailey, D'Lo, Jeff Logan, Kendall Kyndall, James Tang, Fatima Reedy, Graham Shiels, Sergio Calderón, and Rodney To; voice actors Kathy Grable, Chanté McCormick, Thomas Copeland, and Joe Zieja; cinematographers Shane Hurlbut, Michael Goi, Eric Messerschmidt, Jasmine Karcey, Tommy Maddox-Upshaw, Shelly Johnson, Stephen Lighthill, Kira Kelly, Arlene Nelson, Veronica Bouza, and Checco Varese; Foley artists Ellen Heuer, Peter Burgis, Vanessa Theme Ament, Katie Waters, and Andreína Gomez Casanova; Jeff Yang; Chris Smith of the Entertainment Community Fund's Looking Ahead program; Anne Henry of the BizParentz Foundation; Lois Yaroshefsky; Ed Duffy of Teamsters Local 399; writers Gennifer Hutchison, Lucas Brown Eyes, Tze

Chun, Stephany Folsom, and Liza Babin; directors Richard Wong, Sujata Day, Brian Herzlinger, Suzanne Luna, Jake Helgren, Bertha Bay-Sa Pan, Shay Bennett; hairstylists Anissa Salazar, Camille Friend, Susan Lipson, Guyla Wilkerson, and Marva Stokes; makeup artists Jennifer "JQ" Quinteros, Ve Neill, Ashley Hines, Jerry Gergely, and Ally McGillicuddy; production designers Tom Lisowski, David Morong, Jason Kisvarday, Toni Barton, James Connelly, Bill Groom, Judy Rhee, and Desma Murphy; set decorators Brandi Kalish, Andrew Baseman, Rae Deslich, and Rosemary Brandenburg; VFX pros Brittany Piacente, Kaitlyn Yang, Maxine Schnepf, Marcella Brown, Jason Gottlieb, Dylan Sisson, Eliot Mack, Robert Nederhorst, Hoyt Yeatman, and Chris White; AI experts Mike Gioia, Emil Hansson, and Jeremy Toeman; crowdfunders William Yu, Bri Castellini, Kayla Robinson, Jim Cummings, Will Haines, Kerri Pollard, and Ryan T. Husk; stunt professionals Ryan Sturz, Chris Christensen, Mallory Thompson, Banzai Vitale, Alex Daniels, Alfred Hsing, Katie Rowe, Noah Garret, and Olivia Salinas; animation pros Jeffrey New, Ellen Su, Justinian Huang, Kevin Noel, Michelle Wong, Mike Milo, and Bernie Petterson; dialect coaches Leith McPherson, Garrett Strommen, Denise Woods, Junko Goda, Samara Bay, Josh Feliciano-Sanchez Moser, and Jennifer Greer; film festival programmers Lili Rodriguez, Faridah Gbadamosi, Kim Yutani, Martine McDonald, Diana Cadavid, Sudeep Sharma, and Anderson Le; food stylists Brett Long, Caroline Hwang, Anna Lee, and Alyssa Noui; production finance pros Mark Goldstein, Aaron Williams, Paul Steinke, Hilary Wagner, and Melissa Lintinger; animal trainers Ursula Brauner, Karin McElhatton, and Sarah Clifford; unit photographers Warrick Page, Michael Becker, Hopper Stone, and Chara Andrews; social media influencers Eddie Infante, Soy Nguyen, Phillip Miner, Melody Cheng, Helen Wu, and Janet Wang; as well as Romola Ratnam, Rebecca Windsor, Juan Jose Hernandez, Wyatt Muma, Joyce Mehess, Tony Vinciquerra, Franklin Leonard, Thuc Nguyen, Stephen Galloway,

Cheryl Bedford, Michelle Sugihara, Reggie Hui, Jaia Thomas, Zino Macaluso, Rafael Carbajal, Debra Katz, Michelle Franke, Angie Lee, Daniel Plagens, Jen Acker, Brandon Milostan, Brian Torres, Anjali Alimchandani, Jennifer Yu, Betty Ming Liu, Linda Truong, Angilee Shah, and Trang Ada Trinh.

And of course, thank you to our families—Arya Chen, Adelyn Chen, Alexander Chen, Ian Healey, Seth Healey, Margot Healey, David Tseng, Meei-hwa Tseng, and Hsiufeng Tseng—for supporting us on our own Hollywood adventure.

INDEX

INDEX

INDEX

INDEX